MW01275134

# The Story of Sunseed

## And Other True Adventures

FOR JUDITH,

YOU WERE THERE, BACK IN THOSE WONDERFUL AND INCREDIBLE DAYS.

Terry Oftedal

Terry Oftedal

# The Story of Sunseed

## And Other True Adventures

Copyright © 2015 Terry Oftedal
ISBN-13: 978-1522954538
ISBN-10: 1522954538
All rights reserved

Cover Artwork
*"Sunseed's Dream"*
**Cheryl Renée Long**
http://CherylRLong.com

Cover Design & Interior Layout by ***Laura Shinn Designs***
http://laurashinn.yolasite.com

All rights reserved under U.S. and International copyright law. This book is licensed only for the private use of the purchaser. May not be copied, scanned, digitally reproduced, or printed for re-sale, may not be uploaded on shareware or free sites, or used in any other manner without the express written permission of the author and/or publisher. Thank you for respecting the hard work of the author.

***The Story of Sunseed*** *— And Other True Adventures* contains financial discussions as part of the narrative of this author's life story; they are not intended to provide financial or investing advice. The reader is encouraged to consult professionals for personal financial, tax, and legal planning assistance.

# Foreword

There are seventy-seven million baby boomers. Relatively few have written their stories, and none are quite like this one.

I'm of the baby boom generation too—born the same year as Terry Oftedal, in fact. We boomers have lived through hot wars, cold wars, near-wars, integration, the Pill, the '60s counterculture, assassinations, women's lib, Neil Armstrong's moon walk, Woodstock, the draft, *Roe v Wade,* and one of our own generation, Bill Clinton, becoming the first boomer president. Our parents were of Tom Brokaw's "Greatest Generation," children of the 1930s' Depression. They sustained America through World War II and the Korean War, and raised us in the decades following.

*The Story of Sunseed* sails on this sea of global events.

Terry begins the tale before he was born, introducing us to his heritage and successive progenitors a few generations back. This statement in chapter 9 caught me: "If we do choose our own parents, then I chose well." It's an idea that stays with me. Is it true our lives are not random happenings but have purpose, intention, and meaning? This is the *Sunseed* awakening.

*Sunseed* is a name Terry adopted as a young man reaching for reason. He describes "a spiritual wind" at his back, pushing him forward to discover there is more to life than the ordinary. This internal wind moved him to look and learn, to wonder, listen, and be open to possibilities even when he couldn't explain them. Eventually he found he already *was* what he was looking for. His life's arc is an example of the theme of Zen teacher Cheri Huber's wonderful little book, *That Which You Are Seeking Is Causing You To Seek.*

Everything we connect with in our lives comes along with us for the rest of the trip. Especially when there's more road behind than ahead, Terry shows us that we can look back and see it's all right here. A lot may have passed, but it isn't past. It's present. Terry takes us on a recollection excursion, exposing to light the fresh innocence of growing up in Fresno, California; a big-city college experience; a first experience of love and heartbreak; and the spiritual quest for self-discovery.

Along the way we attend frat parties and row with him at UCLA, work his early jobs with him, go on road trips, experiment with drugs, and find kindred spirits at every stage. With Terry and his beloved Kathryn we raise a family, make many life and financial choices, gain timeless wisdom, and reach the vantage point from which *The Story of Sunseed* was written.

In her book *Long Quiet Highway*, Natalie Goldberg says, “Writing is a way to connect with our own minds, to discover what we really think, see, and feel, rather than what we think we *should* think, see, and feel.” Autobiographical writing requires a special willingness to risk, to be open and vulnerable. I hear Terry’s voice clearly through his written words. They ring of caring, honesty, and genuineness. I’ve known him many years, and he really is just the way he writes.

Like all good true stories, *The Story of Sunseed* may remind us of our own. There is a spiritual wind which propels each of us from within if we’ll but let it.

John Clinton Gray, author of *Gift of Seeds* and *If I Die Thursday*
Lake Elsinore, California; October 2015

# Introduction

I always wanted to write a few stories about my life, primarily to share with family and friends. Actually, I just started to write, and this book happened. Along the way I asked myself, "Will anyone want to read these stories?" For those who have crossed paths with me on this marvelous journey, I hope the answer is yes. For those who have yet to meet me, here is your invitation to come along. You will gain a new perspective of me as you read these stories. I believe you will learn something new about yourself as well, because this book is not just about me.

Some may call this a love story. Yes, it is that— and more. I have included thoughts on life topics that come up for every generation, like solving the problems of the world, finding health and wealth, experiencing persistent happiness, and understanding one's own life purpose. To contemplate these fundamental issues, we have to look beyond any one person's story- mine or yours. We have to journey beyond the domain where our minds hold sway, to places inside ourselves where dreams, ideals, prayers, and epic adventures make sense.

Dreams play a particularly important role in our search for understanding and inspiration. So, I have told stories about a variety of people who had big dreams. These people include family, friends, and historical figures; to me they all provide context for understanding my own personal story. In the process of exploration and writing, I realized that the dreams of our ancestors continue on in all of us. They will certainly continue on into our following generations as well. I hope that reading this book will bring you fresh inspiration to boldly follow your own dreams, just as I have been inspired by others along the way.

Over my lifetime, I have been compelled to look into the deepest levels of my own being. What have I learned from my inner journey? I'll talk about that also. I'll tell stories about my spiritual quest and the invisible wind that I became aware of along the way. I assure you these stories are all true. I call them "true adventures." You'll soon find that my life has been colorful in many ways and certainly not dull, particularly after Sunseed's dream.

# Chapter One

## SUNSEED'S DREAM

*"There are two great days in a person's life—*
*the day we are born and the day we discover why."*
—William Barclay, Scottish Theologian

Early one morning a young man awoke from a wonderful and powerful dream. He would never be the same again. As he opened his eyes, he wasn't sure of where he was. The whole dream remained remarkably vivid, particularly the ending. It ended with a man named Sunseed being transformed into a giant fiery bird that was pulling the Earth around its orbit of the Sun.

*"Sunseed's Dream"*

The young man had heard a theory that the Earth's orbit would degrade some day and our home planet would fall into the Sun. That idea was disturbing. It also seemed to ignore possibilities of a living intelligence dynamically guiding creation as we experience it. This dream filled the youth with a strong sense that anything could be possible if he were aligned with that creative intelligence behind our universe. It also seemed more than a dream. Perhaps Sunseed was real, he pondered, and sending a message to him from a different place.

I was that 25 year-old young man. It was my dream. I was living in Ashland, Oregon on that day in 1972, and soon thereafter I took on the name Sunseed as part of a life mission to tell others about my vision of hope and purpose. Even more important, I committed to living this vision.

I studied many old books about finding purpose in life and finding God. I practiced vegetarianism, fasting, cleansing, yoga, meditation, dancing, days of silence, and even tried some LSD. For a time I grew my hair and my beard long. I wore very colorful clothing. Some called me a hippie. But that was just the way I looked on the outside. The dream came in the midst of all this.

In fact, that dream would stay vividly with me for the rest of my life— it would provide a backdrop for many future decisions which would become turning points in my life. Over the following decades I actually did find everything I was seeking, and the realization that I was an intrinsic part of Sunseed's dream has became even more meaningful. This book is now a means for sharing the story of my quest and what I discovered about life's purpose.

But first, this story should start in Fresno, California. Why Fresno? I have asked that question myself many times.

# Chapter Two

## WHY FRESNO?

*"Courage is being scared to death... and saddling up anyway."*
—John Wayne, American Actor

Keep in mind that California was controlled by Spain until 1823 when Mexico's war of independence created a large new country that included the lands we now call Mexico, Texas, and California. In1846 the region today known as California included fewer than 8,000 Californios (immigrants), in addition to an estimated 150,000 native Indians. The Indian population had declined by 50 percent in recent decades, due largely to infectious diseases (such as smallpox, measles, and malaria) that the new settlers carried with them. The immigrants were particularly attracted to the Pacific shores and the Sacramento River Valley, but they roamed the interior spaces and the mountains as well. These lands were far-flung and distant from Mexico's capital, which exerted little government control.

On April 25, 1846 the California war for independence started. Those involved in the skirmishes usually numbered a few hundred or less. Led by men such as John C. Fremont, Kit Carson, and John Sutter, the independent Bear Flag Republic was born in spirit when the first Bear Flag was raised over Sonoma in June. California as an independent country wouldn't last long, because other events were rapidly unfolding. In large part, the success of California's campaign for independence was due to support from the United States, which was fighting and distracting Mexico on other fronts, primarily Texas. By July, U.S. naval forces led by Commodores John Sloat and Robert Stockton came directly into play; they occupied Monterey Bay and its Presidio as well as San Francisco Bay. They declared California part of the U.S., which is what many of the immigrants supposedly wanted.

Colonel Steven Kearney then led U.S. ground troops southward. California was still nominally controlled by Governor

Pio Pico and about 100 Mexican soldiers stationed in the little town of Los Angeles. Kearney's troops, alongside Fremont and the Bear Flaggers, chased Governor Pico out and forced a Mexican retreat in August of 1846. California was again proclaimed a U.S. Territory. This was formally validated in 1848 as part of Mexico's surrender terms at the end of what the Americans called the Mexican-American War. I recommend a book entitled *Bear Flag Rising.* It provides colorful details about the people and the battles. Mostly, it tells a lot of stories about patriots charging around on horses, while they were trying to figure out what was going on. Courageous? I suppose that depends on which history books you are reading.

On January 24, 1848 gold was discovered at Sutter's Mill, in the mountains east of Sacramento, and word spread quickly. People streamed to California by boat, by wagon, by horse and mule. Few became wealthy; most eventually settled and turned to other dreams. On September 9th of 1850, California became the 31st state. The population had swelled to over 90,000 immigrants (92 percent male). Sadly, the Indian population was plunging and would reach 30,000 within ten years— reportedly more than 100,000 were killed during the first two years of the gold rush. This was still the frontier; even statehood did not automatically guarantee order and justice for all. San Francisco emerged as the banking capital and the largest city in the West. Los Angeles was a sleepy little town of 4,000 people.

Situated inland, between San Francisco and Los Angeles, the sprawling central San Joaquin Valley was known for being dry and it was sparsely populated. That all started to change in the 1860s when an enterprising pioneer named A. Y. Easterby invested his money and a lot of hard work to bring irrigation water from the Kings River to his wheat farm near modern day downtown Fresno. In 1871 Leland Stanford, the founder of the Central Pacific Railroad, saw in that farm the potential for further land development and decided to establish a railroad station nearby. This infrastructure investment in California was part of a much larger economic growth cycle being largely driven by the proliferation of railroad lines all over America. In fact the linking of America by transcontinental rail had just been accomplished on May 10, 1869— Leland Stanford himself participated in driving the ceremonial golden spike at Promontory Summit in Utah Territory. It was called "the greatest engineering achievement in nineteenth century America." The connection from Chicago (and points east) all the way to California created new possibilities. The stage was now set in Fresno and the San

Joaquin Valley for another significant economic boom— this time it would be driven by agriculture.

In the early 1880s additional private investors took notice of the area and bought large tracts of land west of Fresno's new Central Pacific Railway Station. They sub-divided the tracts into 20 acre parcels and added a network of roads to access the new train station. They also built a system of canals to deliver irrigation water from the Kings River to each parcel. These arid acreages were now ready to be transformed; they stood ready for the arrival of people with vision— people with big dreams. Developers marketed these affordable parcels in groups known as colonies, each focused on a specific ethnic heritage. Norwegians, who spoke the same language and shared religious and cultural practices, all bought and farmed together in the Norwegian Colony. Other groupings in nearby colonies included Germans, Russians, Armenians, etc. The advertising handbills, distributed through railroads and steamship companies, found their way in letters to relatives in the states east of the Rockies and all the way back to Europe— they proclaimed, "... affordable farmland, and plenty of it." Some 10,240 acres of land were in production in these colonies by the mid-1880s. By 1903 there were 48 colonies with over 71,000 acres in production. The population of California had boomed to 1.5 million people, with over 343,000 of them in San Francisco. The U.S. population was now 76 million.

I trust this sidestep into a little American history helps portray why so many people have been and continue to be attracted to this "land of dreams." The so-called Westward Movement holds particular meaning for me; though the devastation exacted on native Indians during that period was deplorable. At the same time, the ancestors of others were coming eastward from the Orient; they had dreams as well and they played their own part in the building of thc American West. A larger story, however, was just beginning. Periods of even greater economic growth and migration were approaching, and my eight great-grandparents would play a part in it.

# Chapter Three

## MY ANCESTORS WERE DREAMERS

*"The American Dream is a term often used but also often misunderstood. It isn't really about becoming rich or famous. It is about things much simpler and more fundamental than that."*
—Marco Rubio, Senator and
First Generation Cuban-American

Many of my ancestors dreamed of better opportunities and they were willing to risk everything. They left families, to face uncertainty and even physical danger. Mostly farmers, they dreamed of fertile land, where they could farm, raise a family, and experience personal freedoms. America, and eventually California, became part of their dreams. They came to America at different times and in different ways, but there were a lot of similarities. I am telling you about their adventures, because in learning more about them, I have learned more about myself.

My father's father's father was born in 1875 in southwestern Norway, near Stavanger, on a small farm his father had inherited in Oftedal Valley. Descended from a long line of farmers, Martin Toreson (son of Tore) was the second child after an older sister, Melia. Eventually there would be 10 children, but when Martin left for America at age 15, three of those siblings had yet to be born; he would never see them. In those days, family and friends often held an all-night "wake" for the departing adventurer. Though not dead, he or she would likely not be seen again by those left behind.

Martin arrived in America in 1890, probably landing at Ellis Island in New York harbor, as did most Norwegian emigrants at the time. After 1874 all of the Atlantic crossings from Stavanger were by steamship, taking seven to ten days. This was significantly faster and less dangerous than the sailboats which previously took up to four weeks. Martin spent most of his crossing time sitting or sleeping in a crowded room below decks. Upon arrival, the immigration officials wrote the surname "Oftedal" on his papers when he told them he was from Oftedal Valley.

Martin Oftedal made his way to Chicago, joining his sister Melia who had braved the same journey two years earlier. If you are interested in reading some direct accounts of those Pacific crossings and the early days of Scandinavians in Chicago, I suggest *A Long Pull From Stavanger*, by Burger Osland. Martin quickly found work in the city through relatives and saved his money over the next few years. He dreamed of owning his own farm and he had seen the flyers about affordable land in California— soon enough, he boarded a train headed west.

*"Martin and Mary Oftedal with family, circa 1917. My Grandpa Doc is standing back row third from the left."*

At age 21, Martin married an 18 year old California girl, Mary Lashley, in September of 1896. They would live most of their married years and raise their family on a dairy farm in rural Fresno County, at the modern day intersection of Annadale and Westlawn. Martin and Mary sold their milk to a local Danish Creamery, which still operates at the corner of California Avenue and Highway 99. Their farm sat just southwest of the famous Kearney Ranch. Theodore Kearney, an Englishman born of Irish parents, was a successful local land developer and farmer.

Kearney developed and sold 192 twenty-acre lots spread over six square miles of land. I suspect Martin's farm was developed on one of those lots. Kearney's lots sold for $1,000 each with $150 cash down and interest-free payments of $12.50 per month. Martin and Mary no doubt fretted about those "huge" mortgage payments just as we descendants have done when we bought our first homes.

Martin was a leader of his Odd Fellows Lodge. Their philosophy was then and is today "To improve and elevate the character of mankind by promoting the principles of friendship, love, truth, faith, hope, charity and universal justice." Martin was clearly pursuing his own spiritual quest. He never drank alcohol, he was generous to his friends and neighbors, and he followed his dreams. After 30 years of marriage, he died of a stroke at age 51, leaving behind a strong wife and 8 children.

Mary Catherine Lashley was the only one of my great-grandparents actually born in California. Her birth was April 1, 1878 in Centerville, where her parents homesteaded a farm in the Mill Creek area above Piedra. Centerville is a small Fresno County town, in the foothills 15 miles east of the city of Fresno. Even today its population is less than 400.

Mary's father, Seborn Lashley, was born in Kentucky and served in the Union Army in the Civil War. He was a rancher and infamously died in a gunfight— it happened in the middle of the street in front of the Acme Saloon on Mariposa Street in downtown Fresno. They had been drinking and arguing over land rights; a *Fresno Bee* newspaper article reported the story in colorful detail.

Mary's mother, Lizzie Findley, was born in Fresno County in 1861. Lizzie's parents, John Henry and Elizabeth, came from Virginia by covered wagon— the most popular means of westward migration between 1820 and 1870 (before the transcontinental rail link). Elizabeth was pregnant the entire journey, and shortly after reaching California in October of 1859 they stopped at the Mission in San Bernardino to deliver their first child. After crossing the Missouri River, wagon trains typically took another four to six months to reach California. About 250,000 pioneers completed this arduous trek by 1870; others didn't survive. When Mark Twain moved west to Virginia City, Nevada in 1861, it took him only weeks by stagecoach, but he was traveling light, not moving a family. Beginning in 1869 the 1,600 mile train ride from Omaha to California would take only six days.

Lizzie Findley's ancestors had come to America from Ireland

and England in the early to mid 1600s. Some of them landed in New Amsterdam, which was run by the Dutch before the British took it over and renamed it Manhattan. Two of her ancestors, Walter and Ann Wall, married in New Amsterdam in 1648; the population of the U.S. at that time was about 50,000 (immigrants). One hundred and thirty years later David Caldwell Finley, Lizzie's great-grandfather, fought in the Revolutionary War under General George Rogers Clark.

In 1926, a few years after her husband Martin's death, Mary Lashley Oftedal sold their dairy farm and bought a larger 80-acre farm where she would grow grapes and cotton. Her four sons, then in their twenties, helped in the fields. The four younger daughters, in their teens, no doubt helped with the house and cooking. This new acreage was much closer to the city, at the corner of what is now California Avenue and Brawley. According to public records, four years after Mary bought this land, she built a new house with three bedrooms and one bathroom. That sizable two-story house with a large covered front porch still stands; the mailbox reads 4113 W. California. My father used to mention "two palm trees standing out front." Yes, they are still there.

When Mary's third son (my grandfather Doc) married, he and his wife Pearl lived there for a while before moving into the city. My father (one of her 13 grand children) told stories of spending a lot of time on that farm when he was a boy. If any neighbor or friend dropped by at mealtime, Father told us how his Grandma Mary always welcomed them. She would send young Bill outside to catch another chicken and wring its neck; then Grandma would prepare more fried chicken for the table. Unfortunately, the whole slaughtering and cleaning process had an effect on my father— throughout his adult life he refused to eat any sort of fowl.

Mary was an active member of the Daughters of Rebekah Lodge, a female auxiliary to the Odd Fellows Lodge. Their philosophy was "To live peaceably, do good unto all as we have opportunity, and especially to obey the Golden Rule- Whatsoever ye would that others should do unto you, do ye even so unto them." She retired in 1947 and moved into a small house on Hedges Avenue, inside the city. I remember greeting her as a young boy at her eightieth birthday party in 1956, but honestly her stern demeanor frightened me. She died three years later. She did well for her family and lived an upstanding life. Now I wish I could have heard stories of those pioneering days directly from her.

The father of my Grandma Pearl (my father's mother) was named Ossian Milton Button. Sometimes called O.M., he was known to his friends as Kid Button. Kid was born in Chicago and his ancestors came from England. One of them, Thomas Kingston, fathered Elizabeth Kingston, who was born in the Colony of Virginia at Jamestown (the first permanent English settlement in the Americas) in 1614, just a handful of years after its founding. She would marry Thomas Loving, who arrived in 1638 to become the Surveyor General of Virginia and a large landowner. Others of Kid's forefathers were Puritans who settled in the early 1600s around Ipswich, in the Massachusetts Bay Colony— these included Matthias Button Sr. In the 1630s approximately 10,000 Puritans arrived in the colonies, seeking freedom from religious persecution by King Charles I and the Anglican Church.

Kid's great-grandparents Gideon Button and Polly Stone Button moved to Hebron, New York shortly after the Revolutionary War. By 1860, Kid's father Theodore migrated from Hebron to Wisconsin. When the Civil War started Theo enlisted with the 13th Illinois Cavalry and served until he was injured. After one year of recovery he reenlisted with the 11th Wisconsin Infantry and fought with them, mostly on the Western Front in Louisiana and Alabama. He was discharged in September of 1865 in Mobile, Alabama, five months after General Robert E. Lee's surrender at Appomattox.

Kid married my great-grandmother Maggie Hansford in 1903 in Phoenix and they had two children. I heard whispers around our family that he may have been murdered, but no one would talk about it. I eventually found (on the internet) old editions of the Arizona Republic newspaper from 1908 which reported his death in a series of front page articles. He was often drunk and abusive to his wife, which had led to their separation. One evening, eight months later, he appeared at her home and continued his abuse. He then attacked a family friend, who was trying to intercede, and in the struggle Kid was indeed shot. "Button died with his boots on being attired in high laced hunting boots and the genarl working dress of a laborer." The trial drew large crowds, and news headlines made the most of questionable allegations on both sides. My grandmother was two at the time— she was the best thing to come out of that misfortune. He was my only great-grandparent who never made it to California.

Maggie Lou Hansford was born in Kentucky in 1884. Her

family moved to the Arizona Territory via covered wagon when she was a teenager— around 1902. The last leg from Arkansas took 4 months. I heard they encountered Indians along the way in Oklahoma and the cavalry came from Fort Sill to their rescue. An Arizona newspaper reported their arrival, proclaiming the family had 5 children and 35 cents in their pocket. Maggie's father homesteaded a ranch northwest of Phoenix. The Homestead Act of 1862, signed by President Lincoln, provided strong incentive for folks to head west; it allowed any adult citizen (who had not born arms against the U.S.) to claim 160 acres of public land. The claimant could file for a deed after building a dwelling and working the claim (farming, ranching, or mining) for five years. Over time, more than 270 million acres— 10 percent of all public land— passed into private ownership from these grants.

Maggie's father was a genuine Kentucky Colonel named John Henry Hansford, and everyone respectfully called him The Colonel. His father had come from England in the early 1800s. As a young girl living in Phoenix, my Grandma Pearl liked spending time at the ranch with her Grandpa (The Colonel) and Grandma (Mary Catherine)— she told me she would happily sleep on newspapers that she spread out on the wooden floor next to The Colonel's bed.

After Kid Button died, Maggie Lou remarried to Adolph Fuller and she had another six children, half-siblings to my Grandma Pearl. Pearl said her stepfather had dreams of making his fortune in mining— he moved them to Tucson following reports of new strikes in gold and silver in the Pima County area. Many ghost towns from those earlier mining booms still exist, like Tombstone (just east of Tucson) where the Earp brothers and Doc Holliday had their shootout at the OK Corral in 1881. Geronimo and his fierce Apache warriors had surrendered in 1886, and the old chief died in 1909; southern areas of the Arizona Territory were now considered safe from Indian raids.

After trying again in Albuquerque, Adolph gave up his mining dreams. Maggie Lou may have had some say in it. They moved their family to Mexico City around 1913. There Adolph managed a hotel, but it didn't last long. The Mexican Revolution was escalating during the period of 1911-1917 and things were getting risky for "gringos." Pearl was about 10 when her family boarded a train bound for California. Pearl remembered that train ride— she loved to tell how the Mexican Army "Federales" armed with rifles sat on the roof of their train car to protect them from Pancho Villa. Villa was Commander of the Revolutionary

Army's Division del Norte, and he was indeed famous in those years for robbing trains to fund the cause. Adolph, Maggie, and the children ended that trek in the Kearney Park area of West Fresno, where Adolph would try his hand at farming.

Data from the 1930 census shows Adolph living in Southern California and married to a different woman— the same one he married before Maggie Lou. Maggie Lou raised all the kids somehow and stayed in Fresno until her death in 1964. She was a true pioneer of the American West.

On my mother's side of the family, John Barton "JB" Shackelford was born in rural western Missouri in 1866. His grandfather John Shackelford served with a North Carolina regiment in the War of 1812. His ancestors— Shackelfords, Hornbuckles, and Simpsons— came from England and Scotland to the colonies in the 1600s.

Nancy Hornbuckle lived in North Carolina as a young girl during the Revolutionary War. Her mother Nancy Nan-Chi, born in 1742, was a daughter of a Cherokee chief named Nan-Chi. It feels good to know that I have noble Native American blood running in my veins, though in generations past that was probably looked down upon. Nancy Hornbuckle married John Keen, who upon his passing, according to the Will Books of Caswell County 1815, bequeathed an "allotment of negro slaves" to their children. He was not my only slave owning ancestor.

In 1903, at age 37, JB sold his Missouri farm and with his wife Mary (Matthews) and five children left for Fresno County, where Mary's parents had recently moved. My grandfather Leroy was 2 years old at the time. The railroads were advertising about California's beautiful San Joaquin Valley, so they probably traveled by train.

JB worked as a mule skinner, hauling logs needed for urban construction down from the Sierra Nevadas. Though not well educated, he was a founder of the City of Clovis and served on the first City Council. In his latter days he became mentally incompetent and was moved to the State Mental Hospital in Stockton— he likely suffered with Alzheimer's, which was not well understood at the time. JB died in 1932, at age 65, having outlived his wife by 21 years. He literally helped build the West.

Mary Ursula Matthews was also born in Johnson County, Missouri in 1873. Her grandfather Robert Matthews was born in Ireland and came to America sometime in the early 1800s; soon after arriving, he made his way to Missouri. Ongoing waves of people left Ireland in the 1800s due to famine and lack of jobs, but it was also due to religious persecution by the ruling British Protestants. From 1830 to 1940 almost 5 million Irish emigrated to the U.S. Most of them were poor and unskilled, they were Catholics, and for generations Irish Americans endured severe discrimination.

Mary delivered one more child after arriving in California; then she died at age 36 of tuberculosis while summering in the cooler mountains at Shaver Lake. The family brought her body down by horse drawn wagon to be buried in Clovis. She left behind 6 children ranging in age from 3 to 14. My grandfather Leroy was almost 9. We know that Mary's mother Florella lived another 22 years; I suspect she helped raise the children.

My mother's mother's father, Thomas Elmer Hildreth, was born in 1872 in Sherman City, Kansas. His mother, Rebecca Rockefeller, descended from Germans who came to America in the 1730s; most of them settled in Hunterdon, NJ (and many of their descendants live there still). They married Kitchens and Wheelers, who came from England in the 1700s.

Thomas Hildreth married Mary Brown in 1897. Within a few years they moved to Oklahoma, where they had their first child, and then on to Washington State where my grandmother Mabel was born in 1907. Grandma told me (with some embarrassment) that she was born at Nason Creek Switch. It was not really a town, just a tiny railroad siding in the mountains, west of Wenatchee. The railroad to Seattle winds through apple orchards which flourish in that region; Grandma's family likely worked as pickers in those orchards. In 1910 and 1920, according to census records, they lived in Idaho. In the early 1920s, when Mabel was a teenager, they moved to Fresno (though older sister Grace was already married and stayed in Idaho). I was told they lived simply in a tent, pitched in some Fresno cherry orchard where they all worked as fruit pickers.

In his elder years, Great-Grandpa Hildreth lived a few blocks from us until he died at age 82, three years after his wife's death. I remember him waving his cane at me, adding emphasis to his stern voice, whenever he felt I needed discipline. At the time, I was too young to appreciate his courage and the hardships he endured while searching for better opportunities for his family. Years later I would experience a compulsion similar to the one which drove a young Thomas to follow his dreams.

Mary Olive "Matie" Brown was born in Marion, Kansas in

1879. Her father, John Brown, was 22 at the time; her mother, Rachel Miller, was 16. Matie's grandfather, Michael Miller, immigrated to America in the mid 1800s from Bavaria. Matie's grandmother Lydia, born in Pennsylvania in 1815, also descended from German immigrants. They had farms in Indiana, Iowa, and eventually Kansas.

Matie married Tom Hildreth when she was 18, but I have no idea how they met. She died at age 71, after more than 50 years of marriage. I was not quite 4. I have pictures of her holding me as a youngster, but my memories of her are vague. I wish I had asked my grandmother to tell me stories about her mother when I had the chance.

These were my great-grandparents, all born shortly after the Civil War in the 1860s and 1870s. One was born in Fresno County and six more moved to Fresno in their early years. I personally knew four of them for a short while. Interestingly, these four women were amongst the first of my female ancestors to enjoy the right to vote. Although the 15th Amendment to the U.S. Constitution in 1870 guaranteed that "voting rights could not be denied based on race, color, or previous condition of servitude," it specifically related to men only. Finally, in 1911 the State of California extended voting rights to women, after a statewide vote of 125,037 to 121,450 (by the male citizens). In 1919 Congress passed the 19th Amendment to the Constitution, formally granting the right to vote to women in all states; it became law on August 18, 1920 upon ratification by the 36th of 48 states. Equality for women in all things remains an ongoing process. Resolution will take more than passing additional laws, because the problem exists internally. Each of us— male and female— will be required to journey into our own heart and bring forth genuine qualities of respect, appreciation, and forgiveness. When this happens, other inequalities will be resolved as well, and the American Dream will finally be known.

# Chapter Four

## GUNSLINGERS, PLANTATION OWNERS, AND KINGS

*"May the Warm Winds of Heaven blow softly upon your house. May the Great Spirit bless all who enter there."*
—Cherokee Blessing Prayer

We each end up with our own unique genetic blend and our own collection of family histories. Some of the actions taken by one's ancestors may be inspiring, some may be less savory. Learning about both is the risk we take when we do the research. Some of my ancestors in the old west "lived by the gun, and died by the gun." Some were Cherokee maidens and chiefs.

Going back twenty three generations in my lineage we found James I, King of Scotland. His poetry indicated that he had high ideals. Thirty eight generations back we found Alfred The Great, an Anglo-Saxon King ruling from 871 to 899, who was highly admired in England. "Alfred was the 'truth teller,' a brave, resourceful, pious man, who was anxious to rule his people justly." Back forty three generations we found Charlemagne, King of the Franks and first Holy Roman Emperor. He was undoubtedly the most ruthless of his era. They all had serfs to work their fields, soldiers to fight their battles, and priests to grant them absolution. They were deemed heroic after vanquishing large numbers of Vikings, Moors, Moslems, and other heathens— expanding the reach of Christian theology was an important part of "serving God" in those days. The interesting thing is that when you go back that far in time, each generation represents millions of ancestors; try doubling 2 parents 20 or 40 more times (4, 8, 16, 32, etc.). You and I each are one of many, many descendants of many, many ancestors. Were they good people? I can never know what they really felt in their hearts or what really motivated them. I can only know what is in my own heart.

Out of all my digging into the past, the most surprising discovery was that more than one of my American ancestors owned slaves. Some were large plantation owners, more farmed smaller landholdings. An intense sense of guilt washed over me. Most simply put, profiting from human trafficking and involuntary servitude is wrong. The question reverberating in my consciousness was, "Is there anything I can do about this in my lifetime?"

In 1860 thirty one million people were living in the United States, and four million of them were slaves. In the Confederate States, slaves were more than one third of the population. It was a growing problem with no obvious solution; the primary economies of the southern states had become dependent on the institution of slavery. The bloody U.S. Civil War raged from 1861 to 1865, and over one million Americans died in that war. In 1865 slavery was outlawed in the U.S. by the 13th Amendment to the Constitution, but it remains a reality that continues to this day. Too many women, children, and men are still living in slavery. Many are forced into hard labor or domestic servitude; over half are sexually exploited. They are manipulated with fear and deprivation. The "Global Slavery Index 2013" (posted at http://www.walkfreefoundation.org) puts the worldwide number at almost 30 million, including hundreds of thousands in the U.S. Children account for over 100,000 of those enslaved in the U.S.; CNN says globally the number is 5.5 million, including those used as child soldiers- http://www.cnn.com/specials/world/freedom-project. Also check the U.N. site- https://www.unodc.org/unodc/human-trafficking-fund.html.

Much remains to be done. I admire the dedication of individuals like Academy Award winning actress Mira Sorvino, who contributes her time and money to this cause. Ms. Sorvino serves as a United Nations goodwill ambassador focused on the elimination of human trafficking. She travels the U.S. and the world pushing for adoption of trafficking laws on international, federal, and state levels. She also starred in movies portraying these problems- "Human Trafficking" and "Trade of Innocents." Similarly, actress Julia Ormand founded ASSET- the Alliance to Stop Slavery and End Trafficking- and is also a UN goodwill ambassador. Their website is http:www.assetcampaign.org. You don't have to be famous to be part of the solution. Visit http://www.polarisproject.org (an organization started by two Brown University seniors) for ideas on how one person can take action. I also recommend President Jimmy Carter's recent book, *A Call To Action,* in which he offers 23 specific ideas. One is "Adopt the Swedish model by prosecuting pimps, brothel owners, and male customers, not the prostitutes."

What can I do about it? This may sound overly simplistic, but practicing forgiveness is one of the answers I have discovered. Forgiveness happens in our own hearts and in our own consciousness. Those in our world who have been wronged can be blessed with forgiveness. Mostly, each of us can learn how to forgive ourselves— that is a powerful skill. We can speak up and involve authorities whenever we come in contact with anyone who is living in a forced labor situation or wherever we see trafficking in operation. We can support adoption of stronger laws in our own states. Ultimately these exploitive practices need to vanish from the face of the earth, and this will only happen when hate, greed, and violence are eradicated from our collective human heart. I do believe this is possible.

# Chapter Five

## GROWING UP IN FRESNO IN THE EARLY 1900s – MY FATHER'S PARENTS

*"Don't let schooling interfere with your education."*
—Mark Twain (1835-1910), American Author

Those were different times back in the early 1900s when my grandparents were born. Mark Twain left school and became a printer's apprentice at age 12. He still managed to learn what he needed, becoming one of the most famous writers in American history. Fewer than 10 percent of American children born in the first two decades of the Twentieth Century graduated from high school. That does not mean they were ignorant. My four grandparents all came to Fresno as youngsters, and they all spent at least part of their younger years growing up on farms. None of them finished high school but they could all read a newspaper and they could all write, some better than others.

My father's father was named Jasper Martin Oftedal, but everyone called him Doc. Born in 1902, he grew up on a farm, as did most of his ancestors. We found no Vikings in the Oftedal family records, which go back to the 1500s— just farmers. Interestingly, 38 percent of the U.S. population lived on farms in 1900 (down from 90 percent in 1790); today that percentage is closer to 1 percent. Urbanization, a major demographic trend, driven largely by farm mechanization, accelerated in the 1900s. Today it is a special event when children get to visit a farm— so different from the early days of America.

I mentioned in Chapter 3 that Doc's parents met and married in Fresno, but they moved back to Chicago in the year 1900 with two children; I'm not sure why. Doc was born there, but his mother was a California girl and she was terrified of the Midwestern thunderstorms so they moved back to Fresno around 1908, now with four children. Doc was the third of their eight children. He tried farming himself. At one point he raised pigs, no doubt due to his well-known love of pork. I heard there was no part of the pig that Grandpa Doc didn't like. Farming was hard work and I don't think his heart was in it, although later in life he purchased some property in nearby Clovis where he planted an assortment of fruit trees. He found it relaxing to drive out and tend them, watering the trees by hand with some long hoses. Whenever I accompanied him as a youngster, I found it to be insufferably hot and boring. But I did enjoy the fruit.

A significant trend started in the late 1800s with the invention of the gasoline powered automobile, though mass production did not begin until 1908 with Ford's Model T. The first U.S. manufacturer was Oldsmobile; second was the Jeffrey Company, which produced the Rambler. Jeffrey mass-produced 1,500 of them in 1902, their first year of production, the year of Doc's birth. This company became part of Nash Motors in 1917, and some years later Doc began as a car salesman for Dick Parker's Nash and Rambler dealership in downtown Fresno. This seemed a natural career path after previous years as an auto mechanic— for a while he even owned his own gas station. Doc was a natural salesman, being a social and friendly person, and he became well known by people in Fresno.

I heard the story about the earthquake several times. Doc and another salesman were taking a break, sitting inside one of the cars parked in the back row of Parker's Used Car lot. They were sipping from a pint bottle. Kenny Koop and his friend Billy Vucovich happened along at the time, pausing to chat with Doc. When Kenny went inside to buy some auto parts, a rare earthquake rolled through Fresno, bringing down many of the brick walls around them. They hurried outside to see the last row of used cars covered with fallen bricks. Kenny and Billy ran to the car where they had just seen Doc and they began to franticly pull bricks away from the car. A few seconds later, Doc came up behind them and said, "What are you doing?" Thankfully Doc's timing had been good. He was uninjured, but undoubtedly a bit rattled. We have some pictures, and those cars were really crushed. That didn't stop Doc's drinking, but Grandma tried to stop it. Father told me she poured his pint bottle into the kitchen sink whenever she found alcohol in the house.

Doc was often allowed to borrow one of the used cars, which were newer and more reliable than his own car. I have fond memories as a child of him driving Pearl and my family on summer vacation trips to Santa Cruz on the California coast. This required a trek of over 200 miles, a big adventure in those days. The drive took longer then, before the modern highways were built. The speeds were slower as we wound through the mountains on narrow roads, like the one over Hecker Pass, and threaded through the streets of smaller towns. The Oftedal family started enjoying the Santa Cruz beach as an escape from Fresno's summer heat back in the 1890s. They may have gone by horse and wagon, before any of them owned a car, or possibly they rode the stage coach. More likely they took one of two railroad lines that extended to Santa Cruz in the 1870s. This tradition has continued for over 125 years, and is likely to continue for as long as it gets hot in Fresno in the summertime.

Doc never believed in advance reservations or in seeking driving directions. He always managed to get to the right destination eventually, but he often added some extra miles slightly divergent that we called "Grandpa Doc shortcuts." Whenever we talked about going to Santa Cruz, the first question anyone asked was, "Which route will we take this time?"

The best part of those trips was spending time with extended family. We usually rented a small two bedroom unit at the Casa Alta Motel on Ocean Avenue (the street where my great-grandparents slept on rented cots in tents, before the motels were built). Across the street loomed the famous Giant Dipper, a wooden roller coaster built in 1924 at a whopping cost of $50,000. We put four people in each bedroom; others slept on the couch, in a stuffed chair, or on the living room floor. Sometimes someone would sleep in the bathtub or in the kitchen on some lined-up wooden chairs. We played cards in the apartment for hours and ate, and we spent time on the boardwalk and the beach and ate. Relaxing on blankets at the beach one day, Grandpa Doc told me and my younger brother Randy to go across the street and rent an umbrella. I was barely elementary school age. He sent us with no money— simply instructing us to tell the man that I needed to "establish my credit" and that we would pay him when we returned the umbrella. As Randy and I carried that big umbrella back we were met with smiles of admiration for our accomplishment. It was a more trusting world in those days.

I was 8 when Disneyland opened in Anaheim in 1955. Doc and Pearl drove us down to visit relatives in Glendale, and from there we set off for a magical experience at Disneyland. In those days you prepped for a long drive by filling a canvas bag with water and hanging it over the radiator. This helped keep the engine from overheating when climbing up mountain roads such as the "Grapevine" section of Highway 99, which meandered up to Tejon Pass on the way out of the San Joaquin Valley. This was also before seat belts and electric windows were invented. Our car may have had an automatic transmission, which started becoming popular in the 1950's. I'll never forget that first experience on the L.A. Freeways where Grandpa Doc took great liberties with his lane changing, much to the shouted objections of the local drivers. Randy and I still joke about the driver who was so mad that he almost swallowed his cigar while shaking his fist out his window and yelling at Grandpa. Disney's park was so new that the Dumbo ride was not yet operational. This was a disappointment to me, but we had great fun. The next day we stopped at Knott's Berry Farm, also in its earlier days, to see their ghost town with its amazing collection of historical memorabilia. We rode live donkeys and a miniature train, many years before Knott's expanded into a full-scale amusement park.

One day in the mid-50s, Randy and I were awakened before dawn. Doc wanted to drive us downtown to see the arrival of a special train carrying the entire Ringling Brothers and Barnum & Bailey Circus, "The Greatest Show on Earth." We saw an amazing array of animals, including numerous elephants, walking down the gangplanks and into the streets of Fresno, through which they paraded to their big top. Grandpa Doc warned us that morning, "Don't step in the elephant poop." I would later enjoy passing that same warning with a big smile to my own children many times.

Doc died at the age of 56 from a heart attack suffered while napping one evening. He had been lying on his stomach on the living room floor, as he liked to do, in his small leased home near downtown Fresno at 1505 E. Englewood. I was 10 years old at the time and deemed old enough to view his body at the mortuary. It looked like a wax statue to me, and his spirit was clearly no longer present. I remember saying, "That is not my Grandpa." I was not satisfied with the answers to my questions about where Grandpa had gone.

Grandma Oftedal was born in 1906 as Stella Mae Button. She liked to be called Pearl. Actually I didn't learn that Pearl was not her legal name until the day of her funeral. She came to Fresno as a youngster and lived on a West Fresno farm. When asked how she met Doc she would say, "We were kids living out in the countryside; I think I met Doc through his younger brother (Seaborn), who was my age in school." They married young—their first of four children, Betty, was born when Pearl was 16. My father, Bill, was their third child, born just before Pearl turned 20. Raising children, keeping house, and cooking must have kept her busy during her early adult life. I remember eating her homemade enchiladas— Yum! One of her secrets was pre-soaking chopped onions in vinegar (to extract the heat), which she then drained and spread liberally on top of the already baked enchiladas.

When her kids were grown, Pearl got a job at F.W. Woolworth in downtown Fresno. If you haven't heard of Woolworth's or "Five-and-Dimes," you should investigate this part of our history on the internet. In 1932 they started selling things for more than ten cents, but before that everything was a dime or less. Pearl was a sales lady at first and later the floor manager; probably very low paying jobs at the time for a woman with a lot of responsibilities. Standing and walking all day on those wooden floors must have been hard on her feet. "Woolies" sold a wide variety of things, but in my childhood I best remember their candy counter and the lunch counter, which was a precursor to the food courts in modern shopping malls. Eating a sandwich or an ice cream sundae at the counter was a special treat for us. Pearl worked until mandatory retirement age, when she started receiving a very small pension. Doc had no estate, so between her pension and small social security checks I am not sure how she made ends meet in her retirement years. When the U.S. Social Security Administration issued the first old-age benefit check to someone in 1940 it was for the very modest monthly sum of $22.54. Nevertheless, Pearl managed to maintain a spirit of generosity. Every time she dropped by for a visit she brought us a little gift, sometimes a small bag of candy or cookies. She always put one or two dollars in every grandchild's birthday card. Ice cream money she called it.

On one family trip when I was quite young, six of us went by car to Phoenix to reconnect with some of Pearl's long-lost relatives. We drove through the Mojave Desert at night to avoid the worst of the summer heat, but it still felt incredibly hot. Auto air conditioning was just beginning to appear in the 1950s, but our car didn't have it. As we cruised eastward on historic Route 66, all of our windows were rolled down. I could stick my head out the window into the dry and warm air as it rushed past, but I risked being struck in the face by some immense bug. Believe me it happened, and I cried. We met aunts, and uncles, and cousins in Phoenix. During our brief stay I bedded down on a screened front porch with cousin Douglas, trying to sleep in the heat. Like most houses at the time, there was no air conditioning. Electric fans would stir up the dry air— that made it worse.

Years later on a business trip to Phoenix I looked up Ann Rolan, Pearl's youngest aunt and the mother of my cousin Douglas. Aunt Ann regaled me with great stories about growing up in the Arizona Territory. On February 14, 1912, school closed for the day and she told of walking downtown for a big parade to celebrate the day Arizona officially became a state. A 48th star now flew on the new U.S. flags. I enjoyed hearing those stories about my ancestors.

Pearl and Doc always made room in their small home for other family members, and anyone could join in their dinners, just like back on the farm. On Saturdays they often brought food, maybe inexpensive steaks, to our home and Father barbecued in our back yard while we enjoyed a family evening together. Sometimes they took us to a restaurant. My favorite was the old Farmer's Market, where I always chose between a barbecued beef sandwich (with beans and green salad) or a hot turkey sandwich with mashed potatoes smothered in gravy.

Some weekends Pearl and Doc would join us at the home of my other grandparents for a family evening. Amazing how in-laws actually enjoyed each other back in those days. We would all linger on the back patio, visiting in the relative cool of the Fresno evening. After dinner, dessert was always the first topic. Someone might have baked a fruit cobbler or prepared the makings for hand-cranked homemade ice cream. Other times one of the adults would volunteer to go buy a couple dozen donuts; Valley Donut, downtown on Tulare Street, was always open. Painted on the wall, I admired their huge mural of a ship's captain steering the good ship Donatti in a dramatic storm, his hands both firmly gripping the wheel. For his dinner, a donut was spiked on one of the knobs of the ship's steering wheel (thus explaining the reason for the donut's hole). Agonizing over our choices from the wide selection of donuts was great fun, but my brother and I usually picked the chocolate glazed. Other times some of us would head out with one or two quarters to find the biggest watermelon possible. As part of the process of choosing one, we would thump numerous sweet and juicy melons, picked just hours earlier in West Fresno, still warm from the sun. Back then a good price was a half of a penny to one penny per pound. The big ones weighed over 30 pounds; they cost a whopping 15 to 30 cents. What special memories I have of growing up in the warmth of family love and generosity.

Pearl loved playing cards, and she enjoyed a little gambling. After Nevada legalized gambling in 1931, Reno and Las Vegas quickly became popular destinations. Each was only a 4 or 5 hour drive from Fresno. Sometimes Doc would say to my parents, "Let's go to Reno tonight." Father never had much extra money, but Doc always seemed to have a little extra and he was always ready to share it. My brother and I were quickly fetched by our other grandparents, and off would drive Doc, Pearl, and my parents on a spontaneous adventure. Sometimes they even returned with money in their wallets.

When Pearl was 83 she went on one more drive to Reno. On the way home while napping in the back seat, surrounded by family, she lost consciousness. Shortly after reaching the hospital in Madera, she died. It was 31 years after Doc's passing. A simple country girl, quiet, caring, and generous her whole life, I like to say she came home "a winner" from her last Reno trip.

Dealing with the death of loved ones is an important experience. Grief cannot be avoided. In fact, it departs sooner when we learn to embrace it. This is a difficult lesson, which only becomes easier after we come to terms with the reality that our own years are numbered. This is one of life's great mysteries, worthy of further consideration. For now, I don't want to get ahead of my story.

*"Doc and Pearl with grandson Terry, 1948."*

# Chapter Six

## GROWING UP IN FRESNO IN THE EARLY 1900s – MY MOTHER'S PARENTS

*"They do not love that do not show their love."*
—William Shakespeare, English Poet and Playwright

I called him Grandpa Shack, and I know he loved me, even though in those days men were less overt in showing their love. Most everyone else called him Lee or Shack. His given name was Leroy Barton Shackelford. Le Roi is french for "the king," and I later learned he did have kings in his ancestry, but his was a simple life. Born on a small farm in rural western Missouri, his family moved to California in November 1903, when he was two years old. He grew up in Clovis and lived his entire adult life in nearby Fresno. His schooling was limited, but he was capable of reading the newspaper. He always studied the Sports section first. When I brought him the paper from the front porch he'd say, "Pass the Sporting Green, please," because the Fresno Bee printed their Sports Section on green paper in those days.

In the mid-1920s, Lee and brother Otha were living with their father in a one-room house that JB owned; it sat just east of downtown Fresno, at 459 South Backer Avenue. Four sisters had all married. When Lee married Mabel Hildreth in early 1928, they rented a house on Webster Street. At some point, after my mother Patsy was born, the three of them moved back to the house on Backer Avenue— JB had remarried, after being a widower for sixteen years, and moved on to a new home.

Their little house had no indoor plumbing; everyone used an outhouse. Mabel washed their clothes by hand in a washtub and pinned them onto a clothesline to dry in the sun. That washtub was also the closest thing they had to a bathtub. They dreamed of a bigger home, and they were saving part of Lee's earnings. When some foreclosed houses (sitting in the right-of-way for construction of new State Highway 99) went up for auction, they bought one. That must have been a thrilling moment. They moved that house from the Germantown area of Fresno to the front of their lot on Backer, and over time improved and added onto it in several stages. Lee and Mabel built all of the additions, sometimes with the help of other family members. You didn't have to apply for a permit in those days, you just grabbed your hammer and got started. When Mabel found a snake in the outhouse, she set out to add a bathroom with indoor plumbing. I remember that bathroom and being bathed in its small bathtub many times. We could only put about two inches of water in the tub for fear of "flooding the little cesspool" that they had created and buried in the backyard. This was in the days before Fresno's public sewer system extended to their neighborhood.

They moved the little house, which still sat in the back of their lot, by rolling it on a series of logs about 50 feet north; there it became a garage. Inside, Grandpa built a very sturdy workbench along the back wall, adding shelves for his old well-used hand tools— he could fix just about anything. If I became overly dirty or muddy, Mom would bathe me in the garage, in the cement sinks they installed next to their recently acquired wringer-style Maytag clothes washing machine. A large walnut tree grew next to the garage, and every year Grandpa would shake it to bring down the nuts. I enjoyed helping him collect them— for hours he patiently sat on the back porch with a bowl in his lap, cracking the hard walnut shells and placing the freed nuts into glass jars. He loved to cure green olives every season in some large ceramic pots that resided out back. I watched him rinse olives as part of his daily process, and I particularly enjoyed tasting the first ones when they were deemed ready.

In my younger days, when Father was serving in the Korean War, I lived there on Backer with Grandpa, Nana, Mom, baby brother Randy, and Uncle Dale, my mother's younger brother. In later years, Randy and I slept over on many weekends. I learned to ride my first little bicycle in their gravel driveway, and Grandpa would often play catch with me there alongside the house.

Grandpa Shack was a lifelong baseball fan of the major league St. Louis Cardinals, from his native Missouri. He always took his vacation in October so he could listen to the World Series on his radio. After the invention of television, he bought a black and white TV so he could watch weekend baseball broadcasts. Dizzy Dean was his favorite commentator. Dizzy, a retired Cardinals' pitcher, was a country boy from Arkansas with a particularly creative vocabulary, such as "He slud into third base." If the game got boring, Dizz might break into singing a rollicking rendition of The Wabash Cannonball. Grandpa frequently attended the Fresno Cardinals minor league baseball games at Euless Park and each season would take Randy and me with him at least once.

Grandpa also loved the Country Western music programs which he could barely see with snowy over-the-air reception from the Bakersfield and Tulare television stations. He enjoyed performers such as Merle Haggard, Buck Owens, Jelly Saunders, and Dave Stogner; they were early stars of the "Bakersfield Sound" that developed in the San Joaquin Valley in the 1950s. The Lawrence Welk Show and Ed Sullivan Show were other weekly television favorites.

At one Friday night family gathering, after enjoying some watermelon for dessert, while sitting on the grass in the Shackelford backyard, the idea of the brick patio was dreamed up. The next day Grandpa brought in a load of bricks in a borrowed pick-up truck. That evening we returned and someone began to lay out a few bricks, experimenting with possible patterns. In a spirit of "let's just do it," the backyard patio was created that same night. Grandpa Doc Oftedal was there and he played his usual role as "the Supervisor." I was still young; I remember carrying one brick at a time. Work continued into the wee hours, long after I fell asleep.

Lee worked at the Fresno truck maintenance shop of the California Division of Highways. It was the only job he ever had. He worked as a painter, mechanic, and general handyman, but he had started as a blacksmith's apprentice. The Great Depression hit a lot of families hard in 1930 and it persisted for the entire decade. Work was hard to find for many during that severe economic contraction, and unemployment increased to 25 percent in the U.S. In 1939 the federal government started taking Social Security Tax directly from paychecks, and even those who were fortunate to have work felt the impact as they saw their net pay go down a bit. Thankfully Lee's steady paychecks carried them through those rough times. He retired in 1963. Along with many others, I attended his retirement dinner; he was duly honored and friends told colorful stories from earlier days.

Lee lived in that "new house" on Backer for the rest of his married life, and he lived there briefly after Mabel's passing, until he was no longer capable of looking after himself. Grandpa Shack died in 1985 of complications from Alzheimer's disease after living a full life of 83 years. "Vive le roi!"

We lovingly called her Nana Shack. Her birth name was

Mabel Vera Hildreth. Grandpa called her Mabe and others called her Mabel. After coming from Idaho as a teenager, she lived the rest of her life in Fresno. She was fearless and could do just about anything. We have a picture of her standing in front of her brother's old motorcycle, which she enjoyed riding. My mother said Mabel re-roofed the her house on Backer with help from her father, and she was physically involved with all the additions.

Backer Avenue was a gravel road in the early days. There were no sidewalks or curbs, and most of the neighboring families were of very simple means. When the Great Depression started in 1930 Mabel was only 23. Patsy, my mother, had been born two years earlier. Many unemployed and homeless people were roaming the streets and railways in search of work or something to eat. Any family with a steady paycheck was considered fortunate, and I am certain that my Grandparents deeply appreciated their good fortune. I remember being told by a neighbor that my Nana Shack would always provide some kind of food for anyone in need who knocked on her door. I can only imagine how trying a time those days were and picture people wandering through California towns, like Fresno, in search of hope and opportunity. Many of them were so-called "Okies" who had driven west after losing everything when their farms failed and large parts of the Midwest turned into a giant dust bowl. This was only a few years after Mabel's own arrival in California, and the days of living with her family in some fruit orchard were no doubt still fresh in her memory.

When World War II started in 1939, Mabel was in her early 30s. In 1940 she gave birth to a son, Dale. During the War she worked in a classified position for the "Filter Board," somewhere near the current Fresno Fairgrounds. She would only divulge that they helped track the positions of our ships, troops, and aircraft. On a sadder note, the Horse Racing Track at the Fresno Fairgrounds also temporarily served as a Civilian Assembly Center where Fresno's Japanese Americans (some of the 120,000 in all) were assembled before being sent to live in Internment Camps until 1946.

Nana Shack was a very loving woman, and I was blessed to personally experience the depth of her love. She never hesitated for a second to take my brother and me for a weekend stay-over so my parents had time for a getaway or just some quiet time. Even when her arthritis progressed in later life and her fingers became stiff and painful, she would still play cards with us any time we asked. The favorite game in her family was cribbage, and she patiently taught us. She would howl in pretended agony whenever she lost her crib or got skunked.

She passed along to me one of her basic philosophies- "Regardless of how anyone acts, if they are family we love them no matter what." Those words made such an impression on me that I can still picture her face and hear her voice from that conversation.

When my mother Patsy was in the 11th grade she had a good friend, Valera Wrye, who lived up the street. For whatever reasons Val's mother decided to leave town and she left her teenage girls behind in Fresno. Mabel invited Val to live with them and treated her as a daughter; she shared a bedroom with my mother until they finished high school. Shortly after graduation Val married and moved out. "Aunt Val" was always listed in the family obituaries as a surviving daughter.

When I went away to college Mabel frequently sent me letters. Hand-written letters were a primary form of communication in those days, because long-distance telephone calls were quite pricey. Even though they had modest means, Nana was able to enclose a $20 bill about once a month. Often the letters were brief but they gave her the chance to add "Love, Nana" at the end so she could let me know she was thinking about me. Local telephone calls were free, and my mother said she looked forward to talking with her mother by phone every day of every week of every year.

Nana was a competent cook, having mastered a few simple recipes that were family favorites. She cooked a roast every Sunday, and she always put white bread and jelly on the table for dinner. I loved her biscuits and milk gravy (with bits of bacon) for breakfast and mashed potatoes with gravy again for dinner. She decorated fancy cakes for occasional extra income, but our birthday cakes were always homemade and usually pretty simple. She baked from scratch and her cakes always came out dry; my father teased her repeatedly by calling her Sawdust Nelly. On the other hand, her apple dumplings and fruit cobblers were exceptional. She loved to can fruit, and I enjoyed helping her carry the beautiful jars of packed fruit down to their little dug-out cellar, where she would carefully line them up along the shelves she had built. Behind the shelves she had carved out a cleverly concealed niche in the dirt, where a few valuables were hidden; I was sworn to secrecy about that. I was too young to appreciate what a few old coins might mean to a woman who grew up picking fruit while living in a tent, a woman who raised her family during the great depression and yet always found food to share with someone who knocked on her door. She was my Nana, and whenever I was around her all I felt was the fullness of her love; I felt safe, and I knew my world was full of possibilities.

Mabel was a tireless worker and a diligent housekeeper. One day in May 1981, at age 74, she collapsed and was taken to the hospital. A few days later she passed on. She left behind a cleaned house, freshly mowed lawn, and a cake in the fridge. I am forever thankful that I got to see her in that hospital and tell her one more time how much I loved her. I quickly drove up from Southern California with my family. She was unconscious when I entered the room. Her body was agitated, curled up in the bed, as a machine was pumping oxygen into her lungs— but I observed signs indicating she could hear me. As I lightly stroked her head and whispered softly and appreciatively of many precious times together, her body relaxed and her energy field became more peaceful. I didn't want to leave, but as I slowly walked out I felt her spirit resonating inside me. I still do. She was the most loving person I have ever known, and she taught me through her example that actions speak much louder than words.

*"Nana and Grandpa Shackelford."*

Here are a few more words about my Aunt Val. Of course Fresno is famous for raisins. Stories of drying fruit go back to the earliest of mankind's history, but dried grapes and figs became a huge commercial growth engine for Fresno. It started in 1873 when William Thompson imported some grape cuttings to California. The thin-skinned and seedless Thompson grape variety was well suited for the Central Valley climate and produced a particularly sweet and flavorful grape. When some of them unintentionally dried before picking, he sent them to San Francisco for sale and a new industry was started. In World War I the dried fruit, very popular as a portable snack, was sent to our soldiers. During World War II the War Production Board ordered California's entire wine grape crop to be made into raisins for our troops. Still, many people turned up their noses at the funny looking brown things with wrinkled skin, simply because of their appearance. The real surge in worldwide enjoyment of raisins came because of some inventive marketing by the California Raisin Cooperative, called Sun-Maid Growers, which was founded in 1912. It was a successor organization to the first co-op founded back in 1898 by Theodore Kearney, known in his day as the "Raisin King of Fresno." As a young boy, I watched numerous television commercials featuring the dancing and singing California Raisins. Mabel's "other daughter" Val married a raisin farmer named Earl Roque and she worked at the Sun-Maid processing plant. In fact she once appeared on a popular television program called "I've Got A Secret," broadcast from New York City. Her secret was that she worked as a "Raisin Inspector," and she successfully stumped the panel. The last time I saw her, she was in a Fresno hospital dying of cancer. It had been some time since our previous visit, and she was happy to see me. We chatted about her family and shared memories from older times. Her memory was amazingly clear. She seemed to be quite at peace with the process of dying, making the visit a memorable experience for me.

I also need to add a paragraph about my Uncle Dale. He was only 7 years older than I, and he seemed like an older brother. He had a very kind and gentle heart, and I lit up every time I saw him. He would always move to the little bed on the back porch whenever Randy and I slept over in his double bed. When Elvis Presley began his singing career in 1954, Dale was 14 and I was 7. Dale owned a little 45 RPM record player, which played those small vinyl disks with the large hole in the middle. He happily let us listen to the Rock and Roll music coming out of the tiny internal speaker, which was neither high fidelity nor stereo. He would let me sit on his Schwinn bicycle before I was big enough to ride it, and just about anything he did or accomplished was an inspiration to me. He nailed a basketball hoop onto the eve of the back of the garage, and I fell in love with the game of basketball while shooting hoops there with him. I attended his graduation ceremony at Roosevelt High School, a first for me. When he graduated from Fresno State College, majoring in Civil Engineering, he was the first in our family to receive a college degree; I was about 15, and I knew I wanted to go to college, just like Dale. He joined the U.S. Air Force after college and met his wife-to-be Marge while stationed at the San Vito dei Normanni Air Station in Brindisi, Italy. It was a small facility surrounded by artichoke fields and grape vineyards, located on the heel of Italy's boot facing the Adriatic Sea. We heard later from Marge that the base's secret mission was to intercept and analyze radio transmissions from countries in Eastern Europe during the Cold War. Dale was the in charge of maintaining the facilities. She was teaching school. When he was transferred to his next assignment in Texas, she remained to finish her contract in Italy and they corresponded by mail. In December he proposed to her in a letter, and in her next letter back she accepted. They married the following July in a beautiful log chapel overlooking Auke Lake in her hometown of Juneau, Alaska. Dale's parents flew up to attend the ceremony, along with Lee's brother Otha and his wife Rose. Dale and Marge gave birth to two beautiful children- Gina in 1970 and David in 1973. Marge still says with deep feeling that Dale was "the one and only love of her life." Dale died of cancer in May of 1986. He was only 45. When he was in his last days, Kathryn and I drove to Fresno to spend a few hours with him and Marge in their home. Dale was in pain and weak, resting most of the time in his bed. I wanted our visit to be a celebration of love and fond memories rather than a time of sadness, but my heart was very full. All of our hearts were full. I said a prayer out loud and we shared a time of Attunement with my hands at his feet; then a great light filled his room and all four of us were absolutely silent for quite some time. We looked at each other to confirm we were all sensing the extraordinary and powerful vibrations that I can only describe as the substance of heaven. Dale smiled at me; I think he knew that a doorway was beginning to open for his approaching transition.

This was one of several events in my life which led me to KNOW that we are part of a much larger creation, which extends beyond personal perceptions and experiences, and that Life is eternal, with only a portion of it lived in this place and time we call Earth. I can still feel Dale's gentle spirit.

# Chapter Seven

## MY FATHER WAS A HERO

*"I love the heat."*
—Bill Oftedal, favorite saying

Why everyone called him Bill will forever remain a mystery. Even he did not know why. Jasper Martin Oftedal, Junior was born August 29, 1926 at his parents' home on Nevada Street. That was the year NBC began broadcasting over radio waves. People were just beginning to buy radio receivers— made possible by new vacuum tube technology. Ratcliffe Stadium was built in 1926; it was only four years after the Fresno Bee newspaper began publishing, five years after the foundation of Fresno State College, and eight years after the opening of the first Sun Maid Raisin processing plant. Fresno County had a population of 123,000.

Bill would live his entire life in Fresno, where it typically reaches highs of 100 to 110 degrees in summertime, and Bill said many, many times, "I love the heat." It was true, he loved nothing more than gardening in his yard in the middle of a scorching afternoon. In later life he loved sitting in a lawn chair on his driveway while watching the world go by, in the heat.

From an early age, Bill was known for sleeping-in or napping whenever hc could. He grew up in the city, but as a youth he got to spend time outside of town at Grandma Oftedal's farm. He owned only one set of overalls and told us that he had to go to bed and had to take a nap when they were being washed. He thought that was funny, since he loved to take naps. He also told a story of driving his Grandma to town one day when she had a toothache and needed to see a dentist. He assured her that he knew how to drive, even though he was not yet a teenager. She worked the car's crank to start the engine and off they went down California Avenue. Later, after they returned from town and a successful tooth extraction, his uncles were surprised that Bill had done the driving and they asked him when he had learned to shift gears? He replied, "What's that?" The whole trip had been in first gear.

Bill was never a serious student and he shared stories of ditching school. One time he and his friends Robert Hupp and Peewee hitchhiked up to San Francisco to take a look around. I asked him where they slept and he told me, "Oh, somewhere in a field beside the road." When Pearl Harbor was bombed on December 7, 1941 and the U.S. entered WW II, he was 15 and still a student at Fresno Tech High School. Most people heard the news about Pearl Harbor over their home radios. Just after his seventeenth birthday, Bill talked his father into signing for him so he could join the U.S. Navy. His mother had refused to sign. He claimed that his school principal promised to give him a graduation certificate when he returned, but that never happened. Bill felt he could read and write well enough and now it was time to move along and serve his country.

*"Bill Oftedal, 1943."*

He enlisted September 15, 1943 and soon boarded a train to Pleasanton for his basic training at Camp Parks. He spent most of 1944 and all of 1945 on a small troop transport ship, the USS APc-28, in the Pacific. He repeatedly had opportunity to help their one cook on kitchen duty, that is whenever he talked back or questioned his orders. When the cook was reassigned, the ship's senior officer "suggested" to Bill that he take over the cooking duties since he had the most experience in the kitchen of anyone remaining. He spent the rest of WW II and his later tour in the Korean Conflict as a cook in the Navy. He grew to enjoy the cooking, which later led to some jobs as well as many years of cooking and baking at home. Bill spent a total of two years at sea before returning to the U.S. He told us stories of a stormy Pacific Ocean that sometimes sent giant waves to toss their little ship around; no one wanted to eat much on those days. Thankfully his ships were never directly in the heat of battle, but he and the APc-28 were present at the Battle of Okinawa. It was the bloodiest battle in the Pacific, resulting in 91,000 military deaths (and over 149,000 civilian deaths) by the time fighting ended in late June, less than two months before Japan's surrender.

He met Patsy Shackelford shortly after his return to Fresno in mid-1946. They were married in December. He was 20 and she was 18. In November 1947 he was working at his father's Seaside Gas Station in Fresno when I was born. When his second child Randy was born two years later he was driving a delivery truck for Kohlman's Pickles.

On June 25, 1950, Kim Il Sung ordered the North Korean Army to cross the border into South Korea. Less than one month later, Father was recalled to active duty with the U.S. Navy. The USS President Jackson was a 492 foot-long transport ship with a crew of 512 and capacity for carrying another 1,382 troops plus cargo. On September 15 it had been one of 261 naval vessels at the Invasion of Inchon, discharging men from the 1st Marine Division onto the beach. Over the following days they received casualties for return to hospitals in Yokohama and the U.S. On October 11 in San Diego, Bill reported for duty on the Jackson and the next day they sailed with cargo back to Japan. When they returned to San Francisco, Mom took me with her on a bus trip so she could see him. This was one of my earliest memories, though all I remember is trying to see his ship, anchored in the bay, as she held me up to the bus window. After six months on the Jackson, Father was reassigned to the USS George E. Davis, a destroyer escort ship that had been decommissioned at the end of WW II. He reported in April 1951, in San Diego, and cooked for the crew that was working on recommissioning the ship. They sailed October 11, went through the Panama Canal, and delivered the ship to the Newport (Rhode Island) Naval Training Station, where it would serve as a training ship. Bill was transferred from active duty on December 1, and after a bus trip across the U.S. he was home in time for Christmas. He spent the rest of his four year term as a USN Standby Reserve. The Korean Armistice Agreement was signed in July of 1953 and the hot-war changed to a tense standoff on two sides of the Korean DMZ which continues to this day, over 60 years later.

In 1953 Bill and Pat bought their first home. It had 2 bedrooms and 1 bathroom and was located on Fedora Avenue in what was then Fresno's far north end. They secured a low-interest (zero down payment) mortgage thanks to the G. I. Bill, which had been passed in 1944 by Congress at the behest of President Franklin Roosevelt. The house cost $10,900 and payments on their 25-year mortgage, including taxes and insurance, were $68.00 per month. Father was only earning around $250 per month at the time and told us that he would often wake up in the night, nervous about the huge payments and wondering if they had done the right thing.

When my sister Kelley was born in 1959, Bill was working at Drug Service Inc., a wholesale pharmaceutical distributor founded in Fresno by three Stanford graduates. After years of loyal service, he was surprised to receive stock options. When DSI was later acquired by a much larger Bergen Brunswig, gains from that stock provided a substantial portion of his retirement savings. The style of the company changed after that and he decided to leave. He spent some time buying, restoring, and selling antique furniture, working out of his backyard and garage. Later he took a job driving locally for DiSalvo Trucking and joined the Teamster's Union. Pension income from the Union also came in handy in retirement. Dad and Mom paid off that "huge" $10,900 mortgage and later sold the house to my sister Kelley and her family. Our parents moved next door into a smaller house that they built with the proceeds from the sale.

I've mentioned how Father loved going to Las Vegas and Reno whenever he had the chance. He played the craps tables for hours and hours at a time. He would only stay at a hotel downtown, because he felt the Vegas Strip was overpriced. He never liked to fly in airplanes; he always insisted they travel by car. Father felt the scenery en route through the Mojave Desert was quite beautiful. Mom endured the drives, with only a minimum of quiet grumbling, staring at the cacti and dry scrub for hours while praying that the car's air conditioning system would survive.

Bill's favorite vacation spot was Santa Cruz and he drove our family there many summers. He loved to play cards— our favorite game was a three-card game called Knock Poker. It was simple enough for all of us to play, and as many as eight could play at a time. We would each wager three pennies or three nickels in those days, but after inflation it eventually became quarters. Later in life Dad taught Randy and me to play Casino, a favorite card game from his Navy days.

Bill was known for smoking and drinking, which he started as a teenager, as did a lot of folks in those days. He tried to stop unsuccessfully many times, but he made up his mind that on his retirement day he would never drink again. He had already quit smoking shortly before his retirement. He successfully achieved both goals cold turkey, which was an amazing accomplishment.

During retirement his hobbies were golf, collecting golf balls, and going to yard sales. He bought a monthly pass immediately upon retirement and golfed five mornings every week with some buddies. He didn't care about his score; he did care about how many lost golf balls he managed to collect each day as he walked down the edges of the fairway and along the edges of the water traps. His golf ball collection became so extensive that it almost filled his two-car garage. Eventually he donated all of the balls, clubs, and shoes that he had collected to local schools.

One highlight of his retirement days was a trip to Norway in 1996, via a few days in Amsterdam. We hoped to meet relatives we did not know and see the old family farm where Bill's grandfather Martin had lived as a youth outside of Stavanger, before he took the boat to America. Using business miles, I was able to book first class airline seats out of SFO for Dad, Mom, me, and my wife Kathryn. Father was so cheerful, he would frequently strike up a conversation with almost anyone, as if they were old friends, be it the stewardess, a waitress, hotel employees, or distant relatives. We often marveled at how relaxed he could be and at how others took to him so easily. The relatives in Norway treated us like royalty and the trip was unforgettable. Norway is a beautiful country. We had so much fun that, in spite of his dislike of airplanes, the four of us went back again two years later. This time we went through London. We also included a second side trip to the beautiful city of Bergen, Norway.

Norway was occupied by Germany during WW II and many of

our older relatives still had strong memories. Some of them had been evicted from their own homes so that German officers could use them. They wanted to know about Bill's days in the U.S. Navy during WW II, and he told them a few stories. Even though he served on a support ship and fortunately was never directly in battle, one of the cousins spoke up and said very emotionally, "Thank you, you were a hero!"

We brought back some wonderful souvenirs, including warm Norwegian wool sweaters that were gifts from cousin Magnar Oftedal. He owned a sweater weaving factory which we enjoyed touring. Tore Oftedal gave us each an original painting from a large collection of local landscapes he had painted. I purchased some locally spun blue and white variegated wool yarn from a shop in Oftedal Valley and hand-carried a large shopping bag full of that yarn all the way home. Kathryn later crocheted every inch of it into a marvelous extra-long afghan that keeps me warm on winter evenings and is one of my most prized possessions.

Bill suffered a heart attack during his retirement and survived after a triple bypass surgery. This near-death experience was quite humbling and he was a kinder and gentler man afterward-until Alzheimer's Disease began its slow and debilitating progression. He was often very confused in the latter days and sadly could no longer play cards, though he did enjoy sitting with Randy and me while he watched us play. He suffered tragically from this disease in his last years, and eventually needed to be moved to a locked facility where he could be assisted around the clock. His abilities to manage even his basic daily functions eventually waned.

I visited Father for the last time when he had been hospitalized for pneumonia. My brother and I talked out loud about old memories. Father didn't say much, but gazing into the distance he said a few words that indicated he could generally remember the old trips we were recalling. I told a story about us gambling together one time in Las Vegas, when he made an amazing run of passes at a 25 cent craps table. Another gambler at the table, who had done quite well during the run, flipped a black chip to Bill as a tip. We later found out that the black chip was worth $100. Bill made much more from that tip than either of us had from the bets we made with our small stacks of 25 cent chips. He smiled while remembering that one. As I left his hospital room and said my goodbyes I gently kissed him on his cheek and tenderly gave a squeeze to his shoulder. As I told him I loved him for the last time, he said, "Goodbye Terry." I was so moved in that moment that he recognized me and remembered my name. Just down the hallway I began crying uncontrollably and fell to my knees for a few minutes, overcome with knowing that he would soon be gone. Those times were even harder on my mother and sister, particularly on days when he did not remember who they were.

He did his best as a husband and father and was a very faithful provider. It was a very rare day that he did not go to work, even if he was sick. He was buried at Belmont Memorial Park, during a graveside ceremony with many family and friends attending. The U.S military sent an honor guard who performed a 21-gun salute. They took the U.S. flag which had been draped over his casket and with ceremony and dignity folded it and presented it to our family in recognition of his military service. Bill was a member of the "Greatest Generation." He served his country in two wars without hesitation, and yes to me he was a hero.

I learned many things from my father; I admit that some of them are just now beginning to sink in. This realization, that his lifetime is still affecting mine, is quite powerful. I'm pausing as I write this, feeling the full impact of the idea that my words and actions will continue to affect others in the same way beyond my time on Earth— not because I am writing my story in a book, but because the energy behind our words and actions exists in a place not limited by time.

# Chapter Eight

## FOR MY MOTHER, FAMILY WAS EVERYTHING

*"I'm fine, how are you?"*
—Patsy Oftedal, favorite saying

Born in 1928 in a nursing home in the Germantown section of Fresno, she was named Patsy Reabel Shackelford, but she preferred to be called Pat. She lived at a time when there were not many fences around yards. She could walk through neighbors' yards to visit her grandparents, who lived on Recreation Avenue a couple of streets behind her house on Backer Avenue. She attended grades one through six at John Burroughs Elementary, followed by Roosevelt Junior High and then Roosevelt High School. All of them were walking distance from home.

One day in her Senior year she and a friend ditched afternoon classes and took the city bus to Weymouth Pool (in west Fresno near Chandler Air Field) for a swim. There she met Bill Oftedal, who had just returned from his WW II service in the Navy. She graduated from high school in 1946, a first for our family. Later that year on December 28 they were married by Reverend Emery Snider in a ceremony at the home of Bill's parents on North Effie Street. Bill's sister Mary was the Matron of Honor and her husband Lee Amer was the Best Man.

Pat was quite industrious and held several jobs prior to marriage, getting around mostly by city bus. Aunt Myrna, who was managing an Associated Gas Station on Van Ness Street, provided her first job. Pat moved on to work the soda fountain at Kress' 5 & 10; then she became an usherette at the Kenama Movie Theater, working four or five days a week on evenings and weekends. She later worked in the children's department at Montgomery Wards. After marriage she worked with Aunt Val in the office at the Cherry Avenue Auction, which was a flea market and animal auction located just outside of town. I remember her working from home some years doing childcare, phone solicitation for donations to the Disabled American Veterans, and clothes ironing for other families. Finally she worked for almost twenty years at the Fresno City College Book Store, putting away a good portion of that income into a tax-deferred retirement account. Their retirement savings and social security income, along with Bill's pension, successfully lasted them through their latter years— a little remained after Mom's passing, which she asked to be distributed to her children and grandchildren.

Pat loved family and enjoyed any event where she got to spend time with her three children, eight grandchildren, or three great-grandchildren. Birthday celebrations might be a dinner together at the Old Spaghetti Factory, attended by as many of the family as available. Whenever I brought my family to visit, it was a great excuse to go out to eat as a larger group. She liked Mexican food at Javier's and Chinese Chicken Salad at the Shanghai Restaurant. Often we would bring home Chinese food from Fong's or Sun Sun Kitchen. Just being together and visiting was all she cared about and her spirit was infectious, inspiring friendly and respectful relationships around her.

She had her own favorite foods. She loved strawberry soda, a hot dog in a slice of white bread with jelly, and she always had room for a piece of chocolate candy. Sometime after I was born, she got her driver's license, and I remember her driving us downtown to a tiny restaurant called the Coney Island to enjoy a couple of their heavenly chili dogs loaded with chopped red onions. Mom and Dad enjoyed going out for a steak dinner on special occasions— one of their local favorites was The Outpost. Other times we all went to one of the area's Basque restaurants for a multi-course feast which always ended with fried chicken infused with garlic. Anyone walking past us the next day knew what we had eaten; the scent of the garlic would ooze through our pores for at least 24 hours.

She enjoyed cooking, though she didn't learn until after she was married. Growing up she had been looked after lovingly by her mother and had never cooked or done much housework. Food preparations might begin a week in advance for a family vacation to Santa Cruz. When her car arrived, all able-bodied children and grandchildren lined up to welcome Grandma and Grandpa and to help carry the many boxes and coolers of food from the car's big trunk. For years they drove a pink Lincoln Continental. We called it "Big Pink," and that trunk was huge. Mom always claimed to dread that someone might go hungry while on vacation; something that never happened. Family members held friendly differences of opinion as to whether her potato salad had too much mayonnaise, but it always sold out. As soon as breakfast was finished, she would soon say, "What's for dinner?" and joyful planning for the next one or two meals would begin in earnest. Preparation for holiday meals was also a multi-day task, and Christmas cookies were started weeks in advance.

Dad passed first, and his last years were quite emotionally and physically challenging for Mom. After we completed a family intercession and moved him to the 24-hour care facility, she sold their little house and moved into an apartment next to Kelley and her family. Even when you know you are taking steps necessary to providing for the increasing needs of someone with late stage Alzheimer's, feelings of guilt are unavoidable. If you find yourself in that situation, do not hesitate to seek help. More than 5 million people in the U.S. are currently suffering with Alzheimer's and that number is forecasted to triple over the next 35 years. It is the sixth leading cause of death in the U.S.

http://www.alz.org/care/alzheimers-late-end-stage-caregiving.asp

When Mom had a bad fall, we knew she needed more help as well. In her last four and half years, she lived in her own apartment in a wonderful assisted-living facility called The Fairwinds. It didn't feel like home to her at first, but her kind demeanor and outgoing personality led to many friendships. In the last years, her body was in increasing amounts of pain as several of her systems and abilities waned. But whenever she was asked by anyone, "How are you?" her answer was always, "I'm fine, how are you?" She was truly interested in others and didn't want the attention on her. After she passed, she would never have guessed how many residents and staff came to us and told us tearfully how much they thought of her as a friend. They all said she would be profoundly missed.

She lived her whole life in Fresno and, like most of her generation, she grew up in the city rather than on a farm. Her family did not have a lot of money, but she said they always had everything they needed. Her generation saw and experienced many changes. She lived through a great Second World War and other regional conflicts, the breakup of the Soviet Union, the tearing down of the Berlin Wall, and a rise and fall of fears of nuclear war. She lived the change from reliance on buses and streetcars to owning a family car, and she saw the emergence of affordable air travel. She went from party-line telephones to private phone numbers (she had the same number for 56 years) and then to cell phones, networked computers, instant messaging, and video chats. The invention of retirement savings accounts allowed many in her generation to enjoy a decade or two of retirement living without having to depend on others for subsistence or having to work up to one's final day.

Through all the changes in world politics and advancing technology, family was everything for her. She was a bright light; she would be missed by many, but never forgotten. After many years of calling her regularly on Saturday mornings, frequently I still think, "It's time to call my mother." For a few minutes I will sit quietly and commune with her sweet spirit. I can still hear her voice saying, "I'm fine." It feels like she is thinking about me too. Those soul-to-soul connections never go away.

*"Bill and Pat in Norway, 1996."*

# Chapter Nine

## DO WE REALLY CHOOSE OUR OWN PARENTS?

*"My religion is simple. My religion is kindness."*
—Tenzin Gyatso, The 14th Dalai Lama

If we do choose our own parents then I chose well. I was blessed in childhood in many ways, and I was always treated with kindness. My parents loved each other, and I was born in the U.S.A.— a land of peace, security, and opportunity— a land with clear air, plentiful food, and clean water. The United States of America was founded on principles developed by a group of real visionaries and written into a code of law called the Constitution. It defined an innovative approach to government and everyone should read it. The Preamble to the Constitution is a brief statement of purpose worthy of repeated consideration- http://en.wikipedia.org/wiki/Preamble_to_the_United_States_Constitution.

This does not mean that ugly and hateful things have not occurred in our nation. Injustices to Native Americans, slavery and racial injustices, deprivation of women's rights, and limitations of opportunity based on numerous differences have been realities in our society for too long. Unfortunately the quest for truly equal civil rights is still a work in progress.

My experience growing up in Fresno, California seemed one of protected innocence, abundance, adventure, and wonder. I am indebted to my parents Bill and Pat Oftedal, and I later took pleasure in telling them as often as possible, "I love you." This simple statement when delivered from the heart seems to be the most powerful gift anyone can give.

I know that many people have not grown up in a happy and protective family environment. This can make it more difficult in later life to trust and open ones heart or to forgive, particularly relating to those who may have done ill or simply neglected them as a child. Special work is required to heal wounds from childhood days, and it takes time to understand that the longer anyone carries hurt or anger the longer that person himself suffers from it. Fortunately, everyone is born with a heart of kindness. We all have the capacity to experience intrinsic realities such as innocence, truth, and beauty. We all love it when we sense these spirits inside ourselves naturally resonating with something beautiful and true on the outside; something like an inspired piece of music, or a masterful work of art, a rainbow, a flower, or seeing someone perform a caring act.

One interesting aspect of my upbringing was that my parents never sent me to a church. Not once. Later I learned that they both did believe in God, but there was little spoken in our household on that topic. This turned out to be quite a gift. I believe that was their intent. I was free to explore on my own, and let my own sense of the Divine emerge in a natural way. When I was ready, my "empty canvas" would become a unique painting of inner explorations and realizations. But I was never doing it alone. There was always the Spiritual Wind. At first I was only vaguely aware of this powerful force which touches the lives of us all. How I learned more is a story for several later chapters.

# Chapter Ten

## MY EARLY FRESNO YEARS

*"'Pan, who and what art thou?' he cried huskily. 'I'm youth, I'm joy,' Peter answered at a venture, 'I'm a little bird that has broken out of the egg.'"*
—J.M. Barrie: *Peter Pan* (1904)

1947 was a time of hope and new beginnings. The horrors of World War II had ended two years earlier. Thor Heyerdahl sailed the Kon-Tiki from Peru to Polynesia. India gained its independence from Britain after 30 years of non-violent activities led by Gandhi. UCLA graduate Jackie Robinson was named Rookie of the Year in his first season with the Dodgers.

I was born at 12:41 AM on November 5, at Sequoia Hospital in Fresno, and named Terry Martin Oftedal. If it means anything to you, that made me a Scorpio, with moon in Leo, and Virgo rising. The "Martin" middle name was in honor of my great-grandfather who had braved the trek from Norway to become an American pioneer. I was delivered by Pierre LeMunyon, Doctor of Osteopathy. My father Bill and grandmother Mabel were waiting in a nearby room. Family members were not allowed in the birthing room in those days. I was not due until December so my arrival was a month early, and I have been challenged to exercise patience ever since. My mother told me she arrived at the hospital the morning of the previous day and her labor lasted 15 hours, until just past midnight. We stayed there for four or five days, typical at the time, before going home to the house on Backer Avenue where my parents were temporarily living with Mom's parents and brother. Father drove us home in his Nash Graham Coupe, which he had bought "used" from Grandpa Doc. He was working at his father's gas station at the time.

The three of us moved to a tiny one-bedroom house— a rental nearby on Eighth Street just on the other side of Ventura Avenue. Mom said she would often walk me in a pram nine blocks east on Ventura and then the half block up Backer Avenue to her parents' house. After my brother's birth we moved to a slightly roomier house further east, near the new airport. Known as Hammer Field when it opened in 1942, the airfield was operated by the Army Air Force through WW II. In 1947 part of the facilities was renamed the Fresno Air Terminal when civilian commercial flights began.

In July, 1950 Father rejoined the Navy for the Korean War. Mom and her boys moved back to the house on Backer Avenue, and we lived with her family. When Father returned in December of 1951, Nana and Grandpa moved over to live with Nana's parents, the Hildreths (four blocks further east on Recreation Avenue). I was about four when I ran away from home one time and trekked across those four blocks to see my Nana. I remember hiding under their back porch, because I knew I would be in trouble. They soon found me. After Nana fed me a little snack, my mother arrived. Yes, she did tell me not to do it again, but "the talk" was not as bad as I feared.

*"Terry on his first bike, in Grandpa Shack's driveway."*

I was almost five years old when I started Kindergarten at John Burroughs Elementary. Mom walked me to school at first; at some point after I turned five I convinced her I was old enough to walk by myself. She would still stand on Huntington Avenue one block from home and watch me going and coming the rest of the way. We walked together that block closest to our home, but at least I didn't have to endure my friends seeing me being delivered to school by my Mother, as if I was just a child. The next summer, the four of us moved to our very own new two-bedroom home on Fedora Avenue in the north end of Fresno. The population expansion was steadily taking over agricultural land. To make room for our sub-division, the developer uprooted massive orchards of fig trees. For years I would continue to dig up fig tree roots in our hard backyard soil of dirt and clay, while building small cities and little houses for our toy cars. Fig trees remained standing on the other side of Dakota Street, at least for a few more years.

For two and a half years Mom drove each school day to and from Alice Birney Elementary, because it was too far for me to walk. In the middle of my third grade year, a brand new Manchester Elementary opened just up the street on Dakota, and it was close enough for me to walk with my brother. I enjoyed the classroom times and marveled at what we were learning about the Solar System, California history, and a variety of other things. We even had instruction in singing and art in those days, and we still managed to master reading, writing, and arithmetic. I was a slow reader until I received some after-school tutelage by one of my teachers, with the help of some SRA materials that had been recently developed at Stanford University. I had wonderful teachers. I loved practicing and competing with flash cards which showed all of the basic multiplication combinations. During recess in the playground, I learned to play kickball, tetherball, and eventually softball. The city recreation department had budget money in those days for a person to lead us in after-school activities, and I was on softball, flag football, and basketball teams. As one of the youngest in my grade I was always less mature physically, but I played with great passion. It was all about the thrill of competing.

One fact of life in those days was the Cold War and a widespread fear of planetary nuclear annihilation. Between the U.S. and the Soviet Union there were far too many nuclear weapons and far too much political tension. Air-raid sirens, installed all over town, captured everyone's attention with their loud monthly tests. At school we took breaks for air-raid drills—

we were taught to duck under desks, as if that would do any good in the case of a nuclear explosion. Some people built fall-out shelters in their back yards, but I never saw one.

Commercial television broadcasting began in the U.S. in 1937 but the first receivers were expensive and there was not much programming. That changed over the following decade. Shortly after we moved to Fedora Avenue in 1953, my father bought a black and white television and installed it in our living room. Before that we only had radio— I remember listening to radio programs like “Amos and Andy” and “The Lone Ranger.” I climbed up a ladder onto the roof one day with Father; I helped attach a funny looking antenna to our chimney, and he ran some wires down through a living room window. This greatly improved our television picture quality, versus what we had seen using the small antennae that came with the set. Visual entertainment was an exciting improvement, particularly on Saturday mornings when my brother and I were allowed to watch our favorite programs. On weeknights our viewing time was strictly limited. In 1959, when I was about 12, one of our neighbors purchased a color television, the first on our street. Randy and I were invited one evening to watch “Walt Disney’s Wonderful World of Color.” I was impressed.

You have to remember that personal computers and handheld electronic calculators had not yet been invented. The integrated circuit microchip was also yet to be invented— all of the TV sets were powered by an array of vacuum tubes and one large cathode ray (picture) tube. Interestingly, home repair was a possibility in those days. I had watched Father do it. When the picture became distorted, I was allowed to unscrew the cardboard back panel and pull any discolored tubes from the chassis of the set. I put them in a paper bag and rode on my bicycle to the nearby Long’s Drug Store. There I plugged each of the tubes into a tester to confirm which of them might have burnt out. I bought a generic replacement on the spot, pedaled back home, and plugged all of the tubes back into the set. That usually fixed the problem, and we avoided the wait for a repairman. Little did I know that a massive technological revolution was about to begin in a few years. A cluster of cities north of Fresno would soon be dubbed Silicon Valley and play a major role in my future.

My first love was bicycle riding. Our streets were designed in a way that discouraged through-traffic, so it was safe to roam on our bikes for several blocks in any direction. Parents would keep watch from their windows, so even after dark we could play games like hide-and-seek or kick-the-can in the streets. When I started the 7th grade at Fort Miller Junior High School, I qualified for my first paying job as a newspaper delivery boy. I was now able to purchase a substantial bicycle at the Fresno Cyclery— I signed a contract and made monthly payments. I chose a black-and-cream colored Schwinn with heavy duty spokes and knobby tires, flat "Fresno" handle bars, and a heavy-duty rack on the back for carrying saddlebags full of folded newspapers. I served about 60 customers, and if I collected the $1.50 monthly subscription from everyone, I got to keep $25 to $30. BIG money! Every Monday through Saturday, in the afternoon, I rode up Blackstone Avenue to the Fresno Bee's "District 12" shed, where about 30 boys my age received our allotted newspapers. We always competed to see who could fold and rubber band them, stack them into our bag, and depart first. With full saddlebags I rode back to my "Route 1205" on Shields Avenue to throw one newspaper onto the porch of each subscriber. I became quite skilled at landing those papers right on the porch, tossing each one as I pedaled by on the sidewalks without slowing down one bit. I had to memorize which houses to skip; one mistake and I could run short. Finally I rode back home to complete the circuit. Roundtrip took about 2 hours if I hustled. In summertime temperatures often peaked over 100 degrees, sometimes over 110. I suffered but kept moving. On Sundays we delivered early in the morning, and the Sunday editions were extra heavy. On Winter days the morning rides could be really cold and sometimes foggy. I would dress in many layers of clothing, gloves, a pull-over ski mask, and a fur-lined hat. Thankfully snow was rare at our elevation. A McDonalds Hamburger restaurant, their first franchise location, had recently opened nearby at Blackstone and Shields. If my Fresno Bee monthly report card was perfect, I was awarded a coupon for a hamburger, french fries, and milkshake ("The All-American" combo) at McDonalds. That saved me the full price of $.50. I held that job for over 4 years and it provided me lessons in dependability, honesty, and salesmanship. Yes, salesmanship. Once every week I knocked on the door of the non-subscribers on my route.

A major benefit to that job was that I now owned a sturdy bicycle for riding in my free time, for commuting to school, and for speedy runs to the grocery store. I heard immediately when Mike Koop, my neighbor and fellow newspaper carrier, purchased a 10-speed racing bike and joined the Fresno Cycling Club. He encouraged me to join, and I saved money until I could buy my own Bianchi racing bike from Italy. Mine was not as fancy as

Mike's, but I loved it. I also bought my own Fresno Cycling Club bike shorts and jersey. On weekends I went on rides as long as 100 miles, training for category races against others of similar capability. I tried my best to trudge up that big hill on Friant Road in our main annual race, which drew riders from all around California, but my muscles had yet to really mature so it was a struggle. I was a late bloomer. Sometimes club members would gather to simply ride on a leisurely tour of some county road. It was a healthy sport and I made new friends. Bicycling is still my favorite sport. To this day I literally get a big smile on my face every time I pull out of the garage on my Trek bike for a ride up and down the hills of my neighborhood. My heartfelt thanks go to Mike's father, Mr. Kenny Koop, for carting me and my bicycle to all of those events.

Kenny had been on the pit crew for Indy Car driver Billy Vucovich in his younger days. Billy was a very popular Fresnan who won the Indy 500 in 1953 and 1954. Billy was leading on the 57$^{th}$ lap in 1955 when he was involved in a fiery crash and died. Kenny still loved auto racing and I was often invited to join his family on a Saturday evening drive out to Kearney Bowl in West Fresno. It was a quarter-mile dirt track. The noise from the cars was insanely loud in that little bowl, and our adrenaline would really pump. What fun! The most popular drivers of the day were Al Pombo and Marshall Sargeant, who often worked their way to the front of the pack and fought it out at the finish.

During Fresno's HOT summers, swimming was a popular way to cool off. I looked forward to Red Cross swimming lessons held at the San Joaquin Memorial High School pool. I quickly got over my fears and learned to love the water. Over a few summers I progressed through the classes, eventually gaining certification as a Junior Lifeguard. Learning to be at ease in water would open many enjoyable opportunities later in life— water skiing, swimming in lakes and oceans, and even snorkeling and scuba diving. Mom drove us to the pool and encouraged us every step of the way.

Those were wonderful days of youth, joy, and innocence.

# Chapter Eleven

## FIRST A BROTHER, LATER A SISTER

*"Cherish your human connections –*
*your relations with friends and family."*
—Barbara Bush, First Lady of the U.S.

My brother would become my best friend. Randy Lee Oftedal was born December 17, 1949 at Sequoia Hospital, just after I turned two years old. The previous evening Mom knew she was ready to deliver. Nana Shack came to drive me back to her house, and Dad drove Mom to the hospital. Since her labor with me had taken so long, he said he was going to load his Kohlman's Pickles truck for the next day's deliveries and would return shortly. This time labor only took a few hours; Randy was born shortly after midnight. Doctor LeMunyon called Father at work to deliver the news. I don't remember that. In fact, my memories are quite sparse up to the time I started kindergarten. I do remember Randy and I always sharing a bedroom, and we spent a lot of time together. His family nickname was "Baby Doll." He didn't care for that name as he got older; unfortunately a janitor at our school, who was a family friend, found out about it. Too bad for Randy— he was teased a lot.

At Santa Cruz, one of our favorite activities was spending hours at a time in the Fun House on the boardwalk (which really was made of wooden boards in those days). Admission was 25 cents for an entire day. We started with the giant Wooden Slide. After sprinting up stairs high into the rafters, we sat on burlap potato sacks to slide down side by side racing to the bottom. Next was the Spinning Wheel. When it stopped, we ran out as fast as possible to try to claim the spot on the very center. As the wheel reached full speed the centrifugal force would build up and everyone, except possibly the person at the center, would be thrown off into the cushioned rails. In the rotating Barrel, we walked up the wall and sideways at the same time in order to get out the other end before falling down. We enjoyed many other diversions inside the fun house; we ran around from one to another for hours. Our favorite treat on the boardwalk was eating an ice cream "sandae"— a chunk of vanilla ice cream (on a stick) covered with chocolate and nuts. Of course playing in the Pacific Ocean waves was the biggest attraction, along with relaxing and playing cards with family on the beach.

Another annual event was the Fresno County Fair, which took place every October. We saved our allowance dollars (and later money earned with our newspaper routes) so we could pay our own admission, buy whatever food we wanted, and ride those crazy carnival rides. We explored every animal barn and marveled at the people and animals; we always stopped to admire the newly-born piglets. We never raised animals ourselves, except for one pet rabbit named Thumper. Back in those days before any food allergies, I could enjoy corndogs, soft serve ice cream, corn on the cob, soft drinks, peanuts, and other carnival foods with seeming impunity.

Randy also enjoyed riding his bicycle. Many days we just cruised together around the neighborhood. Sometimes we rode to Perry Boys' Smorgy, at the nearby Manchester Shopping Center, to see who could eat the most fried chicken. At least once we happened to have a plastic bag in our coat pocket, so we took a couple of extra legs for a later snack. As we got a little older we were permitted to ride our bikes downtown to a movie theater like Hardy's, The Crest, or Warners. In one of them we watched The Haunted House with Vincent Price. We liked it so much that we stayed for a second showing. Meanwhile, unbeknownst to us, it turned dark outside. When we did not arrive home at the expected time our mother became concerned. She started roaming the streets in her car searching for us. Eventually she got the manager of the theater to find us and pull us out. It had been my idea, but we were both in deep trouble.

On Saturday mornings for several years Randy and I were on a bowling team together at Blackstone Bowl. We had our own balls and shoes and real bowling shirts with the name of our team sponsor on the back. Neither of us was that good, but one time I rolled a 232 and was stunned with amazement as my ball just kept rolling into the pocket and knocking down all of the pins. Father loved to bowl, and we enjoyed cheering for his Drug Service team in a night league.

We learned to golf, with instructions from Ray Forrester at the old Airways course. I never became very good, but a few times each outing everything in my swing synchronized the way it is supposed to and I really connected with the ball. Those are moments that lead you to enjoy the game. It was a healthy sport and we particularly enjoyed it when we got to play with Father. He had a short smooth backswing, and his ball usually lofted down the center of the fairway. He didn't seem to mind that our balls would usually take a meandering path to the green. Later, after he retired, it was a special treat for us to play a round and visit with him when he was so relaxed and enjoying himself.

In the summers, we spent many hours swimming and relaxing at a variety of Fresno's public pools. Our favorites were Blakely's, Airways, and the North Maple Plunge. We loved those big water slides, but the diving towers were too high for me. My fair complexion put me at risk of sunburns, but I had no knowledge of the potential for skin cancer back then. In the warmer seasons, movie drive-ins such as the Starlight, Moonglow, Sunnyside, and the Motor In were all popular. This was an affordable treat for most families, particularly when the price was only $1 per carload. If we arrived early, Randy and I could play on the playground up front and then change into pajamas in the back of our car, since we would usually fall asleep before the movie ended. When I was older I watched several renditions of James Bond and "Woodstock" at a drive-in, but very few have survived. Many have been converted to swap meets over the years or torn down for housing development.

Sometimes Randy and I were left alone at home while our parents went out for an evening. Mom would always tell us, "Don't stick any beans up your nose." This was her catch-all warning, meaning "Please don't do anything stupid." Sometimes that warning worked. One time we decided to watch a scary movie called "The Mummy" on television. The host told everyone to close the curtains and turn off the lights, and we did it. That made the movie even scarier. I think I peed my pants.

Randy's first car was a Volkswagen Beetle. It ran on regular gasoline. Unleaded had not yet been invented. The price of gasoline at the time ranged from 12.9 to 19.9 cents per gallon. He could fill up the tank for two to three dollars. Randy got a learner's permit at 15 1/2, then a real license at 16. He customized that Beetle a bit and took it out for runs on the local drag strip. He still loves to attend drag races and watch them on television.

In high school Randy began working part time at Gong's Supermarket; most of his career would follow in the produce business and retail grocery. His last job was with Frito-Lay, selling and stocking chips in local groceries and convenience stores. There, he was part of one of the most efficient and successful distribution systems in the entire history of the food industry. One benefit of living your whole life in one city is that you can develop long time friendships. Randy still meets up with some of his old buddies for a monthly lunch together.

He attended Fresno City College for one year and qualified for a 2-S college deferment from the draft. One year was all he could stomach. He began working full-time at Gong's Market and lost his deferment. As expected the local draft board soon called him for a physical. He failed for high blood pressure, at least partially due to his not sleeping and other intentional and stressful activities prior to the exam. The same things happened again on several retests, until he received a 4-X permanent physical deferment from the draft.

While working at Gong's he met Judy Blake, a girl who lived just around the corner from the market. Judy's mother, Noreen, thought Randy was cute and frequently sent Judy on errands to the market as an excuse for her to see him. Their first date was a B. B. King concert. In August 1973 they married at the Belmont Christian Church. I took the bus from Ashland to attend. My sister Kelley, who had just turned 14, was wearing a beautiful dress. I was one of the more colorful guests with long red hair, full red beard, and a custom-made long blue hooded robe. More about that later. Great people, great dancing, great food, and great fun. At a later anniversary party, their 25th, I made a surprise re-appearance dressed as a hippie. I no longer had a beard or long hair but Judy's father, George Blake, did a great job with make-up and false hair and I dressed in a sheet tied at the waist with a braided belt. Judy loved it when I made my appearance! We danced for hours. "Thanks again" to Randy's sons, who organized that surprise event. Randy and Judy have been married now for over 40 years and counting. They have two beautiful grandchildren. And they still live on Fedora Avenue.

We were best friends, but we were boys— with the usual sibling wrestling. It was difficult for Randy to follow after me in school. I was the great student from two years earlier, and he was just not as interested. Unfortunately too many people thought he should be more like his brother. He was always looking up to me, but sometimes I was not so kind to him. I later regretted this and brooded about it for years. I knew that older brothers had specific responsibilities to look out for the younger, and I had fallen short too many times. Eventually I had an epiphany and was able to tell him out loud, "I'm truly sorry for every time I treated you badly, I love you." He wisely smiled and gave me a big hug. Today, we are still best of friends. We video-chat once or more every week and enjoy visiting and vacationing together. We enjoy doing genealogy work together and share in new discoveries about our family history. He is a fine man, husband, father, and grandfather.

My sister Kelley Ann Oftedal has always been a different story. She arrived August 18, 1959; I was almost 12 and Randy was almost 10. We were awakened well before dawn and told that Nana was coming to get us, because it was time for the new baby's delivery. In those days there were no affordable tests to determine the sex of the baby before birth. We were all hoping for a girl. Father drove Mom to the Community Hospital in their Oldsmobile Rocket 88 convertible, which he had bought used, of course. He went downstairs to have breakfast, but labor only lasted an hour. Kelley was born around 5 AM, before Father came back up. Men were still not allowed in the delivery rooms. Mother and daughter came home a few days later, and I was thrilled.

I learned how to hold her, how to bathe and dry her, and even got unlimited opportunities to change the diapers. Yes, Sister, I did see you naked many times. With two older brothers, she was quite the tomboy and loved all kinds of sports. Even today she is a bigger sports nut than I am. On weekends in her house the television plays constantly with any and all of the current sporting events.

Some of my fondest memories (and hers) were times when I lifted her onto the back rack of my Schwinn bicycle to take her for a ride to the local grocery store. I slid her legs into my canvas Fresno Bee saddlebags, to prevent any accident with her feet and the spokes. She held tightly onto my waist and squealed in delight as soon as I took off. I also remember the three of us children lounging together for hours in our backyard above-ground swimming pool during those hot summer months. Unlike our Father, none of us EVER said, "I love the heat."

In early 1964, when Kelley was about 4 1/2 and I was 16, I drove her downtown to see a new movie by the Beatles— "A Hard Day's Night." It was crazy; there were SO many teenage and pre-teen girls in the line. They were screaming already. It was packed inside. I made Kelley promise me that when the other girls screamed, she would not scream. She promised. We both loved the movie and there was a lot of screaming, including my sister.

In the Fall of 1965 I left for college and missed much of the rest of Kelley's younger years. Being the only daughter she was dearly loved and no doubt gained extra privileges and leniencies never known by her older brothers. She developed a very warm and special relationship with both Mom and Dad that lasted a lifetime.

Kelley is very intelligent, but she got bored with high school and dropped out. For a while she worked at a local donut shop while still living at home on Fedora. Eventually she decided to become a nurse. Now she had a goal and was motivated. She got her GED, went through college with honors grades, and earned her nursing degree. She has worked for many years at Valley Children's Hospital, first in the O.R. and then in Administration (after adding her Master's degree). She is another example of how you can't force young people to do anything before they are ready. Thank you Kelley for your many years of serving children in need. When I think of you I always remind myself of the importance of timing and the need to honor natural rhythms.

Kelley met Doug Shannon at a party in January of 1978. He was a Fresno boy. On July 13, 1980 they were married in a simple ceremony in Las Vegas at the Silver Bells Wedding Chapel, with just a few friends and family in attendance. This was followed by a big reception party back home in the Fedora Avenue backyard. Over the following years they raised three wonderful sons together.

In January of 2011 Kelley and Doug joined us and a number of family members for a fabulous seven days of vacation in Cancun. We all decided to return the following year. Next time they wanted to bring their three boys. Unfortunately Doug was diagnosed just a few months later with a very aggressive type of liver cancer. He was in a lot of pain as it progressed quickly. It was a very trying time for the whole family. Doug died on August 29, one day before his 55$^{th}$ birthday.

Kelley did return the following January to Cancun with her three boys. We all had a wonderful time. Kelley is still dealing with the loss of Doug, but she continues to gain strength and has been an incredible single mother. We continue to meet up in Cancun. She has always been my favorite sister.

# Chapter Twelve

## FORSAN ET HAEC OLIM MEMINISSE JUVABIT

*"Perhaps one day it will be pleasing to remember even these things."*
—Virgil: *The Aeneid*

When I started junior high school the state of California was experiencing a growth boom. In just 20 years the state's population had more than doubled from 7 million in 1940 to 15.9 million. Fortunately for me the California school system at the time was one of the best, and I had the best teachers— the best of the best. My favorite teacher at Fort Miller Junior High (grades 7-9) was Ms. Robertson. She pronounced it "Mizzzz Robertson." She was passionate about the U.S. Constitution and knew how to make it interesting; she told everyone in her class that we would be required to attain a score of 99 percent or 100 percent on a national Constitution test. And we did! In the process we all gained a more informed appreciation for the privileges and responsibilities of being a U.S. citizen.

I particularly enjoyed my math and science courses. The work seemed easy and I excelled. We are all given different talents and gifts; mine related to numbers and problem solving skills. I was intrigued when first introduced to computers. Father took me to work with him one Saturday, and I saw their recently installed mainframe computer. It was housed in several tall metal cabinets, all sitting together in their own air conditioned room. The Data Systems Manager let me watch as he fed large stacks of key-punched cards into the automated card reader— this was how they input data and programming in those early days. Then I watched lights blinking on the cabinets as the computer performed its instructed functions, until a long paper print-out started spewing from its line printer. In my Junior year of high school, Mrs. Fields took my math class to Hoover High, to see a new mini-computer that had been installed there. This one was quite a bit smaller, but still filled the corner of its room. We received some basic instruction in computer programming, and we were each assigned to write something. It was my first experience in coding, at a very basic level. I wrote a short series of steps that would calculate the factorial number for all of the positive integers. When my program was fed into the computer, the high-speed line printer immediately began spewing out a long piece of fan-folded paper with a list of the integers in one column and the factorials in the next column. The printing might have gone on forever (I had neglected to write in an end command), but the tech stopped it. Mrs. Fields was impressed, which made me happy; she said my concept was "elegant." I wanted to learn more about the possibilities of computers.

I had varying degrees of interest in my other subjects, which were either a necessity for graduation or chosen to help me qualify for college. I was advised to take Latin as my foreign language, which I started in the 9th grade; I quickly learned that languages were NOT my gift. This was really hard work. Mrs. Harter refused to let anyone change to another language, repeatedly assuring us we were all in the right room. The highlight of the year was a weekend Latin Club bus trip to a California Junior Classical League (JCL) Convention at El Segundo High School in Southern California. After that experience, Latin became a bit more enjoyable.

When I started the 10th grade at McLane High in 1962, just before turning 15, I was actually looking forward to more Latin. My new teacher was one of the best— Frances Essley, a recent graduate with honors from the University of Washington. She was smart, she was motivated, and she loved what she was doing. She also sponsored our Latin Club, which was a local chapter of the JCL. I enjoyed new friendships through our club activities, such as car washes, community service, an annual city-wide Roman Banquet (to which we wore tunics and togas), and the much anticipated bus trip to the State JCL Convention. In my Junior year we attended the California JCL Convention in Cupertino and I was elected State President; my good friend Georgia Quick was elected State Secretary. We would be responsible to host the next convention in Fresno.

Inspired by our enthusiasm, Miss Essley decided to organize a train trip from Fresno to the National JCL Convention. It would be held in the summer of 1964 at the University of Illinois campus in Champaign-Urbana. We would sleep in college dorms for five days, attend general assemblies, participate in a variety of interesting contests and social activities, and meet students from all parts of the U.S. I was excited about the idea of traveling outside of California. Eight of us, from three different Fresno schools, purchased tickets on the Santa Fe Railroad. A small crowd of friends and parents gathered to cheer our departure from the local station. We slept in our chairs (we were young, no problem). We discovered the Vista Car, with its panoramic windows, and enjoyed scenery I had never seen before. We roamed all of the cars, striking up conversations with other people. Along the way other cars were added onto our train, and we met students from other states who were also heading to our convention. Needless to say we had a curfew, and Miss Essley enforced mandatory sleep hours. This was in the days when people ate in a real dining car with white table cloths and nice dinnerware. At each meal we would place check marks on our order sheet to tell the cook of our selected meal options, and we were served by a professional waiter who had been doing the same job for many years. The food was excellent— so sad that those real dining cars have disappeared.

*"California delegates to the 1964 NJCL Convention. Terry is front row, third from left; Miss Frances Essley is back row, first from left."*

The biggest surprise of that convention? I was drafted into running for National JCL President and was in fact elected. That earned an article and my picture in the Fresno Bee back home. We Californians would host next year's national convention at

USC. I had to resign the State President position, and we nominated my friend Michael Gromis to take my place. "Mick" did a fine job presiding over the next state convention in Fresno. At our sessions in the Roosevelt High School Auditorium I was a speaker. Public speaking— what a terrifying experience. I knew I would need more help on that in the future.

As a national JCL officer, Miss Essley informed me that she expected me to apply myself more diligently to Latin in the classroom and I would need to score only A's. In fact I became fascinated with the ancient stories we were translating and I even became somewhat expert in Greek and Roman Mythology. One of the other students in our Latin class, Terry Easley, was Senior Class President. He was also President of the local Youth for Christ Club, and he proposed an idea for drumming up more attendance. It was based on the popular TV show The $64,000 Question (which was a huge amount of money in those days). He would host a "64 Hamburger Question" challenge that would take place over several months of weekly YFC meetings. Every week, I was advertised as the expert in Mythology who would have to answer increasingly hard questions in order to double the number of hamburgers earned (or lose it all). The crowds did keep getting bigger every week, and I enjoyed the speakers at those meetings. In front of a huge crowd during that last meeting, I won; and I received 64 hamburger coupons for the local Burger Chef. Terry Easley ended up marrying Marsha Nebblesick, the cutest girl in our school, and today he is an accomplished author and poet.

What an experience I had hosting the JCL meetings and events at USC that next summer! It was August of 1965, just after my high school graduation. USC students are known as Trojans, so the theme of the convention was "Forsan Et Haec Olim Meminisse Juvabit." It is a line from Virgil's *Aeneid* which translates from Latin as "Perhaps someday it will be pleasing to remember even these things." In the story, Aeneas and his men were returning home from Troy after the Trojan War (around 1240 BC) and it turned into a multi-year epic journey full of challenges. His father died in a tragedy at sea and his men had become worn out and despondent, so Aeneas was encouraging them in a funeral speech. Those words have stayed with me over my lifetime. I have reminded myself many times that even in the face of the unexpected and moments of great sadness or stress, surely better days lie ahead; and with perspective, I may later even cherish memories from those previous trials.

Of the more than 100,000 student membership, 1,450 delegates from 34 states attended that convention. Several times each day I stood on stage and hosted our sessions. The colorful array of people seated in the large auditorium before me seemed immense, and I felt my knees shaking more than once. It got easier with practice. I persevered and gained valuable experience in public speaking. All of the attendees had a great time, and I was thanked and complimented for my part. I could feel my self-confidence growing. I also began to learn how to recognize others when they do a good job. I learned that simple acts with just a few well-chosen words can carry great power. Everyone deserves to be recognized and encouraged as part of their growing up experience.

I was a participant at the convention as well. I placed third in the Mythology contest for fourth-year students. We all marched in our tunics and togas over to the Los Angeles Coliseum for a Roman Banquet on the grass football field, where a sumptuous catered lunch was provided by Ringling Brothers. Inside the Coliseum I was interviewed by a couple of local television stations; they would later broadcast clips of the interviews on their evening news along with some colorful overhead coverage of the event they had taped from a helicopter. I even dated a couple of the girls. Linda Buck from Oklahoma was on my staff as National Vice President. She would soon start at Stanford. The next year when some of us drove to Stanford for a football game I arranged to see Linda. I took her to the Purple Onion Nightclub in San Francisco where we watched Miriam Makeba sing. Alice McCown was the President of the Tennessee JCL and I was quite taken with her, as were most of the other guys. She was blonde, beautiful, smart, and as I discovered, also a great kisser. We spent a couple of evenings together after the conference sessions. I exchanged letters with her the next year when she was attending Vanderbilt University, but it was just too far away for anything more to develop.

I attended the following summer's convention as a chaperone. Again we traveled by train, this time from Fresno to Bowling Green, Kentucky, the site of Western Kentucky State University. On the return ride we routed through New Orleans where we stayed for a couple of days and enjoyed a true cultural experience. We took a bus tour of the city. We ate lunch at the Court of The Two Sisters in the French Quarter. We even enjoyed a short ride on a Mississippi Riverboat, where Mick and I ventured up to the wheelhouse and the Captain let us pull the cord to sound the boat's loud steam whistle.

My life was enriched through these activities and I was blessed with many friendships. I learned about gods and goddesses and their connections to the planets and stars, which in various ways has provided me insights into the archetypes of my inner being— this would prove helpful in later years as I began to develop a sense of the cosmos and my part in all of it. I realized that I was learning about myself and my world through the experience of personal challenges, though none of mine would rival those portrayed in the ancient epic stories. At least that's what I thought at the time.

# Chapter Thirteen

## LIVING TO SERVE A GREATER PURPOSE: JACQUES DEMOLAY

*"When you dance, your purpose is not to get to a certain place on the floor. It is to enjoy each step along the way."*
—Wayne Dyer, American Author and Motivational Speaker

I have to dance? My initiation into a youth organization known as The Order of DeMolay provided further formative experiences during those high school days. Founded in 1919, it was a part of a family of Masonic organizations, along with Job's Daughters and Rainbow Girls for young women. Some famous DeMolays were John Wayne, Neil Armstrong, Terry Bradshaw, Walter Cronkite, Walt Disney, and President Bill Clinton. Robert Hupp (a Mason himself I discovered) agreed to be my sponsor. When I needed to start wearing neckties, I was sent to Robert so he could teach me how to tie a double windsor knot. I now had opportunities to dress up for social activities and dances. I increasingly enjoyed them, though I was still nervous interacting with girls. At first, dancing brought up simultaneous feelings of excitement and fear. How can I dance when my knees are shaking? Why do the girls seem so much more at ease? Was I the only one suffering such conflicted feelings? Thankfully I began to enjoy dancing. Understanding girls and relationships? That would take longer.

Important personal values such as patriotism, loyalty, respect, comradeship, and love of God were taught at the meetings and initiation ceremonies, all held in one of the local Masonic Temples. Through the stages of our initiation we learned more about the Knights Templar, a religious order of warriors which was formed around the year 1118 during the Crusades. Their mission was to protect Jerusalem and Christian pilgrims on their way to and from the Holy Lands. While the Knights took a vow of poverty, the Order itself began accumulating great wealth from appreciative bequests. As the last Grand Master of the Knights Templar, beginning in 1298, Jacques DeMolay answered directly to the Pope. A huge and nasty power struggle began, involving Clement V (who became Pope in 1305) and his ally France's King Philip IV, who was particularly desirous of the Order's financial and land holdings. Philip had already gained the cooperation of the increasingly powerful Inquisition. Jacques DeMolay was captured, accused of trumped up crimes, tortured, and burned at the stake in 1314. Knights were rounded up and most of them killed. The Pope, turning a blind eye to all of this, disbanded the order. You can read about it by googling the words "Jacques de Molay." I did not know it at the time but his burning at the stake took place in Paris on Ile de la Cite. It is a small island in the middle of the Seine, which turned out to be the location of my hotel during a later visit to France. At the time I had no idea that some of my own ancestors had fought in the Crusades.

In my college years, Jim Sims, one of my roommates, told me he was also a DeMolay. Jim had done a lot of research into the early days of Freemasonry in the U.S.— I found his stories fascinating. George Washington and most of the earliest Presidents were Masons, and some of the philosophies and symbols of the Masons were important elements in the founding documents of our nation. Look on the back of the one-dollar bill for an example. There is a lot more to those stories, all very interesting. The Catholic Church to this day does not like the Masons, but that is another story.

Inspired by readings of ancient Greek and Latin sagas, and now stories of medieval idealism and heroism, I was becoming even more interested in discovering what could be learned from further research. Over time my life experiences, coupled with learnings about truths revealed in earlier days, would accumulate to form the foundation for a personal quest— to understand life's purpose. Over time I also learned the importance of enjoying each step along the way.

# Chapter Fourteen

## MY FIRST BIG DREAM

*"Every great dream begins with a dreamer. Always remember, you have within you the strength, the patience, and the passion to reach for the stars to change the world."*
—Harriet Tubman, Abolitionist, Humanitarian, and Civil War Heroine

I became passionate about my high school days. I was learning a lot, but I had yet to learn how I might be able to change the world. Besides Latin Club, and later DeMolay, I joined a few other clubs, attended the usual high school classes, and did homework most evenings. I tried out for our high school football team my sophomore year, after giving notice on my newspaper business, but I suffered an injury before the season began and gave it up. One memorable event that year was the Cuban Missile Crisis (in October of 1962). Cold War tensions with the Soviet Union had been escalating. Everyone was relieved when President Kennedy and Premier Nikita Krushchev finally agreed to deescalation after a nervous standoff of military ships in the waters around Cuba.

One year later on November 22, a very popular President John F. Kennedy was shot and killed. This event shocked all of us. I've heard that every American remembers where they were when they heard about the JFK assassination. I remember. I had just come out of a classroom and was at my locker when Alicia DePrima came up to me and blurted out, "Have you heard that the President has been shot?" If there is a collective psyche, it was traumatized that day in a way that I did not experience again until 9/11/2001. Many still believe there was a conspiracy, rather than a lone gunman, behind the Kennedy assassination. Books, movies, and news stories have laid out theories and additional background. At this point in time, it looks like we will never learn the full story.

By my senior year I had a drivers license and a car— a used

1955 Chevy Bel-Air that my father bought from Uncle Dale. Cars of that era had a lot of room under their hoods, and I managed minor repairs and upkeep, such as replacing fan belts, a battery, or generator. I even installed seat belts, drilling holes in the floorboards behind the front bench-style seat and then climbing underneath to tighten nuts and lock washers onto the bolts. I was no mechanic, but I felt satisfied with my little accomplishments. Now that I had my own transportation I started a new job working for Robert Hupp as an after-hours janitor in the Service Department at Fresno Chrysler Plymouth. Most of my earnings went directly into a savings account for college.

I was becoming even more excited about the possibilities of college and consequently even more serious about nudging my GPA higher. In my junior year I took the PSAT exams and scored very high, partly due to the fact that I loved the challenge of taking tests and really concentrated. This contributed to my qualifying for a California State Scholarship which would pay four years of tuition to any university in the state. That year, one of my teachers drove four of us to a math colloquium on the Stanford University campus. I was impressed with their campus and all of the students bustling around. Bob Murphy, my father's boss at Drug Service, was a graduate of Stanford. He said he would recommend me for admission and that DSI would provide a scholarship toward my living expenses. I politely declined; Stanford just didn't feel right for me. I would later receive an acceptance letter from Fresno State University, but I had a strong sensing that I needed to go somewhere beyond Fresno— I had been living there my entire life.

One night on television I watched Walt Hazzard and Gail Goodrich lead a come-from-behind victory for the UCLA Basketball team in the NCAA Championship final game. I wanted to find out more about John Wooden and UCLA. Miss Essley had driven me to USC in Los Angeles during my senior year for a JCL Convention planning session; on the way home we drove down Sunset Boulevard and I had a brief glimpse of the beautiful UCLA campus. By mail I received a copy of the UCLA student handbook, which listed an incredible variety of available courses; many of them sounded really interesting. I was impressed. The competition for acceptance was intense, and it would only become more so in the future. By 2014 UCLA would become the most applied to university in the world with over 105,800 applications— there were only 15,760 freshman slots. The day I received my acceptance letter from UCLA, I opened it without a moments' hesitation. I also qualified for student loans. My dream to become a Bruin had come true. I was ecstatic.

The following days flew by. My high school odyssey was coming to a close. There had been no serious girlfriend relationship, just a little dating with friends such as Georgia Quick, Alana Brown, and Cheryl Nelson. I never even attended a Prom. I worked all summer (except time off for the JCL Convention). I was eager for the Fall trek to UCLA. There I would have numerous opportunities to reach for the stars; perhaps I would even begin to learn how I could change the world.

# Chapter Fifteen

## UCLA – GO BRUINS!

*"Fiat lux."*
*(Latin for "Let there be light")*
—UCLA Motto

It was 1965, and Fresno's long summer was refusing to end. I was almost 18, and I was full of confidence. I had received luggage as a graduation gift, and both bags were packed. Father drove me to the Greyhound station and I fearlessly boarded a bus for Los Angeles. Two hours later as the bus was cruising uphill, out of the San Joaquin Valley, I felt a surge of exhilaration— I even sensed a strong wind blowing at my back. I did not yet understand what it really was.

After collecting my bags at the West L.A. depot, I took a taxi to the hilly western edge of the UCLA campus where several dormitories had been built in recent years. I would live as a freshman on the sixth floor of a modern co-ed dormitory named Sproul Hall. Two to a room, we each had an extra-long bed, a small closet, and a desk. At the end of each floor was a lounge with television and tables for games or studying. Women's rooms were in the other wing, and on the ground floor we shared some large areas designed for relaxation and socializing. To the right of the main entrance was a large cafeteria; three meals a day were included in our fees. One day each week I took bedding and personal clothing down to the laundry in the basement and retrieved them cleaned that evening. My room had a glorious view of the western edge of campus, including the Student Union, intramural athletic fields, and some of the original buildings situated at the foot of Janss Steps. Immediately downhill I could see a large dirt parking lot (later to become a track stadium) and a newly completed Pauley Pavilion.

My days at UCLA were amazing. I learned a lot about how the world functions and a lot about myself. No more parents immediately at hand; I loved the independence. I was in charge of my time and could make my own decisions. What a place to grow into manhood! Years later I would hear about those same days back home— when my mother spent hours in her bathroom with the door closed, crying. Her baby had left the nest.

I discovered that tickets to sporting events were subsidized for students. Football cost $1.00 per game and Basketball was 25 cents. I never missed an at-home football or basketball game. The first game ever played in Pauley was a match between the UCLA Freshman Team (with Lew Alcindor, Lucius Allen, Kenny Heitz, and Lynn Shackelford) versus the defending national champion UCLA Varsity. The Freshman won! The varsity team did not repeat as NCAA champion that year, and we even lost the Pac-8 Conference Championship to an Oregon State team that played an agonizingly slow brand of ball control— there was no shot clock in those days. The next year would be different. Our Alcindor-led varsity team went undefeated, and we were NCAA champions for all three of his varsity years. In fact Wooden-coached Bruin teams would also win the following four years in a row. From 1964 to 1975, UCLA won an unprecedented 10 out of the 12 NCAA championships. Some incredibly talented players came to Pauley, like Pistol Pete Maravich and his LSU team. Even with exceptional defensive coverage by Heitz and Shackelford, Pistol Pete still managed to rain in amazing shots from all over the court. The quality of play in those games was so exceptional that later in the evening we would often watch the tape-delayed replay on television, with Dick Enberg announcing.

UCLA had a newly hired football coach- Tommy Prothro- who always wore a suit and carried a briefcase to every game. No one knew what was in the briefcase, and we never saw him open it. I suspected it was a list of trick plays. We upset a strong USC team that year— my first UCLA-USC game. I'll never forget seeing Gary Beban throw touchdown passes in the last 4 minutes to Dick Witcher and then Kurt Altenberg. We would play in the Rose Bowl! I bought a student ticket the moment they went on sale. I slept overnight with friends on the sidewalk of Colorado Boulevard in Pasadena on New Year's Eve, so we could be in the front row for the Rose Parade the next morning. Beatles music drifted from cars slowly cruising the entire night; Rubber Soul, had just been released. Many of my generation thought it was the best music ever— surely the Beatles would be a rock group for the ages. At the game, Michigan State was close to scoring in the last seconds of the fourth quarter and I was so nervous and excited that I ran from my seat down to the field. I was standing on the grass at the edge of the goal line to watch up close as our

Bobby Stiles tackled MSU's big Samoan fullback, Bob Apisa, right in front of me as time expired. We won, 14-12. Everyone erupted in excitement. I helped tear down the wooden goal posts and I took home a piece as a souvenir. Three years later Gary Beban would become UCLA's first Heisman Trophy winner. I was now a Bruins sport fan for life.

UCLA also organized intramural activities in just about every sport. Over 15,000 students participate each year. I played flag football, basketball, soccer, racquetball, and ran the intramural cross country race. In the primary sports many leagues were formed, and the winners of each qualified for a tournament. One year I played offensive center and defensive linebacker for a football team called The Tall Frogs; we almost made the finals. Another year I played on a basketball team called AMF with my friend Larry Smith; we lost just one game short of the tournament semi-finals.

I attended a lot of classes, and I did a lot of walking from one building to another. I started as a Physics major— I had aced that course in high school and liked it. I soon found that only 10 percent of each class would receive A's, that I was no longer one of the smartest students, and that most of the others would put in a lot more study time than I. Oh well, I got used to B's and C's. I did earn one A grade (besides PE classes) in Psychology of Human Relations— my favorite class at UCLA. This was a wildly popular lecture series taught by Dr. Carl Faber. Each quarter, in addition to hundreds of registered attendees, he allowed anyone who wanted to audit. We filled all the seats in the large auditorium for every lecture, and dozens more sat on the stage and in the aisles. He was quite sensitive in his presentations. He spoke about life, the art of communicating, and the great mystery of male-female relationships. In other courses we were required to read multiple books, but here there was just one text— this quarter it was *Zorba The Greek* by Nikos Kazantzakis. We also heard him speak repeatedly about *Siddhartha* by Hermann Hesse (the text from the previous quarter). I read both books multiple times. Dr. Faber held no tests, in fact the only assignment was to write one paper. For the first time I was writing about my inner feelings and thoughts, and I found more to think about after every class. At the end of his final lecture, all of the papers were brought out in large stacks. I quickly found mine; on the cover was a large A. It felt good.

I took classes in Math (calculus), Philosophy, Psychology, Literature, History, Life Sciences, Anthropology, Foreign Language (Latin and Portuguese), Business (contract law), etc.

The idea was that a liberal arts degree should represent completion of a well-rounded and broad education. Here are some related thoughts from the current-day UCLA Chancellor Gene Block. "Our universities should be a space where the leaders of tomorrow learn the skills that will strengthen civil society— to examine facts without bias; to understand complexity and nuance; to see each other without prejudice. Our students must understand the difference between zeal and zealotry."

Carlos Castaneda was an Anthropology Grad Student at UCLA during this time. I never attended any of his lectures, but I saw numerous posters promoting them. I later read all of his books about his interactions with a Mexican mystic named Don Juan. Those books are still in print and continue to sell, but many news articles later claimed his experiences were a hoax. Due to increasing attacks on his veracity, he became very reclusive from the 1970s until his death in 1998. Accounts available online suggest that his later workshops and closest female associates were recruiting followers into a cult, controlled by Castaneda. When he died of cancer, a number of his followers simply vanished. All very strange; but the books were extremely imaginative. Who knows how much of it was true. I particularly enjoyed my Anthropology classes at UCLA. Through them I gained perspectives from other cultures (historic and modern) that were different from the one in which I had grown up. I wanted to see more of the world, experience other cultures, and visit some historic sites.

My eventual major was Economics. I even learned a few things, like basic supply-demand theory and international trade theory, that would be useful later in my business career. I struggled with some concepts, and the texts required deliberate reading, but it was all part of a high-quality education. I would persevere and earn my Bachelor of Arts degree in June of 1970. Fiat lux? It would take more living before I learned how to invoke the creative power of our college motto- "Let there be light."

# Chapter Sixteen

## I FOLLOW IN THE LIGHT OF CHRIST

*"If thou canst bear*
*Strong meat of simple truth*
*If thou durst my words compare*
*With what thou thinkest in my soul's fee youth,*
*Then take this fact unto thy soul-*
*God dwells in thee.*
*It is no metaphor nor parable,*
*It is unknown to thousands, and to thee;*
*Yet there is God."*
—Ralph Waldo Emerson, "Know Thyself" (1831)

When I was ready to learn more about myself, the lessons usually found me, not the other way around as some might think.

I was enjoying dorm living my first year, but at the beginning of the second term I heard about something called Rush Week. The fraternities were hosting parties every night that week. The fraternity houses, located just down the hill, looked their best. They were filled with cheerful "brothers," and the girls present were very friendly. I had no intention of joining, but I met some people I liked at the Lambda Chi Alpha house. They were one of the older fraternities, and their flag football team had just won the UCLA intramural championship. I returned a few more nights; I felt very comfortable with the people. Terry Ogami invited me to join and I accepted.

I completed my Pledge semester while still living in the dorms. The "hazing" was very light, nothing serious, and the initiation ceremony was quite meaningful. I learned that the Greek letters Lambda, Chi, and Alpha were the beginning letters of three Greek words in a phrase which was the major theme for the fraternity. I swore never to divulge that secret phrase, but look at the title to this chapter for a clue on the translation. I experienced other teachings such as one on forgiveness, based on the story of the prodigal son in the Bible. This side of my fraternity experience would remain with me vividly. Those teachings would have even more meaning to me later in life as I became increasingly intent on understanding life and my life purpose.

My "big brother" was Michael Elley, a wonderful man who was a professional singer in addition to being a full-time student. He volunteered to look after me. When James Lee (one of the brothers) broke an arm, Mick spent many hours holding his hands over James' arm— they believed it was aiding in the healing. Both of them swore they could feel heat coming from Mick's hands and that they actually felt energy moving. Little did I know that later in life I would receive training in Attunement and spend thousands of hours in the same kind of subtle-energy work.

At a rush party the following year we booked an entertainer named Chuck Norris. He was 26 at the time and just starting to become known as a martial artist. He would later have his own television series- "Walker, Texas Ranger." He talked about his personal code of honor, which included positives such as, "I will look for the good in everyone, and make them feel worthwhile." He requested a volunteer, and I was pushed to the front of the big living room. Chuck proceeded to demonstrate some of his martial art skills, and I was suitably embarrassed. He was very quick. Thankfully there was no contact and no injuries. Everyone loved it.

We held a lot of themed parties. One Saturday I decided to attend a costume party as the Incredible Hulk. I painted my whole head and body bright green; I was wearing only some small shorts. That afternoon I had been subjected to a head shaving, but I talked my tormentors into giving me a Mohawk haircut instead. Why not be unique? By this time I owned a 305cc Honda Super Hawk motorcycle, useful for getting to class around the far-flung campus. I joined in a very noisy parade of motorcycles over to Sorority Row where several of us would pick up our dates. My date was appalled at my appearance, but the shock wore off in a moment and she came with me anyway.

At the end of another party I lost a bet, and two of us had to streak naked around our very large block. You better believe we ran our fastest. Something called the Undie Run now takes place every Spring during Finals week at UCLA. Campus police even turn out to control traffic at major intersections. Over five thousand students, both sexes, show up for a jog to reportedly "relieve the Finals pressure." Articles in the UCLA Magazine say they all wear undergarments (or less). Don Craig and I may have started something on our little run.

One other dubious distinction I held was my fraternity's record for chugging a 16 ounce cup of beer. Lance Pugh was my coach. The whole thing was quite entertaining when we did it at a few parties. We began each time with him hypnotizing me in a most dramatic manner, while planting suggestions on how I should optimize the efficiencies of my motions. He made a big production out of it. Then I would start taking a series of increasingly big breaths while focusing my eyes intently on my cup. Lance would entice a volunteer or two to compete, but they were always crushed. My best time, from the cup leaving the table until it touched down again empty, was 1.86 seconds. Jim Sims clocked it with his stop watch. That record may still stand. As I said, a dubious distinction.

I did try my hand as much as possible with dating girls. It wasn't as easy as it might seem. Only one relationship got serious. I'll talk about that one later. If I asked out an attractive co-ed who was Jewish (and there were a lot of them at UCLA), I was usually turned down. She would say that her family and faith wouldn't allow her to marry me so there was no sense in even dating. It also cost money to date; I had to be creative. Movie theaters were particularly expensive. Usually my dates were to fraternity parties or sporting events. In those days the Bruins played "home" football games at the Los Angeles Coliseum, before they moved to the Rose Bowl. Getting to the game was a social event in itself as almost every dorm floor and fraternity rented a school bus for the trek up the Santa Monica Freeway. I went solo most times.

Getting dates was also time consuming. Many Fridays I attended Beer Blasts at one fraternity or another, to celebrate the end of the class week. All of them offered free beer; most featured an inexpensive local band. They all played "Purple Haze" or "Hey, Joe." Jimi Hendrix was immensely popular at the time. I always went solo, talked to girls who I met there, and danced a lot— thinking maybe I would score a date for later. On a rare occasion I would get asked out. One friendly young lady told me she had two tickets to a live play showing in nearby Westwood. The play was called McBird, a satire on the LBJ presidency. I went and we both enjoyed it. Then she invited me backstage to meet the star, who happened to be her uncle. It was Hal Holbrook. I got to chat with one of my favorite actors! I loved "Mark Twain Tonight," his one-man play in which he brought to life one of my favorite writers. I can't remember her name, and I have no idea why I didn't date her again.

I tried out for a popular television program called "The Dating Game," and I was selected. When it was time for the taping I rode my motorcycle to the studio in Hollywood. I wore a green wool blazer over a contrasting green turtleneck shirt, and I tied a paisley silk scarf around my neck. My hair was cut short, in a popular collegiate style. I thought I looked pretty cool, but she could not see the three guys on my side of the divider. The "bachelorette," who was named Penny, asked some pretty silly questions. She chose one of the others, and I missed out on the free date. Every relative in Fresno and beyond watched the evening my episode was broadcast; it was my big television debut. No doubt we were forerunners of today's more convoluted Reality Television dating shows.

We did a lot of "guy" things. One night several of us crowded in a car and drove to a club in Hollywood to see jazz guitarist Wes Montgomery playing at Shelley's Man Hole. Another weekend night Tom Wheeler and I drove to the Anaheim Convention Center to see Ray Charles and his Band, with special guest Billy Preston on organ. Tom was from Atlanta and a huge fan of Ray, so after the encore I said, "Let's go thank Ray." I grabbed Tom's elbow and ran him backstage just in time to meet Ray being guided to his dressing room by his manager. Clearly there was not as much security in those days. Ray flashed his famous smile as we both shook his hand and told him how much we loved the show. An amazed Tom Wheeler told him, "I'll never wash this hand again." One evening five of us jumped in a car and drove to Las Vegas. It was my first time. My driver's license said I was 21. I probably had around $20 to gamble, but the table limits were a lot lower then— even so, my gambling initiation did not take long. We explored the Strip for a bit, grabbed a 99 cent breakfast at one of the casinos, and then drove back in time for classes the next morning.

One of my fraternity brothers, Larry Smith, was a local who initially commuted from the San Fernando Valley. Pamela Jekel was his one girlfriend throughout college. They married after graduation and later she became a very successful writer and painter. Larry and I shared an apartment near campus our Senior year, and Pam was there much of the time. The three of us became good friends. Larry's father, who liked to be called Smitty, was a bricklayer. The previous summer I had lived with Larry at his parents' home in Tarzana while we worked as laborers for Smitty to earn money for our next school year. By the following summer his parents had moved back to their native Iowa, so we flew to Des Moines and worked another summer with Smitty. The pay was good, we got to work outside in the sun, and we thought that carrying and loading bricks and mortar onto scaffolds was great muscle-building exercise. Larry's parents both had big hearts and treated me like a second son. They were very generous in providing me room and board both summers. I could tell many funny stories about Smitty and his good buddy Lowell. They were both colorful characters.

On July 20, I was in Des Moines. Televisions everywhere received live coverage of Neil Armstrong and Buzz Aldrin successfully landing and then walking on the Moon. On the Moon! It was an amazing accomplishment, based on the efforts of many Americans— the culmination of a challenge set forth years earlier by a visionary President John F. Kennedy. That summer of 1969 was also called "The Summer of Love." We did not go to the concert in New York, but we did get to see the movie "Woodstock" in a local drive-in theater in Des Moines. I loved the music of course, but the demonstration of peace and acceptance between so many people became a symbol of hope for our entire generation. So far I have only met two people who were actually there in person at the concert. I heard a joke that said, "If you claim to remember being at Woodstock, you probably weren't there."

When we returned to school Larry and I worked part-time at Woody's Smorgasburger in Westwood, right on the edge of the UCLA campus. We both needed to earn extra money, in addition to our summer-work savings and student loans. We fried burgers fresh to order and then the customers would load them up with any combination of toppings. Woody's was very popular and particularly busy at lunchtime. When the charcoal grill was fully loaded with patties, I had to concentrate to avoid burning any of them. The pay was minimum wage, but I did get one free meal per shift. I made the most of that benefit; it was my main meal of the day. I figured it made up for the low wage. The downside was that I ended each shift with grease all over my body and really needed a shower. The hairs on my forearms were always singed. I learned that I did not want to do that for the rest of my life, so it was another great motivator to stay focused and get a degree.

I should clarify that most of my time was not spent partying and playing intramural sports. More of my time was spent roaming the campus from lecture to lecture, reading, writing reports, studying for tests, and taking tests; if not, the alternative was flunking out and winning a free pass to Viet Nam. I was fortunate however to become directly involved in UCLA's varsity athletic system. This opportunity was unexpected, and it would bring bigger challenges than I had ever before faced. At the same time I would come to know myself in a new way.

# Chapter Seventeen

## THE INSPIRATION OF JOHN WOODEN, J. D. MORGAN, AND JOHN BISSET

*"Make each day your masterpiece."*
—Coach John Wooden

Everyone at UCLA respected Coach John Wooden, and his accomplishments were exceptional. He taught his basketball student-athletes about his "Pyramid of Success," a collection of personal ideals. He was also frequently invited to speak to larger audiences in classes and clubs. His ideas carried power because he lived his ideals. He walked his talk. This philosophy was shared by our Athletic Director, J.D. Morgan, and it pervaded the entire UCLA Athletic Department. I found it to be a lot more appealing and mature than "Go out and beat that other team, or else you are a loser."

Two seasons before my arrival, J.D. hired John Bisset to coach Crew. Bisset had been a coxswain on the University of Washington Varsity Crew, then he was their successful Freshman Coach. Crew (Rowing) was, and still is, one of the most respected Olympic amateur sports. The UCLA boathouse is a thirty minute drive (if no traffic) south of campus. It straddles a manmade jetty that forms a division between Marina del Rey and Ballona Creek. The jetty extends out to the breakwater, and the breakwater protects both the marina and the creek from the Pacific Ocean waves than can become quite strong. It is a beautiful setting for all kinds of water sports. Our boathouse, completed in 1964 at a cost of $47,900, had docks for launching boats into both the Marina and the Creek. UCLA's 2,000 meter races were held in the Creek, and at high tide it was wide enough for three lanes.

The President of my fraternity, Jim Sims, had earned the Stroke seat on UCLA's Varsity boat in the Spring of 1966, my Freshman year. Some of us drove down to Marina del Rey to watch his biggest race of the season. It was a three-boat race against the powerful University of California Crew from Berkeley and USC. Cal had sent crews to the Olympic games and won gold medals. We had never beaten them. As the Varsity boats rowed up the Creek, hundreds of fans ran or rode bicycles alongside on the banks while screaming encouragement to the oarsmen. The crowd was particularly concentrated at the docks, about 500 meters from the finish line. As the oarsmen approached that point they could hear a roar of noise, but for them it was all in the background. They were focused in their boat, concentrating on maintaining rhythm, and struggling to provide more oxygen to muscles that were screaming to their brains. The race lasted about six minutes, but to those in the boat it seemed a lot longer. Our Varsity Eight beat Cal that day for the first time ever and I was thrilled. Jim was really thrilled, and of course his story would be retold in great detail many times for years to come. Craig Bleeker, Rik Cooke, and Randy Grittman were in that UCLA boat, and they would soon become fraternity brothers and lifelong friends. At the end of the season, for the first time, UCLA sent our Varsity boat to Syracuse to participate in the IRA Regatta. We finished thirteenth in a grueling three-mile race that took us almost seventeen minutes to complete.

In addition to everything else I was doing, Jim talked me into trying out for the Crew program in the Fall of my Sophomore year. There would be a chance for a varsity letter, travel, and opportunity to expand both my physical and mental capacities. He promised I would learn lessons that would last a lifetime. He was right. I had the size and a good solid frame, and I worked very hard. We spent many agonizing hours rowing on the water, we lifted weights, ran, and climbed ropes. We did resistance work, pulling ropes through a devilish device called an Exer-Genie. Some early mornings we met as a team on campus to race up and down steps in the new track stadium. Rowing challenges a particular sets of muscles, primarily in the legs, the back, and the forearms. We worked each of those muscle groups in every imaginable way. We also developed our cardiovascular stamina. Of even greater importance was the strengthening of our minds. I was learning how to discipline my mind, and my mind was learning how to discipline my body. I was working to make each day a masterpiece.

Weekdays most of us bused down the San Diego Freeway to the Marina for afternoon practices. It would often be dark and cold by the time we had showered and boarded the bus back to campus. Then we had to endure the L.A. freeway traffic jams. If

I was lucky I might get home sooner by catching a ride in the back of Jim Sims' 1964 MG Midget sports car. There was no back seat in the Midget, it had only a small shelf, and there were only two doors. Bleeker would squeeze into the shotgun side after I had wedged myself behind his seat; the whole drive home I would lie on my side with an arm on Craig's shoulder and a leg over Jim's shoulder. Once home I'd find a meal left on the stove in the kitchen by Florida Taylor, our beloved fraternity cook of many years. Next was nightly reading and study, ultimately followed by eight to ten hours of very deep sleep. Each night my last thoughts were prayers that my sore and aching muscles would recover enough by the next morning so that I could make the walk to my classes.

*"Preparing to launch our shell;*
*Randy Grittman, Craig Bleeker, and Terry Oftedal."*

On Saturday mornings we focused on rowing. Our parade of long eight-oared shells circled Marina del Rey lap after lap doing drills, short match races, or simply putting in miles at a low pace. The marina was lined with thousands of colorful sailboats and the entire setting was gorgeous. Sometimes we heard words of encouragement from the sailboaters, out for a day of leisure. Sometimes we would sneak a peek out of the boat to see a television or movie star in one of the sailboats. Coach was always trailing our boats, bundled in his warm coats, watching from his motorized launch and shouting instructions or technical tips to us through his megaphone. Each lap as we approached our docks, we silently prayed it would be the last lap for the day and that he would shout to send us in. But in the mornings the water was usually still. It was in fact the best time for rowing, so we put in a lot of miles. I had grown from about 5'8" as a Sophomore in high school to 6'3" as a Sophomore in college. I would reach 6'4" in another year. By the racing season in the Spring of 1967 I was rowing in the third boat with other back-up oarsmen; only the first two varsity boats got to race on Saturdays during the season. I still had a lot to learn, but I was showing promise. Coach Bisset wanted me to gain some experience, so he assigned me a seat in one Junior Varsity race against the UC Santa Barbara JV boat. WE WON, by several lengths! I was hooked. My competitive fires were now really blazing. I knew I could do even better the next year. I earned a beautiful blue wool letterman's sweater, which I wore to campus many days. That year's Varsity boat was again successful. They went undefeated in the regular season and won the Western Sprints, beating second-place Washington by four seconds. The Varsity went to the IRA again and improved to ninth place.

In previous chapters I may have told some stories about a few indulgences in alcohol, but every year from January to June during serious training season, I assure you that I never touched a drop of alcohol. We were dedicated to becoming the best that we could be. By my Junior racing season in 1968 my body had matured significantly. I earned the number 6 seat in the Junior Varsity boat. My single oar went out the port side of the boat, so I was always a "port oarsman." At the 6 seat, I was the front man of "the engine room." We sat in the middle of the boat, seats 6 through 3. Usually we were the four largest men in the boat. We had some great victories and some agonizing losses. That year the Varsity, JV, and Freshman Eights all flew from LAX to Oakland, to race Cal in a dual meet on the Oakland Estuary. It was my first airplane ride ever. Big Walter Brennan, who raced behind me in the 5 seat, sat next to me on the plane. During the flight he was the most nervous of us all. We teased him mercilessly whenever the plane hit an air pocket, and each time poor Walter's knuckles turned whiter, clutching the arm rests even tighter. My boat won the JV race and I still have the Cal shirt that my opponent gave me after we returned to the docks. Our Varsity boat was leading their race when the tiller broke. Coxswain Bob Schwartz no longer had a way to steer, but he remained calm, directing one of the oarsmen in the bow to ease up a bit. That rebalanced the power between the port and the starboard oars. The shell straightened back out, and though it slowed a bit, they went on to win. The oarsmen in the Varsity boat were still bigger, stronger, and more experienced than I, but for one race that year I was again given a gift— a seat in one Varsity race. We beat UC Irvine on Ballona Creek in that race and I qualified as a UCLA Varsity Letterman. I earned a blue letterman's jacket with leather sleeves and a big block "C" stitched on the front. I wore that jacket a lot.

The Varsity boat went to Syracuse for the IRA again in 1968, and I got to go along for my first time. This was definitely the high point of our season. I was the port alternate. I was ready to fill in if anyone on the Varsity port side got sick. Otherwise all of the alternates organized ourselves into pick-up boats and held our own informal race. The IRA was the closest thing we had to a national championship back in those days. All of the major universities participated, except for Harvard and Yale. They kept to their own traditional match race instead, on the same weekend. It was hot and muggy when we arrived in Syracuse after a long plane flight. Our team traveled wearing white shirts and UCLA neckties with handsome light-blue colored team blazers; we were certainly visible moving en masse through the airports and proud to represent our university. Upon arrival, a reserved bus took us to the Fairgrounds where a lot of oarsmen would sleep in bunk beds lined up in rows in one big room. Our meals in the Fairgrounds Cafeteria were pretty basic, it was not the fanciest of facilities. But the rowing was gorgeous. We rowed in borrowed wooden shells, to save the significant expense of having our's shipped all that distance. In the days before the prelims, everyone practiced by rowing up long canals that stretched for hundreds of miles. The waters were perfectly still; both banks were lined with mature trees and draped with gorgeous greenery. It seemed a bit surreal— the scenery was so different from the modern man-made sailboat marina back home. Many universities brought three to five teams (Varsity 8,

Freshmen 8, Lightweight 8, etc.). At nine men per racing shell (eight oarsmen plus one coxswain), it added up to a lot of people running around. Throughout the day, men holding their boats waited in line to get into the water at the busy launch site. We observed many traditions and also some pranks. The University of Wisconsin rowers would go out late one night and paint a huge red "W" on the train trestle bridge that overlooked the docks. The next night the Washington men snuck out and overpainted the same "W" with purple or white. And on it went through the week.

We raced on a 4.5 mile-long Lake Onondaga which had plenty of width. In fact, up until 1967 there was just one big 3-mile long race for each category, and all of the boats took off together lined up far across the lake. Beginning this year, 1968, in order to help our American teams become more competitive internationally, the IRA switched to the shorter 2,000 meter Olympic distance. This was more of a dash. That was fine with us. It was the distance we had been racing all year. This made the IRA into an even bigger and more complex event. They now ran a series of preliminary races and consolation races before the finals (in each competition class). With six boats maximum in each race, it amounted to a lot of races spread over more than one day. On the day of the finals, thousands of family and fans attended, picnicking for hours along the grassy shores. Our Varsity won the Petite Finals race that year— seventh place overall. Another improvement over the previous years.

By my Senior season in 1969 I had matured significantly and gained a lot of muscle mass. We had ropes hanging from the boathouse ceiling, and I could now climb them to the top as many as five times in a row just using my arms (no legs). I still hated to run, not my favorite form of exercise, but I could row for hours. John Bisset had retired to take a better paying position in UCLA Administration, and Jerry Johnson was our new coach. He had been a stroke at UW. I rowed the 6 seat in the Varsity boat for almost all of the races that season. Our Varsity boat finished second to Washington in the Western Sprints. We sent our top two boats to the IRA, but my Varsity boat struggled. I'll skip the details except to say one of our oarsmen was unable to finish in our last race. Our Junior Varsity boat, with Duncan Henderson at stroke, was at their peak and they did great in their Finals. I earned a blue wool blanket with the UCLA block "C" letter stitched onto the center of it, and I was named Most Valuable Oarsman at the Crew Banquet. I really was learning about capabilities of endurance and fortitude that I never knew I had. I felt great physically. I also had a lot of energy in bed, but that is another story. I said I wasn't drinking; I didn't say I wasn't dating.

In those days the NCAA required that Freshman participate on a Freshman team and then you had three years to participate on a Varsity team. But in 1969 the NCAA changed that rule and said everyone had 4 years of Varsity eligibility. Because I had not competed as a Freshman, I was awarded a fourth year of eligibility. I was one of the first two athletes in any sport at UCLA able to compete for a fourth Varsity year. I'll call it my second Senior season. The internal competition was intense that year. Duncan Henderson moved up from the JV boat to become varsity stroke, and Jim Jorgensen moved from stroke back into my 6 seat. I spent most of that racing season in the Spring of 1970 in the 6 seat of the JV boat. We flew up to Seattle that year for a match race against the University of Washington. We raced up the Mountlake Cut on "Opening Day." Rowing to the starting line, we saw hundreds of sailboats and powerboats everywhere. My JV boat lost in a close finish to an outstanding UW JV; their guys were huge. UW's Varsity had not been beaten in Seattle since 1947, but our Varsity boat was very strong and in a thrilling finish we won by inches. UCLA's Varsity also later won the Pac-8 championship at the Western Sprints in Long Beach. I was certain that my JV boat helped make our Varsity faster that year, after we pushed them hard in all those many practices—my JV boat would consistently win in side-by-side 500 meter sprints during practices, which drove Coach Johnson crazy. I did get in at least one Varsity race early in the season and earned another blanket. Unfortunately our Athletic Director decided that UCLA would boycott the IRA that year; he was making a point that the timing of the event was unfair to the schools on the quarter system. Those of us on the quarter system had to take some of our final exams out in New York, when we would have preferred to concentrate only on racing. I was honored as Most Valuable Senior. In the best shape of my life, I wanted to continue rowing, but my attention would soon be driven in different directions.

I recommend the book *The Boys In The Boat* to learn a lot more about crew and what a terrific, wholesome, and challenging opportunity it is for young men and women. Now UCLA has a Women's Varsity Crew. For financial and political reasons the Men's program has become a club sport, and it is now dependent for funding on donations from alumni, parents, and the oarsmen themselves.

I still played a bit of intramural sports every year. In the Fall of my last year I was playing goalie for an intramural team when some of the UCLA Varsity Soccer players came over and invited me to play goalie with them, saying they were short handed. I was stopping everything they kicked my way— they even used some trick plays. I didn't know it, but they were in need of a new goalie due to an injury. After what they were seeing as a successful tryout, they invited me to join the UCLA Varsity Soccer Team. I thought about participating in both Soccer and Crew, but I had a lot of irons in the fire, including two part-time jobs. I turned them down. I later regretted my decision, as our Soccer team won the NCAA championship that year. This experience stuck with me, and I resolved in the future to sleep at least one night before making any important decision. Isn't it amazing how things can seem so complicated one day and then be so much clearer the next day?

# Chapter Eighteen

## MY FATHER'S ADVICE

*"Dissent is the highest form of patriotism."*
—Thomas Jefferson, Third President of the United States

I thought of myself as a patriot— I definitely supported the U.S. Constitution. In 1968 I turned 21 on election day, qualifying on age on the last possible day, and I most certainly would exercise my right to vote. Congress had not yet lowered the voting age to 18. LBJ announced that he would not seek re-election, pressured by growing sentiment to end the war in Viet Nam. Bobby Kennedy appeared likely to become a popular Democratic nominee after he won the California primary in June. Unfortunately he was assassinated moments after his victory speech at the Ambassador Hotel in Los Angeles. I watched recordings of the actual shooting being played over and over on television. It was shocking, hard to believe. Vice President Hubert Humphrey gained the Democrat party nomination at the convention. I was one of the 20,721 Californians who voted for Senator Eugene McCarthy as a write-in candidate in the general election, because of his strong commitment to end the Viet Nam War. Richard Nixon, the Republican, won. The war continued.

The war was on the front page every day in the '60s and '70s, on television every night, and it seemed to influence everything. It lasted 20 years from 1955 to 1975, and that was after a previous 10 years of fighting led by the French, which they called the Indochina War. The fighting was supposedly about more than the defense of the local people in South Viet Nam. The political "Domino Theory" of the day held that if Communism took over South Viet Nam it would then spread to the rest of Southeast Asia, like cascading dominoes. From there it would gain dominance over greater parts of the globe. This theory was later proven wrong, because indeed the North did eventually prevail.

Due to the draft laws in effect from 1940 to 1973, I was

required to register at my local draft board by my 18th birthday. During this period 2.2 million men between the ages of 18 and 25 were drafted and most of them ended up fighting in Nam. An estimated 100,000 fled the U.S. rather than serve during the Viet Nam War— many moved to Canada. Of the 72,000 who registered as conscientious objectors, nearly 6,000 were sent to prison, along with 16,000 alleged draft evaders. Richard Nixon had campaigned in 1968 on a promise to end the draft, but that did not happen. It would become only one of many controversies surrounding Nixon. When all of the dirt came out later after the Watergate Scandal, my father was so disillusioned that he swore to never vote again.

Thankfully I was granted a four year 2-S Exemption to attend college. Meanwhile a number of my friends were sent to Nam. Some returned healthy, some returned with psychological or medical issues, some were killed in action. My friend Randy Grittman returned with an ongoing case of malaria. My friend Bob Smith returned after being exposed to Agent Orange.

Just days before traveling home for Christmas holiday break in 1966, a fraternity brother named Terry Maas talked me into accompanying him to the Marine Corp Recruiting Center in L.A. He wanted to take the officers candidate school test to see if he would qualify. He dragged me along with him. He argued that taking the test was non-binding. We both scored near the max and the recruiter got very excited, making all kinds of promises about training us to fly jets or helicopters. I said that I would discuss it with my father, a veteran of two wars, and then decide. I took the Greyhound bus home to Fresno for the holidays. One evening I explained my thoughts to my father and then seriously asked his opinion. He looked at me silently for a moment and then quite bluntly said, "I try to avoid telling you what to do, but that is the stupidest idea you have ever had. Yes, I served, but it was a different time and those were different kinds of wars, and I joined voluntarily. Please do whatever you can to avoid going into the military and fighting in Viet Nam."

The following year I learned that my friend Terry Ogami had died in Viet Nam; a roadside bomb exploded under his truck. I was stunned. On campus, people would stand silently along Bruin Walk each weekday between noon and 1 PM in protest of the war. It started with a few, but the numbers were growing. Some held signs, most simply stood in silence. After days of agonizing debate in my own mind, I decided to join them for the first time. With my conventional haircut and clothing I stood out. I felt quite uncomfortable— a steady stream of students glanced my way as they passed, but the silence was good for me. During those hours of contemplation I thought about the responsibility of the individual to speak up or act when facing a situation that was not right. I had been moved by stories and movies about people committed to non-violence, people who had shown courage in their individual lives when confronted with social injustice. Not only was I opposed to the war and the draft, I also felt deeply that those fighting on my behalf needed to be brought home safely and soon. I still thought of myself as a patriot. More importantly, I realized that I had changed— going forward I would nurture in my consciousness a more focused awareness of my part and my responsibilities in the world drama. This would be an ongoing contemplation.

Years later I visited the Viet Nam War Memorial in Washington D.C. and found Terry Ogami's name on the wall. It was an incredibly moving experience. Not only could I sense my own long-buried emotions surging up to the surface, it also seemed I was feeling the psyche of a nation of people with powerful and troubled feelings still unresolved. It felt as if an invisible cloud of energy was hanging over the entire monument. I suspect it is still there. We never thanked our veterans when they returned from Nam and many of them were actually shunned. They all deserved better.

I didn't graduate from UCLA in four years; at one point in the second term of my Freshman year I had withdrawn from all my classes, due to a severe case of infectious mononucleosis. I became incredibly weak and landed in the UCLA Medical Center for a miserable stay. My four-year draft deferment was running out in 1969, and I still needed part of a fifth year to finish the requirements for my degree. I was about to become draft eligible.

Many people complained that the draft system was unfair, so in 1969 the Selective Service Agency invented a draft lottery. They said it would be totally random. Men would be drafted in the order of their lottery number until the draft requirements for the year were fulfilled. If my number was not reached, I would be exempted from the draft. On the evening of December 1, I walked to my favorite neighborhood bar in Westwood; it was called Mom's. I planned to have a few beers while watching the lottery as it was broadcast live on national television. If my November 5th birth date came out early, I would probably keep drinking in misery. Thankfully my number came out 310th. I thought I would be safe, but the next year I got rather nervous as my board was drafting an unusually large number of people. By December they were approaching number 290; the "current number" was printed in the newspapers every day. Fresno's board stopped at 295 and I was permanently excused. I felt as if I had been given a gift that I would need to pay back in some yet to be discovered ways.

My friend Jim Sims participated in Army ROTC during his undergraduate years. This allowed him to continue his education, including Law School, before he had to report for duty. He would also serve as an officer. He always hoped the war would end before he reported. It didn't. He ended up in Nam. He didn't believe in that war either, and he didn't approve of the draft. He returned safely after a few years, but as with many others those were bitter years. He explained that many soldiers believed their service was a form of involuntary servitude. He felt as if years had been taken from him; he felt personally disempowered. We need to respectfully hear such stories. Thankfully the war ended in April, 1975 with the fall of Saigon, though I know it brought tragic consequences to many people living there. A few years later the draft was abolished, hopefully never to return.

I was never called. At the same time I am grateful to those, including my own family members back along the way, who did serve— motivated by hopes that their descendants could enjoy the benefits of freedom and liberty. The great American experiment in democracy continues, and despite the noisiness of its processes, it thrives. If Thomas Jefferson could be here today, I believe he would be amazed at the challenges we as a nation have faced and overcome. I think he would be gratified to see that his dreams, and his words in the Declaration of Independence, remain very much alive in us.

# Chapter Nineteen

## I THOUGHT I WAS READY FOR MARRIAGE

*"Many a man in love with a dimple makes the mistake of marrying the whole girl."*
—Stephen Leacock, Canadian Economist, Writer, and Humorist

The idea of marriage had never crossed my mind— rather, I didn't think about it until just prior to my graduation. Maybe I should back up to my Freshman year and tell you about the first time I met Mary Gandsey. It was at a social exchange between our two dorm floors— called a mixer— where we moved about the room introducing ourselves and talking. She was a Psych major, somewhat quiet, but very self-confident. She looked straight into my eyes when we talked. I couldn't take my eyes off of her. She had long brown hair, and I thought she was beautiful. Mary was from Palos Verdes, an experienced horsewoman, and an excellent tennis player. On our first date I took her to see The Association, a concert in Pauley Pavilion. She became my first serious girlfriend and she was definitely more experienced than I in male-female relationships; I was eager to learn. Our relationship seemed perfect for a while, then it seemed to change. In the following years, we each pursued other interests and our dating became sporadic. By my fifth year she had already graduated and secured a job with Los Angeles County Social Services— later that year we reconnected and started dating again.

That fifth year was a year of transition for me. I leased an apartment farther off campus in a community called Palms, near Culver City. It was a two-bedroom unit on the ground floor in a quiet fourplex. Jim Sims was my roommate. I commuted up to the UCLA campus on my Honda motorcycle for morning classes, then for lunch I rode back south to work a couple of hours at the Woody's Smorgasburger in Culver City. From there I went on to the UCLA boathouse for afternoon workouts on the marina. We had no rowing scholarships at UCLA, but there was one student part-time job. I asked for it and got it. I was hired by the UCLA Facilities Department to be the Boathouse Janitor. I mopped and cleaned the boathouse before every workout, and on Saturdays I put in extra time trimming the grounds. After workouts, I rode back to the apartment on city streets, avoiding the freeways. Jim was now attending Loyola University Law School and he spent a large part of his time studying in law libraries, but we did eat a late dinner together most evenings. I was the primary cook, but I was always exhausted after workouts so I kept it simple. For the fun of it, I would often stage theme meals. Our favorite was "Trail Hand's Delight," which featured chili and cornbread— we dressed in cowboy hats and boots (plus underwear). Most nights, after a full day of classes, reading, two part-time jobs, the grueling workouts, and cooking dinner, all I could think about was sleep.

As June approached, Mary and I were spending more time together. I decided that instead of going directly into the job market after graduation I wanted to attend Graduate Business School. Fresno State had accepted me, and I was warming to the idea of returning to Fresno for a couple of years. Mary knew about my plans and we talked about our options. One evening at my apartment I told her I wanted her to go with me, and I asked her to marry me. I was somewhat surprised when she immediately said, "Yes." I was 22; I thought I was pretty mature. After all, I had been on my own for five years and soon I would be a college graduate with a degree from a major university. Only later, after life has brought us many surprises, do we come to realize that in our twenties we are just getting started. Before I knew it, my last quarter ended. There would be no trip to Syracuse for an IRA Regatta this year— an intense four years of rowing had come to an end. I skipped the formal graduation ceremony and picked up my diploma at the UCLA Administration Building. Mary had recently moved in with me. We started planning our move to Fresno.

Our wedding would take place July 18, 1970 in my parent's backyard. Mary and I wrote the words for our vows. Larry Smith conducted the ceremony (he had a mail-order Certificate of Ordination from the Universal Life Church). He and his wife, Pam, came from Del Rio, Texas where he was currently stationed in the Air Force. Jim Sims was my best man, and Craig Bleeker stood up with me as well. Several rowing buddies including Duncan Henderson and Dennis Phelan drove up to surprise us, arriving just as the ceremony started. Mary hired some L.A. musician friends to play for the ceremony— as she marched down the aisle wearing a simple short white dress, they played

"Little Wing" (by Jimi Hendrix) with singing by John Valenzuela, the lead guitarist. After the ceremony they played rock and roll tunes well into the night. The cement patio Father had installed years before served as a perfect dance floor; dancing continued non-stop. Our guests brought a lot of food, a tradition in Fresno, and it was a fabulous party. Most of us imbibed a bit, and we were honored with a champagne toast. Finally a distant neighbor complained and the police came to shut down thc party.

The next morning Mary and I departed on a road trip around the U.S. and Canada, expecting it to last several weeks. The Canadian Rockies were quite impressive. We stopped for a few days in Banff National Park in Canada, where we enjoyed some hot springs and a wonderful massage. After enduring the Great Plains, we crossed the border and headed to Chicago, where Mary's parents were currently living. After a short visit, we crossed the border again to catch a glimpse of the Canadian National Rowing site in St. Catherine's, Ontario, and from there we drove to Niagara Falls. Boston was our next strop— I wanted to see the boathouses along the River Charles. We explored some historic sights, but I became hopelessly lost driving around the confusing mass of streets in downtown Boston. When we eventually found our way out of town, we headed south to Washington D.C. The monuments and museums were quite fascinating, but that summer the entire East Coast was experiencing a severe heat wave. We were told it would become even hotter the further south we ventured; we decided to skip Florida and head home. We were young, so why not see how many miles we could cover each day. We reached North Texas on the second day, only to have Mary's little Triumph Spitfire sports car break down in Shamrock. We limped to a garage and learned it would take a couple of days to get a replacement water pump. Texas was unbearably hot, cvcn worse than D.C. We checked into a tiny motel room with a cranky air conditioner that could not keep up. The motel had no pool— we took turns floating in the bathtub trying to cool off.

We eventually reached Fresno and found an apartment near First Street and Ashland, just around the corner from a fast-food called Munchies. They served the cheapest (and smallest) hamburgers in town. My Business School classes were held in the evening, so I got a day job substitute teaching at the high school level. I was working for the Fresno Unified School District, thanks to Mr. Reid Gromis (my buddy Mick's dad), who was the Superintendent. I qualified to substitute in English, Math, Physics, Chemistry, Civics, and Latin. I received a call to work most days. Mary got a job, through my Grandma Pearl, working at a Woolworths that had just opened. Everything was wonderful for a while, but Mary increasingly missed her friends and family back in L.A. After six years I was also getting tired of the college routine. When I completed my first year of the MBA program at Fresno State, we agreed I would take a break. We moved to Pasadena, where she started a quilting company, Rags To Riches, with her friend Andrea. I got a job with the American Glass Company in downtown L.A. We bought a used VW Van from Mary's grandmother, which I used for my commute on weekdays. On the weekends Mary used it to sell quilts at craft shows.

Our relationship became more strained, for a lot of reasons. I'll skip the details. I wanted to keep trying; she decided we should split up. I was a Scorpio and she was a Leo— I guess it just wasn't meant to be. The marriage lasted a little over a year. I moved to a small studio apartment in Eagle Rock. In January of 1972, I was served with a Judgment of Dissolution of Marriage. I was heartbroken at the time, but intellectually I wanted to believe it was best that our break was clean, coming sooner rather than later. This was my first experience with such deep emotions, and for years I wrestled with questions like "What did I do wrong?" It would be many years before I could look back at all of this and see it as a learning experience; I did come to recognize how really different women are from men and how we all change, particularly in our early adult years. Back then I could only hope that Aeneas was right, and that someday it would be pleasing to remember even these things.

# Chapter Twenty

## "... AND THAT'S WHY THEY CALL IT MUNCHIES."

*"Keep on truckin'."*
—R. Crumb, American Cartoonist and Satirist

I was pretty confused. I quit my job and moved back to Fresno. My brother invited me to take a spare room in a house which he was renting with another friend; it was Robert Hupp's old house, on the back side of the same block where my parents were still living. I wasn't working; I just wanted to take some time to let my head and my heart settle. Those were tough days, and my brother was a great friend. I enjoyed that gift of time with my family— they were all concerned about me of course.

In recent months in L.A., I had been smoking marijuana more frequently. I didn't consider it harmful or addictive, but it could impact whether or not I would be very productive, if that was of concern. These days I understand there are some strains of marijuana that actually help people to focus and be more productive (in addition to providing numerous medicinal benefits). At the time, that was not my experience. I also often said, "I trust Timothy Leary more than I trust Richard Nixon," and I knew I was not the only one. I had met a man in Echo Park who supplied me with some LSD. He encouraged me to never use it frivolously; he said it should be used for a conscious purpose— only when I was ready to learn more about myself and my connection with God. I did learn some things, but knowing what I know now, I would not recommend LSD these days. The learnings will appear.

Anyone who has ingested marijuana knows about "the munchies"— a strong urge for snacking, or more than snacking. Even Fruit Loops will work if that is all you can find in the cupboard (which was the case for me my first time). The Fresno hamburger stand named Munchies was always appreciated as a righteous solution for any munchies attack. During a New Years Eve party that year in Randy's house, a bunch of us piled into my

VW Van. I was NOT driving, and Fresno's tule fog was particularly thick, which only added to the surreal nature of this magical mystery tour. We were searching for something to solve a particularly serious case of the collective munchies. We arrived at Munchies and found them closed. I don't remember where we eventually found a convenience store that was open, but we persevered and acquired a broad variety of snacks which we took back to the party. It remains a memorable event whenever my brother and I reminisce.

I attended some great rock concerts with my brother. Elvin Bishop rocked downtown Fresno in a small club. Manassas, recently founded by Steven Stills, played a spectacular concert in the Selland Arena; Boz Scaggs, a well known Texas bluesman, was the opening act. I'm sure we were stoned, and I seem to remember having prepared hashish brownies.

After a few months, I decided I was ready to move on with my life. I thanked my brother and headed once again to L.A., where I intended to touch base with some friends. I found that my graduated college friends had spread to different parts of the city and beyond. I visited a few; I was looking for ideas. For a while I volunteered as a roadie for some friends in a band— the ones who had played at my wedding. John, Richard, and Ernie now called themselves Gold Seal. I had plenty of time for music and I attended all of their gigs. I was still not ready to commit to a job. I began sleeping in the back of my VW Van at the end of a road on the edge of Griffith Park, where the band guys shared one floor of a rented house. I bought a Fender electric guitar and started to learn how to play. I even wrote a couple of songs. Eventually I realized that I needed a total change of scene— I was tired of driving the L.A. Freeways, and I was ready to get away from the drugs. I had been drifting; I needed to find a purpose. The wind at my back was definitely building.

# Chapter Twenty-One

## ARE YOU A HIPPIE?

*"Imagine there's no heaven, It's easy if you try,*
*No hell below us, Above us only sky,*
*Imagine all the people, Living for today."*
—John Lennon, "Imagine"

I was growing my hair longer, and I remember the first time a teenage boy asked me, "Are you a hippie?" It was a bit of a derogatory term to some people in the 1960s and 1970s, but it didn't bother me. I had never thought of myself as a hippie. That term originally referred to the flower-power folks, like those living in alternative lifestyles in the Haight-Ashbury district in San Francisco. They wore wild tie-dyed clothing, grew and smoked marijuana, and reportedly practiced "free love." That was all pretty radical at the time and it greatly concerned the older generations.

What was really happening with young people at that time and what was the protesting all about? What was the "counter culture", and who was in it? Great questions. Yes, it did have to do with our music, and the War in Viet Nam, and some major cultural differences between my Baby Boomer generation and our parents' generation. They had been raised to obey their elders without questioning, they joined the military when they were needed, and they trusted the government. We questioned everything, we felt the war in Viet Nam was a painful mistake, and no way would any of us buy a used car from Richard Nixon. My generation was on a quest for independence and self-determination. We wanted to try new things, like marijuana and LSD. We wanted to experience new modes of communal living and pursue idealism and utopia, not just intellectually but in day-to-day living. We felt that living was all about today. This perspective was coming through the popular music of the day and we played it constantly— Hendrix, the Doors, the Grateful Dead, the Byrds, Neil Young. We wanted to "Make Love, Not

War!" I attended a lot of music concerts. The Pasadena Civic Auditorium offered $1 concerts and I saw a young Doobie Brothers Band in one of their first public performances. Over time I rocked with Earth, Wind, and Fire; the James Gang; Leon Russell; Redbone; and Dr. John the Night Tripper. I danced to the Byrds at the Hollywood Palladium and The Grateful Dead at several venues. I caught Loggins and Messina in their first public appearance at the Troubadour, before their first record came out; they were a surprise opening act for Curtis Mayfield. I sat right in front of Bill Withers as he sang in a very small club in the San Fernando Valley. I went to free concerts in Griffith Park and saw Santana.

When I decided I was ready to leave L.A. again, I committed to making a fresh start. It was time to lighten up. I gave away almost all of my possessions, including all of my college textbooks. I pulled the rear seat out of my VW van and built a double bed with mattress into the back. I stitched a sheet, which I had tie-dyed with bright colors, into the headliner above my bed and put tie-dyed curtains over the windows. Everything else that I owned, mostly clothes, fit into three cardboard boxes neatly arranged side-by-side under the bed. This was my home and I was mobile. I didn't know where I would go first, but I began calling all of my friends to tell them that I was heading out, to somewhere unknown. When I called Lance and Annette Pugh, they told me they had just quit their jobs with the May Company and tomorrow they would be moving. We were amazed at the synchronicity of our decisions. They invited me to come help them open a new business which his parents were bankrolling in downtown Ashland, Oregon. It sounded like an excellent idea. I told them I was already packed and I would see them there in a week.

I headed north on I-5 and stopped in Fresno for a brief family visit. Nana sewed patches of colorful fabric over the holes in my blue jeans, and I pinned some bells onto the legs so that I jingled when I walked; I was definitely looking like a real hippie. I quickly caught up on the latest news with my brother, who was getting more serious in his relationship with Judy. Mom gave me some canned foods to add into one of my three boxes. I knew that my parents and grandparents were concerned about me, but I had unshakable confidence that good things would lie ahead. I could feel the Wind.

I headed north again toward the Oregon border, ready to discover something totally new. It was quite hot in the Valley, even though it was technically still Spring. I should have checked the oil level more frequently. Heading uphill just past Redding, while climbing out of the north end of the 500-mile long Central Valley, the engine overheated. I heard an audible "ping" as it blew out. Somehow I found a local mechanic and he towed my van to his yard. He said I could leave it there until I earned some money. I would then call him to proceed with an engine rebuild and I would come back to retrieve it (and the rest of my belongings). I slept that night in the back of thc van, and the next morning I left with a bag of clothes and my electric guitar to hitchhike the rest of the way.

I caught a ride pretty quickly with a man who wanted to talk about conversations he had out loud every day with God. This man assured me that God was always listening and He was interested in everything we thought and did. That certainly gave me something to think about. Lake Shasta was gorgeous, and it was full of precious water (though sadly those water levels are much lower these days). I couldn't believe how beautiful it was winding through the mountains surrounding Mt. Shasta and how much relief I felt from the heat of the Valley. Both sides of the road were covered in lush green colors; stately pines and cedars extended in all directions. If I had a good sense of smell, which unfortunately I do not, I would no doubt have smelled the changes as I moved into this new forested region. I caught other rides and continued heading north for the Siskiyou Mountains, through towns with funny names like Weed, Yreka, and Hilt.

I was about halfway between San Francisco and Portland when we passed over the state line from California into Oregon. Then, just past the Mt. Ashland summit, I-5 starts winding downhill. We exited the freeway just as Emigrant Lake appeared on the right. Soon we passed a picturesque Southern Oregon State College campus and a grand old public library, as we continued toward downtown Ashland. It was April of 1972. I was dropped off at 47 North Main Street, in front of Lithia Grocery, and I went inside to see the new venture. Everything I thought I knew was about to change.

# Chapter Twenty-Two

## WHO AM I? – THE ASHLAND YEARS

*"Be here now."*
—Ram Dass: *Be Here Now*

Lithia Square was a small plaza at the entrance to Lithia Park. The park itself was beautiful, with trimmed grassy meadows and mature trees surrounding Lithia Creek. The creek flowed (usually at a gentle pace) down from the mountains through this rather long and generous park setting and then continued right through the oldest section of the downtown. In those days the park was always full of hippies playing guitars, dancing in colorful clothes, or relaxing with friends on blankets. It seemed that someone was always throwing a frisbee or playing with a dog. Lithia Square had free parking, and the cars and trucks parked there were mostly of an older vintage. Across Main Street, the Ashland Food Co-op had recently been established and New Age folks regularly came in and out after shopping or volunteering. I donated time there as a member, cutting large wheels of cheese into smaller chunks which I then wrapped in plastic, weighed, and labeled all by hand. Casa del Sol, next to the Co-op, was a pottery studio run by a quiet and very creative fellow named John Conners; you could watch him through the front window, as he worked at his craft. Around the corner was the Pillars Coffee House. In the other direction from our Grocery was a small health food store and then the Log Cabin Bar, which was often rowdy and loud with old timers and folks from the hills. Positioned next to the bar was Rare Earth, stuffed with imported items of colorful clothing, hippie home decorations, and many other items of interest to young people. Lithia Grocery was tucked in the middle, amidst these tenants who together were inhabiting a row of older and stately one and two storied brick buildings.

On the other side of Lithia Park sat the world-renowned Oregon Shakespeare Festival's Elizabethan Theater. In those days it was an outdoor stage, open air to the night sky (and sometimes rain). The theater had no amplification and the actors worked hard at projecting their voices, just like back in the day of the Bard himself. The acting company had been established in 1935, and young actors from all parts of the country rotated through the company for a few years to gain some experience and add to their resume. I remember one young actor named Powers Boothe, who had a particularly clear and booming voice. He was just six months younger than I was at the time; recently graduated from SMU, he had secured his first gig in the lead role of "Henry IV, Part 2." He later starred in movies, won an Emmy on television, and performed in some plays on Broadway. It was quite common to meet and befriend young actors and directors as they also enjoyed strolling the stores on the square and relaxing in the park. Sometimes you could hear one of them midday rehearsing his lines loudly amongst the trees.

Ashland was much smaller then, and its residents felt a real sense of community. The quiet town was home to a mixture of many folks whose families had lived in the area for generations, plus students at the smallish Southern Oregon College, the colorful actors, and a lot of hippies. Some of the pioneering families had lived there since the days of covered wagons and the Oregon Trail, and they didn't want to see their town changing from the old ways. They had no idea what to do with the long-haired hippies who had seemingly invaded their little town.

Prior to our arrival Lithia Grocery was struggling, due to competition from the new Pioneer Supermarket situated only a few blocks away. But loyal old-timers still walked to Lithia to shop for their basic food needs or tobacco or wine. We soon discovered that under the previous ownership our grocery had been a gathering place for local residents to commiserate about the changes. Onc day one of the older locals came in and said to us, "What are we going to do about the hippies?" It was as if we were still the old owners. Lance and I looked at each other's appearance, confirming that indeed we looked like hippies ourselves. Lance turned to the man and said, "I think we need to accept them."

I borrowed some money from Lance and got a ride with a friend back to Redding to retrieve my van with its newly rebuilt engine. After staying in a room at Lance and Annette's rented house, I was happy to be sleeping once again in my own van, though I still had bathroom and showering privileges.

Have you ever done something just for the love of it? I thought of it as my "Karma Yoga"— sharing in the creating and operating of Lithia Grocery with Lance, Annette, and others. After paying back my loan with hours worked, I refused a salary and worked for a draw of $20 per month (to buy gas for my van) plus meals. It was truly a labor of love, and for a while I would be genuinely disinterested in money. We turned the dusty old store into a "very hip" vegetarian deli and New Age grocery that we invented as we went along. Local artists consigned works of art to hang on the walls; I loved the batik paintings by Linda Novik, all very colorful. Hand-filled bags of herbal teas, nuts, beans, pasta, spices, and other dry goods filled the wooden shelves along both side walls. One of the most popular bagged items was dried seaweed; we usually sold a couple of varieties. We wrote the prices by hand on unique and artsy Lithia Grocery labels. Interspersed on the shelves we placed a variety of hand thrown tea pots and tea cup sets (on consignment from Casa del Sol). We sold milk and cheese from a large old commercial refrigerator— we had spent hours stripping white paint to reveal its original oak beauty. In front of that stood a wooden rack displaying all manner of local Manna Bakery granola, whole grained breads, and other baked goods. On the opposite side of the front door Lance had built a counter from old barn wood; on it sat an old fashioned cash register, which we used for all of the transactions, and a large antique scale (also well used). Toward the rear we installed a giant potbelly stove, which we had rescued from an old barn; that stove heated the entire store in the winter. In the off-season Annette cooked split pea soup on top of it (her grandmother's recipe) which she sold at a low price— our customers were mostly local folks in the off season and some of them were financially challenged. We stopped selling alcohol, tobacco, and meats. We were changing too— we had all become vegetarian. I swore off alcohol.

Our best selling deli item was the Super Deluxe Avocado and Cheese Sandwich. We started by hand slicing two pieces of freshly baked Manna Bakery bread. Add mayonnaise, then load on slices of fresh avocado and locally made Rogue Valley Creamery cheese. Pile on a handful of fresh alfalfa sprouts and sprinkle with some soy nuts and Annette's Lithia Blend Seasoning. Slice the sandwich in half and put it in a basket. Add a few Dr. Bronner's Corn Chips and an orange slice on the side. You could eat yours at one of our vintage tables inside or on the bench out front, or take it for a picnic at the park just steps up the street. Yum! I had learned how to grow alfalfa sprouts back in Los Angeles, but not on the scale we would soon need at Lithia. I borrowed a shopping cart (later adding another) and filled it with a lot of one gallon glass jars, each with cheesecloth stretched over the mouth. Every morning and evening I rinsed the alfalfa seeds and started soaking more seeds for the next one gallon batch. When they were almost fully sprouted their growth accelerated— the mass of them expanded so much that I would need to split them into separate jars, and then finally I exposed them to sunlight for a day so they would “green up.” After each five or six day cycle I was able to harvest at least one fresh batch each morning. They taste quite refreshing, are low in calories and rich in magnesium, iron, phosphorus, and zinc. They contain Vitamins K, C, B1, B2, B5, and B9, plus Saponins which reportedly help lower your LDL (bad cholesterol) and increase your HDL (good cholesterol). I believe my sprouts in that sandwich introduced the health benefits of alfalfa sprouts to thousands of people.

*“Lithia Grocery, 1972.”*

Our signature over-the-top sandwich was called the Rogue Zeppelin. We built it on a twelve inch torpedo roll and overloaded it with many kinds of deli meats and cheeses. It was too big to fit into your mouth and plenty of food to be shared. Though it was our highest price item, I did a cost analysis which showed we were losing money on every one we sold. Lance didn't care. He loved making them and loved seeing the wide and amazed eyes when he handed them to the customer. He insisted we keep them on the menu. Raise the price? No, that might hurt the volume.

Our old building had overhead fans but no air conditioning. During summer months it got warm inside, as we stood for hours making sandwiches non-stop for people lined up out the door. Business was heaviest in the summer, during the peak of the Shakespeare season. We also saw a lot of folks, on their summer vacations, who were just pausing a bit in our town before continuing on north or south on the I-5 freeway. When the days got really hot, out on the back porch we hand-cranked homemade ice cream, flavored with some local in-season fruit like sweet peaches. We sold it until it was all gone, usually within an hour or two. The hand cranking was fun at first and definitely a conversation starter, but it soon became tiresome so we relegated it to special events.

One weekend Lance drove his VW Van, with several of us in the back, up to Springfield to hear Ram Dass speak. He was previously known as Dr. Richard Alpert, a professor at Harvard, as was his close friend Dr. Timothy Leary. They were pioneers of LSD usage, but Dr. Alpert had left it behind after going through an amazing transformation and changing his name to Ram Dass. In 1971 he published his first book, *Be Here Now.* I read it so many times that my copy fell apart and I bought another. We loved hearing about his experiences of personal transformation.

Jerry Barnes, another fraternity brother from UCLA, arrived in Ashland. He blazed into town in his bright orange Mustang Mach 3, with the car stereo blasting his favorite tape— Jimi Hendrix and the Band of Gypsies. Seemingly overnight he mellowed into our much more relaxed rhythms. He sold the monster, bought a VW Van, and was soon concentrating on growing his hair longer and playing acoustic blues guitar with Lance. Later that year he and I decided to take a road trip back to California. We took my van. I somehow missed the signs and made a wrong turn in Sacramento. We figured it out when we picked up two lady hitchhikers, who we thought we had magically conjured after starting to chant just moments before.

They told us they were headed to Tahoe. We dropped them at the next stop, rerouted, and eventually reached Fresno, where we spent a night with my family. We continued on to L.A. and visited a few old friends, but very quickly we were dazed by the air congestion, traffic, and noise. We promptly headed north along the coast. Part of the purpose for our trip was to meet with a music booking agent, which we then did in Santa Cruz. We heard from him about an outdoor concert in the Bay Area, so the next night we stopped at the Berkeley Amphitheater to see Stevie "Guitar" Miller perform. That was where I donated my Fender electric guitar to someone in greater need than I, as I discovered when we returned to the van. The side doors had been forced open and my guitar was gone. We made it swiftly back to Ashland and tried our best to forget California.

A group of us had been talking about producing a rock concert. We invented a company named True Moon, and I reserved the Medford Armory just up the highway from Ashland. After calling our new acquaintance in Santa Cruz, we booked Albert Collins, Papa John Creech, and John Mayall as co-headliners. That was too much overhead, we later learned. After weeks of organizing and promotional work, I enjoyed the show along with all those who bought tickets. My face was a work of art, painted that afternoon by Lavell Foose (a local artist who created the sign hanging above the front entrance of Lithia Grocery). The Medford Chief of Police and a plethora of his men showed up as well. He tried to shut us down, but I successfully resisted. We were in fact really loud, and there were rumors, he claimed, of marijuana illegally on the premises. Medford was a sleepy and conservative little town in those days, even more so than Ashland. The Chief did not know what to make of me, my long hair, my painted face, or my Birkenstock sandals. The concert lost money. My backers decided that we had learned our lesson; we agreed to forget that whole business idea.

I returned to an increasingly quieter lifestyle. I offered a series of evening nutrition classes at Lithia Grocery; I told my story about "Why did God make vegetables different colors?" I was reading many nutrition and health books, when I realized that none of us needed to memorize vast amounts of nutritional facts— we could simply make the combination of foods on our plate as colorful as possible. God knew it all, and He provided us a simple color coding system for all the vitamins and minerals. While talking, I demonstrated some of my healthy snack ideas, like sliced apples topped with a mix of nut butter, raisins, seeds, and bits of dried fruits. It was fun, and dozens of people attended.

At the back of our store was a mezzanine, previously used for storage. I cleaned it out in my spare time and began to sleep up there on a mat I rolled out nightly onto the wooden floor. It was a welcome alternative to sleeping in the back of my van, as winter was approaching and temperatures would soon drop below freezing. I practiced yoga first thing every morning and meditation every evening. I did a lot of silent walking, and I read a lot of spiritual books. I kept asking myself and the universe, "Who am I?" I sensed very deeply that there had to be meaning and purpose to such an amazing creation as I was experiencing. I would soon receive some answers.

# Chapter Twenty-Three

## THE APPEARANCE OF SUNSEED

*"... If a part of me is of the earth*
*Earthy*
*A part of me is also of the sun*
*And it is the largest part*
*So that I could say, and speak truly,*
*I come from the sun.*
*I carry the light that shines in the sun*
*I bear the fire that burns in the sun...*
*I just dwell in the earth*
*For the moment."*
—Chris Foster, "Bearers of the Sun"

The first time I walked into the New Age book store, up Main Street near the college, I found *Autobiography of a Yogi* by Paramahansa Yogananda. I loved that book. The purity of his intent in life was inspiring. I read it more than once. I felt on fire inside. I wanted the focus of my daily living to become a search for God and my connection to him. I wanted to live a life of selfless action. Other books like *The Tibetan Book of the Great Liberation* and *Tibetan Yoga and Secret Doctrines* gave me many ideas for my yoga and meditation, on that mezzanine above the Grocery. I practiced some evening meditations meant to help me stay conscious in my dreams and to intercede in chaotic moments of dreaming. It worked, and my dreams did become more peaceful.

Vegetarianism, fasting, and some periodic cleansing, as well as the yoga and meditation all helped my body and my mind to calm remarkably. Some weeks I would eat only two meals a day. One was a potato salad with raw vegetables, lots of sprouts, miso, kelp, seeds, and brewer's yeast; the other was a huge fruit salad with nut butters, honey, and seeds. I used chopsticks, to insure I would eat slowly. For a while, on my day off, I fasted one day each week drinking only water, after drinking a quart of prune juice the day prior. That routine will clean you out nicely. Some fasting days I remained silent for the entire day. Silence is an acquired skill; it helped me to observe my busy mind which if left unbridled would love to spew its every thought out into the world.

In front of Lithia Grocery, in the center of the plaza, stand the famous Lithia Water drinking fountains. Those waters come from a nearby spring and are rich in lithium and other minerals. As part of my daily routine I stopped to drink my fill. Lithia Water has an unusual taste that is unforgettable; many people never come back after their first taste. Needless to say, I experienced some physical changes from my new lifestyle— I lost a lot of weight, became quite flexible, and with my long red hair and beard, plus hippie clothing, I had an unmistakably unique appearance. I was also beginning to cultivate a stillness about my body and mind that I had never experienced before.

*"Sunseed, with water and chopsticks (tools for healthy living)."*

I started taking modern dance classes at a local studio, because I wanted to learn new types of movement and to improve my sense of balance. The sessions were held at night. I was the only man in the classes. All of the women had danced for years and had their own colorful assortments of dance clothing. By mail-order from San Francisco, I bought a size-tall white leotard and matching white tights. I enjoyed those classes, and I participated for most of a year. Sometimes, during free dance time at the end of the class, our teacher liked to take off all of her clothes. The rest of us followed along; I didn't mind. She said we were developing freedom of expression. We did a few public performances (clothed), I made friends, and I know it contributed to my self confidence. Many nights I left in a very zen frame of mind. Yes, I was feeling a new freedom of expression.

I met an amazing assortment of people on their own spiritual quests; people that the Spiritual Wind had also drawn to Ashland at that particular time. Some lived in alternative communities with names like Ascendington, Glory Be Farm, and Rainbow Star. Some pitched tents beside the Applegate River, moved in with a new acquaintance, or just moved around. Some rented houses together. I later rented a house behind Lithia Square on High Street and invited several friends to share it with me. In one bedroom was Yogi Ron (Ballesteros), who was a devotee of Kundalini Yoga as taught by Yogi Bhajan. Just across the hall lived Spaceman Ron and Tria, who were awaiting the return of space brothers from somewhere. In the third bedroom was Deborah and her daughter Zanna. Deborah was a seamstress. She made me some colorful yoga pants as part of her rent payment; she also created a beautiful long blue robe that I would wear to my brother's wedding. I used the empty dining room as my bedroom. I slept on blankets on the floor at night, and rolled them into the closet in the morning to create an uncluttered floor for practicing my yoga and some dancing. Other fascinating friends I fondly remember from those days had names like Amana, Sonny Blue Boy, Brother Lee Love, and Rosebud. What I remember most is their gentleness, sweetness of spirit, and warm smiles.

A woman named Andreleria was hosting spiritual meetings in Mount Shasta City and they always attracted a variety of interesting folks; I enjoyed the singing and the stories people told of their spiritual quests. Sometimes I made the trek over the Siskiyou Summit and down into California for one of her evening meetings. Then, if it was not too cold, I slept in my van parked on the side of that great mountain. The silence up there made for colorful dreaming.

Ravi Shankar came to our local college to play a concert. The audience was mellow and relaxed as we waited for him to appear on stage. Many of us were sitting on the floor of the bare auditorium. Some were chanting softly. It was a very colorful crowd. Ravi was a little late. Then a man came on stage to say, "He is here but a little delayed; please remain calm and do not panic." This provided a visible lesson for me— though his words were simple, the spirit behind them was agitated. The energy of his agitation affected the crowd more than the opposite intent of his words. Many people became concerned and started buzzing, saying to their neighbor, "Why did he say we should not panic?" Soon Ravi appeared and stood at the front of the stage. From his presence and simple greeting spread a great calming wave. I could see everyone relax immediately. In both cases, spirit was clearly at work behind the words.

I had the pleasure of meeting Swami Satchidananda at a home in Ashland. He had been the opening speaker at the Woodstock Festival. His message was about joy, peace, internal discipline, and unconditional love. With a long white beard, pure white hair, and the most amazing piercing eyes, he had a striking appearance. You could feel emanating from his calm demeanor waves of intense stillness and focused power. After speaking to our small group, interspersed with periods of silence, he performed a small blessing while moving about and briefly looking directly into the eyes of each of us. He was a yogi master teacher and founder of an organization called LOTUS. http://lotus.org.

Other swamis came through town that year; then I had an interesting personal experience. After meeting real swamis and reading that Gandhi had been celibate for his last 42 years, I decided that I would emulate them and give up sex for the rest of my life. It only lasted about a month, thanks to my friend Christine. She asked if she could join me for an early morning yoga session at the Lithia Grocery loft, when I was still sleeping there. I led the session, but when we finished she crawled on top of me and then she did some rhythmic leading in her own way. I think it was premeditated on her part. It was definitely one of my favorite meditations. She was the only woman I knew who literally purred afterward when she was deeply happy. I also think it was God's way of telling me that I did not have to follow an ascetic lifestyle that had worked for some of those from the East.

I continued to teach yoga lessons in Lithia Park and in the

basement of the public library. I would continue to dance in that beautiful park by myself and talk to God out loud. When did Sunseed appear, and when did I start being known by that name? I don't remember the exact date, but it was one day in 1972 in the midst of the events of this chapter. I already told you about Sunseed's dream and how it affected me. Consciousness of the Sunseed identity continued growing quietly inside me for weeks after that dream. Then, one day, I simply told my best friends, "From now on my name is Sunseed; please call me Sunseed." Each of them looked at me for a moment, smiled appreciatively, and said something like, "Of course." I was not the first in the area to discover a new name, and it seemed they all felt this name suited me well. Other friends were equally accepting; but when I told people who did not know me, I always saw a puzzled look and they asked questions. I didn't mind. It gave me a chance to tell stories about realizations that were important to me; stories like those I am retelling in this book. In a later chapter titled "Working With The Invisible," I will say more about the name Sunseed and what it has come to mean to me.

# Chapter Twenty-Four

## MEETING THE LOVE OF MY LIFE

*"We are stardust, we are golden, and we've got to get ourselves back to the garden."*
—Joni Mitchell, "Woodstock"

She definitely caught my eye. I saw her walking down the street in Ashland wearing a simple but lovely blue dress, and I thought she looked like springtime. With brown hair and blue eyes, she was a little taller than average; she was walking briskly with a confident posture. This was in the Spring of 1972, just after I had arrived from California and Kathryn had arrived from Portland.

*"Kathryn, 1972."*

I later discovered she was also moving on from a recent divorce. As well, her early years had not been as easy as mine. Her father had also been a cook in the Navy. Late in World War II (January, 1945) his aircraft carrier, the USS Salamaua, was providing air cover in the Philippine Islands when it was struck by a kamikaze pilot. The flight deck and below decks were set ablaze and 95 men were killed or seriously injured. He would say that he had experienced some gruesome sights in the war, but he refused to talk about any of it. Kathryn found these details many years later on the internet. She suspects her father suffered post traumatic stress disorder for the rest of his life. This definitely did not contribute to a stable family situation for Kathryn or her brother Charles when they were young.

Upon arriving in Ashland, Kathryn found an apartment which she shared with her 4 year old daughter— Jennifer had been born in Seattle, a couple of weeks before Kathryn turned 21. Kathryn got a job at The Pillars, the coffee house on Lithia Creek. Jennifer started Head Start and later attended Montessori Pre-school. Jen was smart and strong-willed. My friend Jim Sims saw her for the first time through the window of his home on B Street. He saw a determined young girl with a suitcase marching briskly down the sidewalk. Then came a woman, apparently her mother, hiding behind trees while sneaking along behind. He later learned that Jen was upset because her health conscious mother would not buy Fruit Loops for breakfast. She was determined to move in with a young friend whose mother did allow that kind of thing. Jim loved telling that story, always laughing because he could not decide which was a more humorous sight— the marching girl or the concerned mother.

From the time she was a young girl, Kathryn wanted to become a nurse. She began classes at the local college, while also working as much as possible. It wasn't easy, with household duties, raising a daughter, and trying to have a life of her own at the same time. Single mothers are some of the hardest working people on the planet. Later she would earn her nursing degree at nearby Rogue Community College.

I was teaching yoga in the basement of the Ashland Library when I first met Kathryn. She came to a few classes with friends; I enjoyed a warm hug with her at the end of each session. When I was giving nutritional lectures in the evening at Lithia Grocery, Kathryn attended with Jennifer and we chatted afterward. At a wedding celebration for our mutual friends Steven and Debra Bochinski, I kissed Kathryn for the first time. Captivated by the sparkle I saw in her beautiful blue eyes, I thought I felt something special moving between us. She was not yet sure what to make of me.

Kathryn had moved into a communal house; there were a number of them in Ashland. This one had a spiritual orientation. One day I accepted an invitation to dinner from Sandra Lindley, a wonderful employee at Lithia Grocery, who lived in that same communal house. I brought a big bowl of my potato salad. Everyone raved over it, including my soon-to-be good friend Rory Boyle. It seemed they all knew about Sunseed. Several of them were frequent customers at Lithia Grocery, and I was pretty unusual, so of course talk about me spread from friend to friend. Actually I discovered they were occupying two houses, together functioning as a small community. It was coordinated by a fascinating man about my age named Carl Romaner. Carl and his longtime friend Les Spivak lived in one house, as did their dogs Tonka and Hosea. Between the two houses there were a number of other people, mostly young adults. Some were single mothers. The Bochinski's, who lived in the second house, had a natural childbirth at home and were joined by a daughter, Gabrielle.

Carl and Les were the ones that introduced me to the process of Attunement and a perspective that was called the Spiritual Expression Approach to Living. I made some return visits to their house on A Street in the following weeks to learn more. They maintained a spiritual purpose and focused intent to their daily routines that really resonated with me. In a few weeks, I asked to become a part of the community and I was welcomed with open arms.

Rory was my new roommate in an attic room. We were both tall and the ceiling in our room was about five feet high, at the highest point. We looked pretty funny up there walking around bent over, which made the youngsters laugh when they climbed the stairs to spy on us. I had been in Ashland for two years and I was ready for more changes. I decided to cut my hair. I walked into the old-fashioned "Modern Barbershop" next door to Lithia Grocery and took a chair. The longtime owner was stunned. I had chatted with him many times outside his shop, but hippies with long hair were a rare sight inside his shop. He was so delighted to shorten the hair of a hippie that he refused to charge me. He only took off a few inches, but I felt pounds lighter walking out with a real spring in my step. I felt energized and was indeed ready for more change. At home that evening I let it be known that something unusual was about to happen, and a few interested friends were mingling. I came out of the bathroom with NO beard. I offered "free kisses with a clean-shaven man" to all of the women who were there, and Kathryn jumped quickly to be first in line. I remember that kiss too.

Carl soon figured out a way to purchase an unusually large two-story house with a lot of bedrooms. It was further from downtown, on a quiet hillside, with more of a country feel. We vacated the two houses in town and moved into our new communal home. All of us were vegetarian, which made cooking for so many people reasonably practical. That is, until Big Al came for his next visit. Big Al Romaner was Carl's father, a no-nonsense successful businessman from Florida. He was physically a big man, and he was easy to like. He respected the spiritual basis of our community, but he argued that it had nothing to do with vegetarianism. Big Al announced that he was buying organic hamburger, enough for everyone, and it would be available on the dinner menu that evening. Needless to say, that sparked a lot of conversations. He was challenging each of us to reexamine our most basic principles. I sensed a need to determine which ones really resonated with my core and which ones did not. When dinnertime arrived, we said our blessing and the plate of little hamburger patties was passed around. Every one of us chose to take one. Honestly, they tasted delicious. The old routine had been reset, and we started seeing non-vegetarian options on the menu several times a week. I knew it would make things simpler for me in the future. I also found I had more energy. My experiences with different approaches to eating would continue over the years and even lead me to some unexpected surprises— I'll talk more about those surprises and what I learned in another chapter.

Kathryn and I went on a few dates that year, but a serious relationship would not begin until a bit later. We both felt a need to take things slowly— each of us were still dealing with emotions from terminating a previous marriage. That was probably the right thing for us; sometimes it takes years to resolve certain past experiences. Sometimes we are part of larger creative cycles which seem mysterious at the time but make sense when we later reach a point of resolution. I'll give you a clue as to how things eventually worked out for us— the title at the beginning of this chapter gives it away.

# Chapter Twenty-Five

## THE SPIRITUAL EXPRESSION APPROACH TO LIVING

*"Thankful are we now to be*
*filled with praise Lord to thee.*
*So shall our living bless the Earth.*
*Thankful are we, Holy King."*
—Martin Cecil, "The Blessing Song"

In the Spring of 1974 I took a train with some friends to the small town of 100 Mile House in central British Columbia for a one-month Spiritual-Expression-In-Living class. The town got its unusual name during the Cariboo Gold Rush in 1862 when a roadhouse was built there as a stopover for stagecoach passengers. That site was 100 miles up the Old Cariboo Road from Lillooet, which was the farthest north that steamships could take you. Along the way up, you hear town names like Kamloops, Lac La Hache, and 70 mile House. William Cecil, an English Lord, purchased the old roadhouse and 12,000 acres of land surrounding it in 1912. He hired a local agent to establish a cattle ranch for him. In 1930, at age 21, a well-educated Martin Cecil (William's son) moved there from England and took charge of the ranch. He would play a significant role in the growth of the town over the following years and later donated some of the acreage to the township for public use. He built a good sized log-wall Lodge just off the main road. It served as his initial home, and he also rented rooms to travelers. Years later he built a more modern and much larger motel and restaurant, The Red Coach Inn, in front of the Lodge and even closer to the main road.

Martin Cecil began his own spiritual quest in the 1930s and started searching for others of like mind. In 1948 he established an intentional community on the grounds of his expansive cattle ranch. Over the following decades a variety of people on their own spiritual quests moved there to join him. Now in 1974 there were about 60-80 residents, spanning all generations, who would serve as our hosts during the class sessions. Indeed we were hosted with great generosity. The food was amazing, and the cooks utilized local freshly picked products as much as possible. Have you ever eaten steamed lamb's quarters? It was a nutritious and prolific local weed with a surprisingly pleasing flavor. Have you eaten steamed beets freshly dug the previous day, or enjoyed goat's milk freshly milked that same day? They were incredible, and the free-range beef from Martin's ranch was indescribably tasty and tender. The old Lodge was now serving as a gathering place. A modern kitchen and large communal dining room had been added onto it; a few people resided in the rooms upstairs. Yes, there was opportunity for each of us to volunteer with the washing of dishes and clean-up.

I remember the first time I met Martin, I found myself standing next to him in the Lodge as we quietly awaited dinner together; we chatted briefly. He was a man of amazing accomplishments and substantial means. It became clear to me that embarking on a quest for spiritual awakening was not reserved solely for hippies and baby boomers.

The class drew about 30 attendees from different parts of North America and a few who had travelled even further. Our ages ranged from the early twenties up to what we called seniors. We met for sessions in an old log chapel situated right on the edge of the cattle ranch. The adjacent field, growing a variety of grasses that would provide winter feed for the cattle, extended as far as we could see. The class faculty was composed of Michael Cecil, Nancy Rose (Meeker) Cecil, and her brother Lloyd Meeker, Jr., all of whom resided there in the community. To say that I was inspired by the thoughts and experiences they shared with us would be an understatement. We also received some instruction in Attunement, which I will talk more about later. In my free time I was inspired to begin a reading of the Bible. A friend had recently given me a copy of the King James version as a gift. I had never read it before. Within a few months I completed it— every page. Certainly, amidst the colorful stories, it contained significant life lessons that would serve me well in the future. I was 26 years old and finding myself in the midst of my own increasingly colorful story.

Much of class time was given to consideration of "the spiritual expression approach to living." Here are the basics. We experience what we express. The energy released through conscious self-expression is much stronger than the chaotic sea of events floating around us. Each of us is the master creator of our day, and we each determine the quality of our own experience. As we cultivate our abilities to sustain this practice of mindfulness, and consistently reveal life-spirits such as Blessing and Thankfulness, we begin to recognize essences of the Divine within ourselves. Along this path each of us has the opportunity to more clearly understand our life purpose. In the absence of creative expression, we feel impacted by external forces and may accept a belief that we have no control over our lives— that is literally the experience of Hell. In each moment we choose. All of this reverberated deeply within me. The more I practiced it, the more it felt real and true.

One afternoon I was on a stroll and decided to turn toward Martin's home. There I found him sitting quietly in his driveway. There was an empty second chair; he invited me to join him. Mostly we sat in silence, watching brisk winds blowing through the tall trees lining the far side of his front yard. I asked him about his spiritual quest in his younger days. Without hesitation he told me that he had been voraciously reading spiritual books whenever he could find the time. He was also looking into different spiritual groups. One was called The Brotherhood of the Sun, but it proved to be of only passing interest. He did not sense any significant resonance with the people. Then he encountered an American, named Uranda, who happened to be speaking in Vancouver. They immediately felt a strong connection. That was April of 1940 and Martin was 31. A deep friendship developed, and they found numerous ways to collaborate over the following years. The rest, he said, was simply living day by day and learning as you go.

We were in a region known as the Cariboo Plateau. One of the community residents, David Oshanuk, owned a small single engine airplane and took each of us for a short tour of the area from above. It was my first experience in a small plane and the overview of the area was absolutely gorgeous. That ride served as a memorable allegory, reminding me of the power of perspective when trying to understand events in my world. Such things always become clearer when viewed from a little altitude, usually achieved only after we stop wrestling emotionally with the parts we do not like.

I remember fondly another resident named Chris Foster. He was a witty and warm-hearted Englishman who had pursued a career in journalism in England, Rhodesia and New Zealand, before leaving it all to continue his own spiritual quest in the "wilds" of Western Canada. He wrote poetry and published a newsletter called "Integrity International"— people from various parts of the world were moved by inspirational ideas they found in it. Some of the responses, many from people in developing nations, were published each month. Chris developed a correspondence with as many of these people as possible, and he loved traveling on speaking expeditions, when funds would allow, to meet some of them personally.

As I was standing in the dinner line one evening, I began to chat with a gentleman named Ross Marks. It turned out he was the town's Mayor. He had a smile and a natural exuberance that rivaled a thousand-watt light bulb. With him it was not a political affectation. He was the real deal. He was a wise gentleman, and he had a manner that put others around him at ease. I am happy to say that in future years we would have opportunities to work together in a businessmen's organization which I'll tell you about later. We would also collaborate on a financial advisory committee for some non-profits.

Those four weeks flew by quickly. During this brief retreat I was continuing to develop a personal sense of purpose and direction. I contemplated how I might communicate this increasing sense of consciousness with others. I now knew that the answers would come each day through the quality of spirit I released in each moment; words would only serve as the outer clothing.

# Chapter Twenty-Six

## WALKING MY TALK

*"I am the Universe, cleverly disguised as Deepak Chopra."*
—Deepak Chopra, Author and Physician

Shortly after my return to Ashland, I realized that my karma yoga experience at Lithia Grocery was complete— I sensed that new and different adventures were awaiting me. I took the city bus to Medford. The engine in my van had gone out again after an increasing number of other mechanical problems, so I had given it to a local mechanic friend. Montgomery Wards sat in front of the first bus stop on the edge of downtown Medford; I stepped off the bus and went inside. I aced an impromptu interview with the General Manager, and he immediately hired me to manage the third floor— the Carpet, Furniture, and Draperies Departments. I had no background in any of these products, but he assured me that I could learn as I go.

James Danks, another resident of our Ashland community, was working at the other end of the same block selling carpet. We began to commute together to Medford in an old Plymouth Valiant that we bought for $100 each. It emitted an annoying grinding noise in the transmission whenever we got it up to freeway speeds, but it was quite dependable. Sometimes we chanted out loud, resonant with the transmission, as we cruised along I-5. In those moments the grinding didn't seem annoying at all. A few months later, James bragged to his store owners about how I was performing miracles with Ward's carpet department. Soon Jerry Kurtz and his partner Dean, owners of the Oregon Carpet Exchange, marched down the street to steal me away with a better offer. My GM refused to match the offer. It was an easy decision for me. Rory Boyle also came to sell at the Carpet Exchange. Rory was a natural actor and comedian, and he appeared in some hilarious local television commercials with Jerry and Dean. They portrayed the super-heroes Carpet Man and Shag, always fighting and vanquishing the villain Evil Prices, played by Rory. I came to enjoy selling carpet, and I learned some sales fundamentals with Jerry's coaching. Unfortunately, Jerry was also known for unexpected highly emotional outbursts. His face would get so red sometimes that I expected it to explode. I would watch in fascination as his head seemed to grow bigger and bigger, his yelling louder and louder, as if it were a cartoon. I knew I needed to save some money and move along to something else.

One of my friends from Ashland was shocked by my change in appearance and my return to the conventional business world. He told me with great concern that he could not understand me, because "You used to be so spiritual." Actually I did not think I had changed at all, except for my appearance. I was now going again by my old name of Terry Oftedal, but I was still Sunseed inside.

As stated in *Be Here Now*, "Before enlightenment, chopping wood and carrying water; after enlightenment, chopping wood and carrying water." Regardless of where anyone is along the spiritual path, we still have to operate in the world in the midst of all of mankind. It was a challenge, but I believed it was possible to experience the turmoil and stresses of the world while living internally in a totally different and calmer space. At least I was trying to maintain that inner calm and peace. When I was in that space, I could honestly say, "I am the Universe, cleverly disguised as Terry Oftedal." Sometimes Sunseed was the disguise. I was trying to consciously walk my talk.

When several of us agreed to purchase Manna Bakery from Baker Bill, on easy payment terms, I was happy to change my work venue back to Ashland. Bill was a well-known hippie in the area who had developed some delicious and wholesome products at his little bakery. He made everything by hand. He did the sales and distribution as well, driving each week as far as the towns of Cave Junction and Wonder. He called me "Seed" or "Mr. Seed," in his attempt at humor. Manna was such a great name; it was the food that fell from the heavens when the Children of Israel were wandering in the wilderness after they left Egypt. We had been one of Bill's biggest customers at Lithia Grocery, and all of the sandwiches we made at our deli in Lithia were on his handmade breads. Bill lived in a bedroom behind the baking room, in a rented building on A Street across from the railroad tracks. Like other bakers he would rise and start the baking process before dawn in the wee hours. He was simply tired of getting up so early after many years. The lease, his equipment, and the recipes were included in the purchase. I still have copies of all those recipes— whole-wheat bread, rye bread, and whole-wheat bagels, granola, cinnamon rolls, brownies, sesame bars, and yummy fruit bars with fruit paste (date, apricot, peach, or apple) between layers of an oat crust. I took the lead and became the new baker in town, assisted by James Danks. In this work environment, maintaining an inner calm was certainly more feasible. We looked for ways to make our days as fun as possible. We could sing as loud as we wanted, play music, tell stories, or chant while we were going through our daily routine. Meanwhile the early mornings got old quite soon, and the income was not impressive. I had a next step in mind.

I met George Emery several times on his visits to Southern Oregon. He was a retired Christian minister and a charismatic speaker. He was on his own unique spiritual quest. He loved public speaking and he held forth frequently, at any venue at any time. He spoke in coffee shops, in libraries, at colleges, and in residential living rooms. His message frequently included statements about the importance of "being who I am, and doing what I came to do." We were all encouraged to do the same. He had a lot of stories to give as examples. Yes, a lot of stories. His lovely wife Joelle was tireless and full of life herself. They wanted to inspire as many of us as possible to follow our own callings and discover our own life purpose. It was easy to say that he was walking his own talk, which gave his words impact. Perhaps it was even more true of Joelle. George recommended a class at Sunrise Ranch, which I had already heard about from Carl.

I wanted a clearer understanding of my purpose in life; I wanted to develop new skills in Attunement and bio-energy work. So instead of finding a better job, I decided to take a break and attend a Spiritual Leadership Class for three months at Sunrise Ranch in Loveland, Colorado. I was accepted for their July class. After a few more months of baking I passed my part in the bakery to James Danks. I packed one small bag, and gassed up the Plymouth Valiant (after buying out James' share for $100). I spent the next night in Portland, at the home of Eric Dunn. There I had prearranged to meet with four other people headed to the same class. I remember the names of three- Beth Van Skoik, Joyce Ellering, and Moira O'Connell; we would become good friends. We stuffed four additional sets of clothing into the trunk along with mine, shared the cost of the gas, and traded off driving as we headed east toward the Rockies. It was cozy with three in the back seat, but everyone was friendly. By the time we left Oregon, the grinding sound coming from the transmission somehow had become a reassuring and relaxing melody. The Wind at our backs felt quite strong.

# Chapter Twenty-Seven

## WHAT IS SPIRITUAL LEADERSHIP?

*"At the heart of each of us is a very specific story.*
*Why are you here on earth at this specific time?*
*What are the gifts that are yours to bring?*
*To unlock this information each of us*
*has to journey to our core."*
—Andrew Shier: *Attunement, A Way Of Life*

When I first arrived at the Ranch that summer of 1975, the air was warm and dry. The cottonwood trees lining the entrance road provided sparse bits of shade. White cottony masses, which carried their seeds, were floating about in the air and covering random patches of the ground. I pulled my trusty Valiant to a stop in front of the building marked "Administration," and we got out to stretch our legs. I was assigned a bed in the two-room Men's Bunkhouse. I shared this living space with three other classmates about my age, including Chris Jorgensen and Larry Johanson, who I would find myself working with again in later years. We had a fully functional outhouse nearby, adjacent to a large hand-tended organic garden. Meals were provided for us communally in a dining hall, a short walk past the laundry building which contained showers we could use. As I strolled about, I observed various-sized houses and apartments spread around the property, which retained a peaceful country charm. I was delighted to come upon their Sanctuary with its beautiful stained-glass windows; it contained a reading room and a few Attunement rooms, which were filled with people for hours on most afternoons. The entire property had a tangible energy about it, and the atmosphere inside the Sanctuary was exquisite— a place of deep rest and healing.

In the afternoons, when taking a break from our classes, we did chores for a few hours with the residents. It was an opportunity to move our bodies and give our minds a rest. I volunteered to work at the Dome Chapel project. It was a large geodesic half-dome, which overall took about two years to complete. It sat against the Rimrock, beside a peaceful hayfield and a quiet pioneers' cemetery, in this picturesque little Eden Valley. The dome was quite a structure; even Bucky Fuller would have been impressed. I was on a team tasked with installing sheetrock into the ceiling structure, a sub-project which took us months of afternoons to complete. I became a team leader when I invented a process for capturing the actual dimensions of each unique triangle in the ceiling structure and then cutting a set of sheetrock pieces that would fit precisely. A team of us would then haul each piece of cut sheetrock up the scaffolding and screw it into its intended triangle. Jim Wellemeyer was the coordinator of the community at Sunrise Ranch and he had overall responsibility for this project. He enjoyed stopping by every afternoon, always contributing words of appreciation.

I saw Andrew Shier my first afternoon at the Dome. We had met the previous year in British Columbia, where we attended the same one-month class. He wasn't on the faculty for my class; he was one of many people who happened to be there living communally while on his own spiritual quest. Like me he was in his mid-twenties. He seemed to always be smiling, and I felt a warmth and gentleness of spirit about him. Andrew was working on the Dome Project, and in his spare time he was practicing Attunement, which would turn out to be his life focus. Thirty three years later he would write his book, a distillation of learnings and perspectives gained along the way. It is an amazing book; I've read it numerous times. Thirty nine years later I would run into him again at an Attunement weekend in Portland, Oregon. The Spiritual Wind would have us crossing paths again and again.

Lloyd Meeker (Senior) had founded Sunrise Ranch in December of 1945. Earlier, in September of 1932, he experienced what he described as a spiritual awakening, and that's when he took on the name of Uranda. He was 25 at the time. He began touring the country while sharing his experiences, all part of his very colorful spiritual quest— along the way he inspired others to embark on their own journeys of self-discovery. Even earlier, in 1929, as he was becoming increasingly aware of patterns of energy in his own body, he began to develop the process which he named Attunement. He said he was not the inventor of this kind of work, rather he remembered it. It felt so natural to him; surely others in the past must have known all about it.

At one point Uranda came in contact with some chiropractors who were experimenting with the idea of "no-force adjustments."

They would hold their hands near the area where the cranium rests on the top of the spinal column and allow "innate" to make the adjustment. In other words they didn't physically manipulate the spine, they were beginning to perform bio-energy work through what they called the spiritual substance surrounding the body. They found this substance to be quite tangible (once they had taken time to develop their innate sensitivities). Uranda invited several of these chiropractors to Sunrise Ranch to share their learnings and together to further develop the practice of Attunement. My bunkhouse had been the original classroom where they spent many hours together. Uranda died in 1954 while piloting his small plane, 21 years before I arrived at the Ranch.

I met many interesting people that summer. One had been in MI-6, the British Secret Service, during World Wars I and II. He had a most unusual name— Conrad O'Brien-ffrench. In his autobiography, entitled *Delicate Mission, Autobiography of a Secret Agent,* he claims to have been the inspiration to his friend Ian Fleming for the literary character James Bond. His designation was Agent Z3; not as catchy as 007 in my opinion. He grew up in Europe and later lived in many parts of the world. When just 17 he moved to Canada to become a Mountie. His later war experiences included time as a prisoner of war, during which he sent information to MI-6 in letters interspersed with messages in invisible ink. He loved to climb the high mountains of the Alps and Himalayas, and his book contains some colorful stories about those adventures. During his second stint in Canada, he met Martin Cecil, and together they drove down to California for a workshop with Uranda. In Conrad's latter years he moved to a lovely home called the Chalet, which he built on the side of Green Ridge. He lived out his years there painting, exhibiting (nearby), and lecturing. You can google his name and read more about his fascinating life. After his death in 1986, our friends Bob and Judy Hollis took over residence in the chalet, and Kathryn and I had opportunities to stay there as guests.

Another fascinating resident was a tall and gangly ex-chiropractor from Huntingburg, Indiana named George Shears. Born in 1890, he had briefly been a pitcher for the New York Highlanders in 1912, before they were renamed the Yankees. Following an unfortunate accident that ended his baseball career, he began chiropractic training under the famous B. J. Palmer at the Palmer School of Chiropractic in Davenport. George later founded the GPC (God-Patient-Chiropractor) Chiropractic movement in the 1930s. It was based on his strong belief that the healing flow of life current moving through the practitioner and the patient was originating from God. He began increasingly to validate the effectiveness of no-force adjustments through his practice and to document his increasing use of "the sensory functions through the hands, and the flow of life through the fingertips." Attunement became his primary modality and he practiced for years on Sunrise Ranch. He died there in 1978 at age 88, a few years after my time with him. I remember sitting on his porch listening to his old stories as often as I could. I treasure my signed copy of his booklet, *Innate Analysis, Innate Adjustment*. I can still hear his deep voice lovingly sharing his favorite saying, "In all things, give Thanks."

Our classes, held in the Old Chapel, were led by Alan Hammond. Born in England, and previously a school teacher, Alan would meet with us almost every morning for three months. He was not earning extra pay; clearly it was a labor of love for him. We would listen to audio or video tapes of class presentations from previous years or have guest speakers in the first three hours of each day. This was followed by a one hour extemporaneous talk by Alan or others. Grace Van Duzen, who had been Uranda's secretary for many years, came for one week to our fourth hours and presented her "Story of Man." Based on a brisk walk through all the books of the Bible, she painted a picture of the history of mankind in a way that made a lot of sense. Her talks seemed applicable to our current day as well. She generously shared her beautiful spirit and her vision of life purpose. She was an amazing woman.

One of the most valuable gifts I received in my spiritual quest was several weeks of instruction in the Attunement process, to the degree that it had been developed so far— it would be a field rich in ongoing discoveries for all involved over many years to come. Alan began our instruction with a few hours on human anatomy and physiology; then we enjoyed experiential sessions working with each other. We later had opportunities to practice afternoons in the Sanctuary with community members and visiting guests. Knowledge of anatomy was useful to start, but when sufficiently still, I could let my hands guide themselves from focus point to focus point in the energy field of my partner, as each session progressed. Soon I discovered my own energy field was reflecting what I was feeling through my hands. We learned about physical and energetic functions of the Endocrine Glands and how to locate their focus points. We also learned about other energy systems and contact points related to the major organs, the skeletal system, the central nervous system, and the chakra systems.

For the final week of our three months, Martin Cecil arrived and spoke at each fourth hour. In one of those hours I remember quite clearly hearing him talk about the need to avoid idolizing any one person in our spiritual quests. He said, "Look up to the heavens, there are many stars." He told us that he was motivated to assist others to think of themselves each as an emissary of divine purpose, regardless of organizational affiliations or beliefs. I found his vision to be refreshing, eye-opening, and compelling. The fact that he had lived a life based on that vision made it even more compelling. Just standing within a few feet of him I could feel the vibrancy of his bio-energetic field.

While there I was called Terry Oftedal, but Sunseed was loving every second of it. Those three months seemed like a journey to my core, like a time of remembrance. I now had a new vision of how my living could be a blessing to others, and in the same moments how those blessings might contribute to returning our world a bit closer to its original natural state. Two days before I left, a commencement ceremony was held with all of the residents attending. I was invited to represent our class, along with Tessa Welch. Originally South African, her current residence was in England. This was just days prior to her marriage to Rupert Maskell. I spoke from my heart and gave thanks to our hosts, for what they had provided and even more for their inspiration as fellow journeymen on our spiritual quests.

# Chapter Twenty-Eight

## THE GIFT OF ATTUNEMENT

*"We are designed to make the invisible visible. The awareness that layers of energetic fields or auras surround the physical body is certainly not new. The body is simply a reflection, and an accurate one at that, of what is present in the field. Change the field and the body changes. Attunement is focused on the dynamics of the field. Learning how to discern what generates and enhances our energetic fields and what dissipates them is one of the most important and ongoing practices of Attunement."*
—Andrew Shier: *Attunement, A Way Of Life*

Attunement is a gift. No beliefs or religious affiliations are required, but every practitioner comes to perceive that we are facilitating the flow of life energy and that it comes from a sacred place. The Attunement current moves through a cloud of spirit substance and into the earth of our human bodies, and then it flows back again to that invisible place, in an ongoing natural cycle.

Why offer to share an Attunement with someone? This question is like asking "Why do I breathe?" or "Why do I say, 'I love you'?" It is a pure expression of giving, coming from the heart, engendering no sense of gain in return. To me, it is "the spiritual expression approach to living" applied. I start each Attunement session by focusing my consciousness on the still place within me. I like to offer a brief silent prayer; sometimes it is simply, "O, Lord"— it is both a calling and an offering, conveying "Here am I, and I am ready." Then I listen to the silence. An amazing thing happens next, sometimes quite quickly. It feels like the opening of an invisible window. Invisible to the physical eye that is; to my energetic senses it is quite tangible. If I have a partner, we share that window, whether or not he or she has any experience in remembering this process. This opening ability exists within everyone. Then subtle energy begins to flow naturally— it comes through that window from another place. The hands can serve as a means of assisting the flow through focus points in our energetic fields, with the fingers or palms usually resting a few inches above the physical body. In the process, our bodies are given an opportunity to remember a more natural state. It seems these memories reside in a deep place within us, and they are always available. There is no need for talking. There is usually no physical contact, but there can be an experience of blessing, of balancing, or perhaps of healing— a return in some measure to that more natural state. I always finish with a silent prayer of thankfulness. This may all sound a bit abstract or mystical, but that is not my intention.

This may help. I recall a day just after Kathryn and I started spending time together in Ashland. We were enjoying some herbal tea, seated silently across a table from each other in Lithia Grocery. We gazed into each other's eyes for minutes at a time, and it felt like each of us was touching something deep inside the other. Have you ever known that kind of experience? We were not touching physically, but it felt like we were. As I came to learn, some touching happens with the physical body but even more of it happens in our consciousness. Have you ever felt someone you know come into your consciousness, someone who was not in the same room? Perhaps they were even far away at the time, and you felt the contact? Actually this happens all of the time whether or not we take notice of it.

A highlight of my class at Sunrise was time spent with a wonderful gentleman named Roger DeWinton— he was a master Attunement practitioner. His generosity of spirit and dedication were inspiring. Attunement was his life, and he was available 24 hours per day. He would regularly receive phone calls at his home from people in various countries of the world. Often the callers were working with some particular health situation in him or herself or in another who they were assisting. It might be real-time, during a hospital or surgical event. Roger and his wife Dorothy were always interested and always welcoming. They had amazing sensitivities to facilitate bio-energetic contact from great distances. As we learned and practiced ourselves, there is no dimension of distance in the realm of our subtle energy fields. I am not the only one who has come to perceive that the energetic body of mankind is in fact one connected body. Some call it the Christ body, which provides each of us a direct connection to God. On a number of later occasions I invited Roger's partnership from over a thousand miles away, and the power and immediacy of his presence was amazing.

I am not comparing anyone to Jesus, but there is a marvelous story in the Book of Matthew. "There came unto him a centurion, beseeching him, and saying, Lord, my servant lieth at home sick of the palsy, grievously tormented. And Jesus saith unto him, 'I will come and heal him.' The centurion answered and said, Lord, I am not worthy that thou shouldest come under my roof: but speak the word only and my servant shall be healed... And Jesus said unto the centurion, 'Go thy way; and as thou hast believed, so be it done unto thee.' And his servant was healed in the selfsame hour." Sounds like Attunement to me. If the "healing" word bothers you, think of it as "facilitating change" or "assisting a return to the natural condition."

The power of the spoken word can be substantial. I was beginning to understand the reality of creative commands, like "Fiat lux" (Let there be light)! I had been pondering that one since my UCLA days. I was beginning to understand how I could change the world. I have seen wonderful things happen in physical bodies when life energy is flowing abundantly and there is a clear connection between spirit substance and the physical body. Many opportunities to put these learnings into action would appear as life soon took me in new and unexpected directions.

# Chapter Twenty-Nine

## OFF TO THE NORTHWEST

*"We live in a wonderful world that is full of beauty, charm, and adventure. There is no end to the adventures that we can have if only we seek them with our eyes open."*
—Jawaharlal Nehru, First Prime Minister of India

I moved to Seattle in the fall of 1975; I had heard of a job possibility. I was also eager for a new adventure. I took a room on the upper floor of a communal house in the Ravenna District, not far from the University of Washington. Here I saw no hippie trappings, as had been so prominent in Ashland. I was living with an assortment of singles mostly; there was also one couple with a young child. A short walk up the street, we participated in meals at a second communal home. We all shared an interest in spiritual expression based living, and several had spent time in the same classes I had taken. The residents, and many of our guests, were also interested in Attunement; I had opportunity to practice my art there several times each week.

We all took part in maintaining the physical operations of the household. Some took turns with the cooking and I enjoyed some new recipes, but a few things got boring. One was a Saturday dinner tradition, enjoyed by the children, consisting of popcorn, cheese, and fruit. That was it— popcorn, cheese, and fruit every Saturday night.

After some electronics tutoring by a friend named David Husky, I secured a job at Tek-Electric, a Portland-based electronics distributor. I was assigned a desk in their Seattle sales office, in the Ballard District, and became responsible for sales in half of the state. The pay wasn't great, but I covered my basic expenses. Then, one day, as I was walking past a used car lot on NE 65th Street, my attention was captured by a bright yellow Mazda RX-4. It was a two-door, with black leather interior, a peppy rotary engine, and lots of zoom-zoom. I had no savings, so I took on monthly payments. I easily found a new owner for my trusty Plymouth Valiant— someone who would appreciate her.

Seattle was a friendly place, for a large city, and at that time before its huge technology boom it was a lot less crowded and congested. The Emerald City, as it is known, is situated along a beautiful Elliott Bay, with gentle hills, lots of trees, and several lakes of different sizes. The largest is Lake Washington where the UW Crew rows and a good many sail boaters and power boaters abound, particularly when the sun comes out. Did I happen to mention the rain? Yes, it does rain a lot there. Even when it wasn't raining, there were often days with gray skies when I did not see the sun for a week. That didn't stop me from playing basketball indoors some evenings. I'm not sure how he found me, but my old friend Larry Smith gave me a call— he had moved to Seattle, and of course he was eager to join our basketball games, just like the old days playing intramural ball together at UCLA. He and Pam had separated and, you guessed it, he had followed a woman to Seattle. Sandra was stunning and extremely intelligent. He soon married her. Larry had completed his tours with the Air Force and wanted to become a commercial pilot; he ended up flying the big jets for United Airlines. In his spare time he finished law school and eventually left the airline to join a Seattle-based law partnership.

Living in the Northwest made it easy for me to venture up to British Columbia. I got to see a bit of Vancouver and its neighboring towns. I made a few trips back up to 100 Mile House in the interior of BC. It really was a drive of exceptional beauty through the Fraser River Valley. The highway, passing through gorges surrounded by high rock walls, followed along the edge of a rapidly flowing river. I caught glimpses of adventurers in big rubber boats braving the rapids. Then everything became flat and plain for some time, until I arrived in the beautifully green forested Cariboo. Of course everyone up there speaks their brand of English with a distinctive difference.

After a year, for a variety of reasons, I left my job at Tek-Electric. I began searching for something with more of a future. To fill the gap I briefly worked a few steps from my home at an old-fashioned bakery- the Tasty Home Bakery- calling on my previous experience in Ashland. "Baker Bill" Schumacher was the owner, and his bakery was quite popular. To keep up with demand, his high volume back-room operation started early and continued for many hours. Friends Steve Bodaness and John Heard worked there; they coached me in this high speed style of hand baking. I learned how to make a lot of new pastries. It was also exhausting. Fortunately I soon happened upon an opportunity with substantial potential. I'll tell about that interesting and significant experience soon enough. For now, I want to return to a favorite part of my story.

I was not dating, because, quietly in my heart, my feelings for Kathryn were growing. An adventure as a single man was progressing externally, while a love story was developing internally. She was still in southern Oregon, but in the midst of our busy weeks we had been exchanging letters since the time I left Ashland. I loved hearing her voice on the phone, but I didn't know what to say; there were often long pauses of awkward silence. Mostly we wrote. In her written words I felt a current of deep connection; she indicated that she felt that connection as well. One day an idea popped into my mind— it was a like a spring flower that suddenly broke above ground into the sunlight— I invited Kathryn and Jennifer to come live with me in Seattle. Why did it take so long? That's hard to explain. All I can say is the timing was finally right. One day they appeared at my doorstep, with huge beaming smiles. Kathryn took a job nursing at Swedish Hospital, where she had worked years before. Jennifer started at Ravenna Elementary School. A few months later I proposed. It was five years after our first kiss, and she finally agreed to marry me. Some cycles require patience. I had some ideas about how marriage would change my life, but our next adventures together would be full of surprises.

# Chapter Thirty

## A PROMISE TO GOD

*"Where wast thou when I laid the foundations of the Earth?*
*declare if thou hast understanding.*
*Who hath laid the measures thereof, if thou knowest?*
*or who hath stretched the line upon it?*
*Whereupon are the foundations thereof fastened?*
*or who hath laid the cornerstone thereof;*
*When the morning stars sang together,*
*ands all the sons of God shouted for joy?"*
—Job 38:4-7
*(As shown on the wedding announcement for Terry & Kathryn)*

When I asked Kathryn to marry me, I said that I felt a Spiritual Wind was bringing us together, that God was bringing us together. In fact, we tried to express our intent by including a quote from the Book of Job in our unusual wedding invitation. It was our way of "declaring something to God."

Have you ever made a promise to God? A promise to God is a serious act, not to be taken lightly and not to be forgotten. I vividly remember making such a promise when marrying Kathryn. The ceremony was conducted by Michael Cecil in a little chapel in the small town of Aldergrove, British Columbia. It was a Sunday, February 13, 1977. A small collection of guests were present. Sigrid Kirsch played some peaceful cello music. Ken and Diane Ghirardi stood up with us. Michael spoke some beautiful words, and we made our promises. Then we felt a spiritual fire falling from the heavens, totally engulfing us in a bright light, and it felt as if God had blessed us with his presence. Honestly, that is exactly how it felt.

We held a reception in Seattle the following weekend at the Ghirardi's home. Friends from around Washington and Oregon were able to attend this time. In fact it was quite heartwarming to see how many friends came to show us their love. We wore the same clothes we had worn at the wedding. My outfit was a brown polyester leisure suit, which was quite popular for a brief number of years, though no one would be caught dead in one today. Kathryn was beautiful in a long dress with a lovely flowing pattern of rust and cream colors. We cut into another cake, made by Baker Bill himself.

Many times in my marriage I have felt a wind at my back—everything seemed to flow easily. But in some days of some years it felt like that wind was blowing in my face. At times along the way I wondered how I ever put myself in such a situation. Marriage is not for wimps; it requires work and humility. Humility helps when I feel wind on my face, because it is highly likely that I am the one going in the wrong direction, not the Spiritual Wind. Patience can come in handy; it is a skill that requires practice however. I have many times thought of my promise to God and felt reassurance that everything works out for a purpose, sometimes exceeding my limited powers of understanding. Of course it also helps to practice "giving thanks in all things." Thankfulness brings stillness. In stillness sometimes I really can hear the morning stars singing together and the sons of God shouting with joy.

# Chapter Thirty-One

## SHOULD WE HAVE MORE CHILDREN?

*"Love is always patient and kind.*
*It is never jealous.*
*Love is never boastful or conceited.*
*It is never rude or selfish,*
*It does not take offense,*
*And it is not resentful.*
*Love takes no pleasure in other people's sins,*
*but delights in the truth.*
*It is always ready to excuse,*
*to trust, to hope, and to endure,*
*whatever comes."*
—I Corinthians 13:4-7

I love the wedding ceremony in the movie *A Walk To Remember*, which starred Mandy Moore and Shane West. It is particularly meaningful because in the story they know their marriage will be short lived, due to her cancer, and they were marrying anyway for beautiful and deliberate reasons. In one of my favorite scenes her father, a minister played by Peter Coyote, read the beautiful words shown above (from the Book of Corinthians) during the wedding ceremony.

Marriage causes one to think about a lot of things and hopefully to become more deliberate. Perhaps the biggest decision anyone ever makes relates to bringing a new life into the Earth. Some decisions can be changed, but when a new life is brought forth, the responsibilities never go away.

In the 1960s and 1970s I had serious concerns about the booming world population and whether we as a whole would be able to produce adequate amounts of food. Books like *The Population Bomb*, by Dr. Paul Ehrlich, painted a concerning picture. Global population in 1968 was 3.5 billion, and it seemed incomprehensible that even that huge number could double—which it has as of 2014, reaching 7.2 billion while still growing

1.14 percent per year. Birth rates were increasing in the U.S. in the 1960s and projected to rise even higher in other parts of the world. It seemed that child bearing decisions deserved consideration on a scale beyond just desire and a couple's financial means.

We already had one child, Jennifer. She was eight and a half years old when I married Kathryn. Prior to the wedding our minister, Michael Cecil, asked us whether we intended to have more children. We honestly had not talked about it out loud, but that started us talking. At the time I thought one more child might be about right, Kathryn thought maybe two. In less than a year we would know the answer. One day, after she had gone for a check-up with her doctor, when I returned home she asked me, "Guess what?" I immediately blurted out, "We are going to have twins." The thought had just spontaneously come into my mind. Yes, we were being given a double gift.

I felt even more motivated to find a job that had more of a future. It happened one day as I was walking in the University District near the University of Washington— I came upon a frozen yogurt shop that had just opened— it was called The Yogurt Stand. Frozen yogurt was a new concept and it was particularly appealing to people concerned about health and nutrition. Hardcore ice cream lovers usually avoided yogurt, certain that it tasted awful. The frozen yogurts I had previously experienced actually were awful. They left a sour taste partly overlaid with some weak flavoring notes. The Yogurt Stand guys had done their homework— their yogurt tasted incredibly good. I asked, "Who do I talk to in order to get a job here?" The next day I met Dave Hanna, who with his brothers, Jim and John, were the founders and owners. This was their flagship store and they had big ideas about franchising and expanding the chain. They wanted someone like me to manage their shop, develop new yogurt flavors, create an operations manual, and help them open new stores. I was soon hired as the new Operations Manager. This job would prove quite interesting over the coming months, as well as further in the future after the company became known as YoCream International. I'll tell a lot more stories about YoCream in later chapters; for now I want to continue the story about our twins.

The good news is I now had health insurance. The bad news was the twins were considered a "pre-existing condition," and the insurance would not help at all with the hospital and doctor bills to come. We moved to a more modern house in Mountlake Terrace, just north of Seattle, where we had more space. We painted the bedroom between ours and Jennifer's, and in it we assembled two brand new cribs. We took classes together in the Bradley Method of natural birth and practiced our breathing and relaxation techniques in preparation. I was very excited about helping with the delivery.

With twins inside, Kathryn was getting quite big. I frequently assured her that she was more beautiful than ever; it was the truth. On a date night we went to see the newly released mega-movie *Star Wars*. The line was so long that it stretched around the block. Kathryn's back soon began to ache from standing, so I took her to our car to lie down until just before our saved places in line reached the front door. Pregnant women were respected and given extra consideration in those days. One evening we went to a small club where B.B. King was performing. Upon seeing her condition, the host walked us directly to a table immediately in front of B.B. What an experience— the King of the Blues!

At her six month check-up, we learned that Kathryn was partially dilated. Concerned about risks related to premature delivery, Dr. Donahue ordered her to spend the last trimester of pregnancy in bed. She could get up for the short trip to our bathroom, and she was allowed to sit in the wooden rocking chair next to the bed. She had a bell, which she rang when she needed something. She ate breakfast in bed, as well as lunch and dinner. We shared a lot of Attunements. For hours I would lie next to her in bed, my hand on her belly, enjoying the warmth and radiance that was naturally building; we would talk quietly together about our dreams, past and future. I rubbed her feet. I whispered "sweet nothings" into her ears and covered her in soft kisses. She made it two more months.

# Chapter Thirty-Two

## A TRULY UNFORGETTABLE EXPERIENCE

*"There are two ways to live:*
*you can live as if nothing is a miracle;*
*you can live as if everything is a miracle."*
—Albert Einstein, Theoretical Physicist and Philosopher

After a couple of false-alert trips to Swedish Hospital, one morning Kathryn told me she knew the babies would definitely be coming today. With great calm we grabbed her pre-packed bag and started the short walk to our car, when the doorbell rang. It was two recent acquaintances who just happened to be driving through Seattle and stopped to say hello. We invited them in for a cup of herbal tea. As we were sitting in the living room and I was serving tea, one of them asked how soon we were expecting the babies to arrive. When we said that we were preparing to leave for the hospital just as the doorbell rang, their eyes opened wide in surprise. They quickly finished their tea and said their goodbyes. We were calmer than they were.

We made it to the hospital by early afternoon and were admitted. Contractions were still at least 10 minutes apart, so we played cards for a bit. Mostly I held her hand, and we talked and waited. We called our trusted friend Roger DeWinton to touch in and he encouraged us to remain patient— no need to rush things. A few hours later the time between contractions did start to shorten and her dilation increased. We prepped and went into the delivery room. She was only one month early, the date was September 25, a Sunday. Kathryn became quite energized, to put it mildly. My job was to coach her breathing and help her stay as calm as possible. It turned out that the delivery bed, which we had not seen on our prior tour of that very modern hospital, was not designed for natural childbirth. A nurse strapped Kathryn's legs into stirrups, which clearly made it very difficult for her to simulate a natural squatting position. I had to physically lift Kathryn's back into a vertical position. I got plenty of exercise supporting her back for some time, but she was doing the really big work. Thankfully the breathing exercises did prove a useful tool for maintaining focus, for both of us.

All along we felt it was the boy who was in the big rush to come out, and we were right. What an unforgettable experience! When he came out at 9:34 PM and quickly took his first breath, a powerful energy and light filled the room. We were participating in a cosmic event, the crossing over into this world of an eternal spirit into a new life form. Within minutes I got to hold him briefly. He was beautiful. So tiny, yet so strong with life energy. He weighed 5 pounds and 8 ounces, not bad for a preemie. We were hoping they would each exceed 5 pounds.

Kathryn was given five minutes of rest and then told she needed to get back to work; we didn't want to risk oxygen deprivation with the second baby. Kathryn was now fully dilated, of course, but due to the lessened crowding in her womb her stretched abdominal muscles were slacked and it was hard for her to use them for pushing. Applying external pressure, Dr. Donahue, our obstetrician, tried to turn the second baby from her breech position, but he was unsuccessful. Then he discovered that the umbilical cord was wrapped around her neck. This caused some concern, but we gave our permission and he gently reached inside to unwind the cord. This all happened very quickly and just 6 minutes after the first birth, at 9:40 PM, the girl backed out butt-first. She would have liked a few more weeks, but her brother had changed all that. She did not breathe immediately because she was not really ready. Our pediatrician, Dr. Adkins, carefully massaged her until she began to breathe. Then we felt another rush of spirit and light, but this was much gentler and had a sweeter feminine-energy feeling to it. When she was handed to Kathryn, she was smiling. We have a picture of that moment, but I can still envision it all in perfect clarity without the picture. She weighed 5 pounds and 5 ounces. We got to hold both of them and softly offer words of welcome, but the doctors wanted to get them into a warm incubator as quickly as possible. Thankfulness for these two precious gifts and for Kathryn's continuing health filled my heart. We had experienced two miracles.

We had names in mind but we wanted to meet these new people first; then we thought it would become obvious which names were meant for each of them. Brian Jasper Oftedal was definitely the right name for the boy; the "Jasper" in honor of his grandfather. We named the girl Tracy Elizabeth Oftedal. I realized we were now responsible for the care and raising of

THREE young angels, but it was more than that— I felt changed by this experience, as did Kathryn. We were new people ourselves now. I made another promise to God.

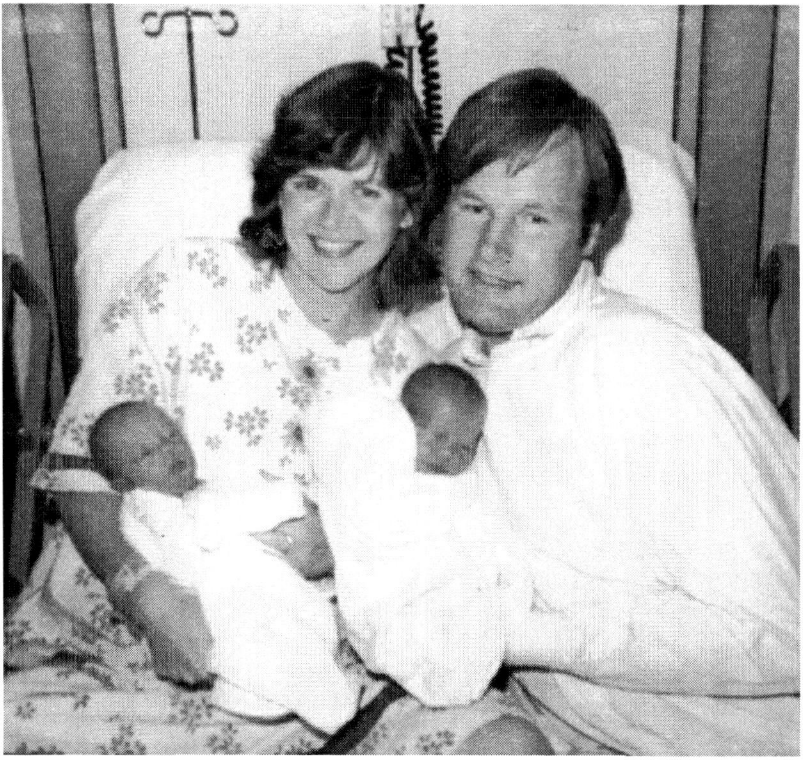

*"A truly unforgettable experience."*

Each of the babies gained a few ounces over the next few days. Kathryn reminded everyone that she was a nurse and promised to keep in close touch; this helped her talk the doctors into releasing us sooner. The meter was ticking and we had to cover all of the hospital and doctor bills. A pre-existing condition, remember. We drove home to Mountlake Terrace in my little Mazda RX-4. Because it was a two-door sedan, putting the babies into their car-seats in the back seat was quite awkward. I would quickly need to step-up to something bigger. Shortly thereafter I did trade in my zippy little car for a slightly used VW Van, with a large side door.

Because we had no health insurance coverage and no savings, we set up monthly payments of $15 to Swedish Hospital, $15 to Dr. Donohue, and $15 to Dr. Adkins until they were each paid off. Meanwhile we were still paying student loans, $50 per month combined, a few monthly credit cards, and a car payment. My take-home pay was $865 per month, after taxes and insurance. Needless to say we were frugal in those days. We agreed to co-mingle our money and our debts, and that month we created a budget in a black ledger book, listing all of our expected income and expenses by category. One month per page, we have continued through all the years of our marriage to agree in advance on a monthly budget; a lot of potential disagreements are avoided when there are no surprises.

I tried to negotiate with the Hanna brothers for a significant raise. They felt that even though we were achieving some significant successes, the business was still too leveraged. They started the company with a small investment of $10,000 each, and there was simply not yet enough cash flow to help me. It was clear I would have to move on. I did not want to burn any bridges, but having a degree from UCLA I felt confident I would find a higher paying job. I was ready for another miracle.

# Chapter Thirty-Three

## BACK TO CALIFORNIA

*"Your family is God's gift to you, as you are to them."*
—Desmond Tutu, South African Social Rights Activist

It had been way too long since my last visit with family in Fresno. None of them had seen the twins yet— none of them had met Kathryn or Jennifer either. When the babies were almost three months old, all five of us boarded a United Airlines flight to Fresno for a Christmas visit. We settled into three seats in the bulkhead row and found in front of us two baby-sized baskets hooked onto the wall. Brian and Tracy slept for the entire two and a half hour flight in those baskets. Parents, grandparents, brother, and sister were all lined up and waiting for us right at the door as we walked off the plane. We enjoyed much hugging and many tears of joy. Over the next few days we were stuffed with a wide assortment of foods, home-baked cookies, and pies. We were blessed with many gifts. Everyone patiently waited for a turn to hold a baby. We took a lot of pictures. It was a wonderful reunion and it ended too quickly. Thankfully our return flight was a quiet one again.

We moved from Mountlake Terrace to Seattle's South Park area, and Jennifer changed schools again, after our landlord terminated the lease early. We were certainly not eager to move again, but I was not uncovering any quality job opportunities. The wind at my back was gathering power quickly; I was unable to stand still. With Kathryn's agreement, I gave two weeks notice to the Hanna brothers, who understood my situation. I began handing off responsibilities to my capable assistant, Rhoda Thorpe. I was leaving on good terms, which turned out to be a very good thing— setting the stage in fact for a fortunate turn of events that would take over twenty years to evolve— another long cycle.

We began packing for a move to Los Angeles, where I would look into some job possibilities I had uncovered through some friends. My Fresno family was thrilled that we would be back in California. We purchased a new Mazda GLC, which got exceptional gas mileage and actually felt spacious inside for a little car; I traded in my VW Van because it had developed a mysterious habit of shutting off its own engine while I was trying to drive in the middle of traffic. One morning we rose early, ready to head south. Some friends gathered at our driveway to wish us a bon voyage. I was driving a rented truck with Jennifer on the bench seat beside me; in the back were all of our belongings. Kathryn followed in the GLC, with two babies and some house plants. If the babies needed attention, she would flash her lights and we would all pull off the road for a rest stop. Everything went surprisingly well actually. Along the way we stopped in Auburn, California— in the old Gold Rush country— where we spent an overnight at the home of Rick and Karen Toal. We knew them from our Ashland days. The next morning Rick demonstrated for us his secret recipe for the world's lightest waffles. Mumble, mumble, whipped egg whites, mumble, secret, secret. Of course we stopped next in Fresno, continuing to retrace the route I had taken north in 1972.

Once in L.A., we lived for a few months in a communal apartment complex in South Gate. It was coordinated by my old friend Chris Jorgensen and his wife Donna. We found ourselves surrounded by friends old and new. This is also where we met Francine Ladd, a lovely young woman just out of high school, who would become a dear family friend. Jennifer started at Tweedy Elementary for yet another short stay.

I began selling soft-serve yogurt machines; it would be the first step in an interesting progression of jobs. Commissions were sparse, but I was able to lease a two-story house in Cerritos. Cerritos? Situated on the eastern edge of Los Angeles County, rent prices there were more affordable. It was previously named Dairy Valley, before the dairy farms moved out to the desert in search of lower overheads. The farmlands were quickly being transformed into freshly-built new suburban neighborhoods with new shopping centers. One of the great things about Cerritos was our proximity to Knott's Berry Farm. All of us loved Mrs. Knott's chicken dinner, complete with fresh hot biscuits and marionberry jam. Our children were growing and they loved the rides in the park, so we bought annual passes. We drove over to Knott's many times— Kathryn and I would relax on a bench, chat together, and enjoy watching kids running from ride to ride. I'll admit, we had a few favorite rides as well. Knott's had grown significantly since my first visit with Grandpa Doc.

I found a job with steadier pay (through an ad in the L.A. Times), selling industrial electronics for The Hundley Company. Hundley was a distributor of products similar to those at Tek-Electric in Seattle. With offices in Glendale, my new commute was a challenging drive up a crowded I-5 Freeway through the heart of downtown Los Angeles. After one year I had yet to receive a single commission check; the commute was becoming even more stressful.

I signed with a recruiter on Wilshire Boulevard who quickly secured me an interview with a New Jersey company, oddly named Indiana General. They wanted a western-based regional salesman for their ferrite products, which were ceramic magnetics used in a variety of industrial and high-tech applications. I boarded a plane to meet their Sales VP and their General Manager in Chicago's O'Hare Airport, where the three of us would converge from different directions. I found them in a small meeting room in a United Airlines lounge; they had one hour to talk. I thought the interview went well, the company sounded fascinating, and I felt good chemistry between us. Before I landed back in LAX that evening they made an offer through my recruiter, who immediately called Kathryn. Kathryn then immediately called our realtor and signed a late-night offer to buy our first home, conditional on my approval. I found out about all this when I arrived home. The next morning I was offered a sales job with Memorex, but I declined. I made my commitment to IG.

My new take home pay would be $2,625 per month (the most I had ever earned). In 1980 inflation was spinning out of control. Interest rates ballooned and unemployment had risen to 11 percent. We bought the house on Ashworth Street in Cerritos for $98,000, with $726 per month combined payments on $88,000 worth of mortgages. The first mortgage was at 12 percent interest; we secured a second at 18 percent, and the sellers carried a third at 15 percent. My parents loaned us $10,000 for the down payment. We had been looking for a home to buy but everything seemed so expensive, as it always does to first time buyers. The house was sturdy, and the neighborhood was quite attractive. The house, however, had been abused by renters, and the sellers were motivated to dump it as-is at a discount. Kathryn heard about it from a realtor neighbor, who knew that it was going to be listed the next day and that it would surely attract numerous offers. He called and they immediately met for a quick walk-through, while I was still on my airplane. Kathryn's quick actions that night and the timing of my new job coincided perfectly. We invested our own sweat and labor totally gutting it. We painted every inside surface, and installed new doors, new flooring, and curtains. At the same time we were packing. Within a week we moved into our new home; I was amazed at how magically it all came together.

I developed a great relationship with my new boss, John Breickner, who lived in New Jersey. It was a challenging time for Indiana General. He liked to remind me that when he hired me he told me, "The faint of heart need not apply." I was up to the challenge, and I learned a lot from John. We still exchange emails every few years. Back then I often received business calls at home, and frequently one of our family would answer the phone and then sing out, "It's John Breickner calling." We made a joke out of it. Often times I would answer the phone and then fib to the kids, "It's John Breickner calling." Sometimes Brian would call from a neighbor's house and disguising his young voice try to convince me that he was John Breickner calling. I set up a small one-man office with a part-time secretary. It was located only a few minutes from home; a much improved commute. Some days I would go home to enjoy a quiet lunch with Kathryn, often talking about when we might be able to get away for a date, just the two of us. We felt young, and we were very much in love. Dates became more feasible when we joined a babysitting co-op. We could drop off the twins with someone we trusted, but also on short notice we might be required to look after the children of another co-op member. It was a good system actually and everyones' hours balanced out.

I was meeting a lot of people and absorbing a lot of technical knowledge, while gaining a broad perspective of the many high-tech companies operating in the the Western U.S. I called on companies like Intel and Motorola Electronics, who were each making bubble memory data storage devices at the time. We were supplying them a magnet assembly which was essential for their device to work. I frequented power supply companies, the U.S. military, telecommunications companies, and the rapidly growing disk drive industry.

A couple of years down that road, one of my customers recommended me to Hitachi Magnetics, a company that was searching for someone like me. They were much larger than Indiana General, and they could afford bigger salaries and better benefits. I declined their first approach, but shortly thereafter I ran into Joe Betts and Frank Shiraki (both from Hitachi Magnetics) at Powercon, a High Tech event in Dallas. Joe made a strong pitch to me while we were standing in a very crowded bus on the way to the DFW Airport. The next day, after talking it over with Kathryn, I called Joe to arrange a flight to Michigan for interviews at their U.S. headquarters. I liked the people, I liked their broad technology base, and I really liked the idea of traveling to Japan while working with such a well known and respected company. I would be their sole U.S.-based salesman for a variety of high-tech ceramics they were producing in their Japan factories, where the parent company was called Hitachi Metals Corporation. A separate sales force would continue selling the magnets being produced in their Michigan and North Carolina factories. I accepted, and after gaining the blessing and well wishes of John Breickner, I started commuting south on I-5 to an HMC sales office in Newport Beach. I would continue to drive around Southern California, interspersed with short flights to Northern California and surrounding states, and now I was adding some international travel.

*"Terry with Joe Betts and Hitachi Metals Managers in Tokyo – an evening meeting."*

Hitachi was more advanced in their abilities to produce ferrite ceramic parts. I learned even more about magnetics and worked my way even deeper into the disk drive business. My first assignment was support for an existing business— we were supplying recording heads for floppy disk drives (FDD), and Tandon Magnetics was our primary customer. We were working even harder to develop recording heads for hard disk drives (HDD). Few personal computers at the time came with HDD's internally installed, but I believed that percentage would grow over time and eventually become a standard data storage device within all PC's.

Hitachi Metals was producing a precision machined ferrite part called a slider, which carried a transducer for reading and writing data onto a rotating disk. In the FDD, the slider would physically slide on the rotating floppy disk— that's how it got its unusual name. In the HDD, sliders were actually flying about one or two millionths of an inch above the more rapidly rotating hard disks. We sold both monolithic and composite type HDD sliders to companies that turned them into HGA's (head gimbal assemblies), which were then sold to the disk drive manufacturers. My main customers were Information Magnetics (Infomag), Applied Magnetics (AMC), and Acton, all located in Santa Barbara. Sunward Magnetics of San Diego soon emerged as another key HGA provider. They all had large manufacturing operations outside the U.S.

I spent a lot of time traveling on business. I also treasured my time with family. In the midst of it all, inside I was still Sunseed. I was still seeking ways to share my most personal thoughts and realizations with others. I was still focused on living a meaningful life, while dealing externally with emergencies and alligators snapping at my heels. The trick is to stay awake— with vision focused above the swamp— and avoid making a habit of wrestling with those pesky alligators. It helps if you have friends who are living their lives with similar intent.

# Chapter Thirty-Four

## BEING AWAKE IN L.A.

*"The path to salvation is narrow and as difficult to walk as a razor's edge."*
—W. Somerset Maugham: *The Razor's Edge* (1944)

We became friends with a fascinating young woman named Barbara Kaufman. She was working as an Associate Dean at Cal State University Long Beach. She knew many interesting people and would travel to share her vision in places as far away as Moscow and Kazakstan— all part of her spiritual quest. Barbara liked to share Attunements; she also hosted weekly meetings in her Long Beach home, discussing topics relating to our shared interest in the Spiritual Expression Approach to Living. Barbara organized one particularly memorable meeting in the home of our friends Stan and Sonia Gabrielson, with guest speakers Bill Ury and Bruce Allyn. Both were active in the Harvard Negotiation Project, and Bill was a co-author of the best-selling 1981 book *Getting to Yes- Negotiating Agreement Without Giving In.* We were fascinated by their stories of coaching high level officials in both the U.S. and the Soviet Union and of how the project had helped with the advancement of nuclear arms treaties. The same principles applied in the private sector and between individuals. The simple ideas defined in that book have stuck with me for many years and have proved quite useful.

Buckminster Fuller was a renowned 20th century inventor, philosopher, and futurist. I first heard about him in the 1970's when I came across a used copy of his book *The Dymaxion World of Buckminster Fuller,* which explained the concept of tensegrity. This was the functional basis for the domes for which Bucky had created the term "geodesic" and for which he was awarded one of his many U.S. patents. As it happened, the City of Long Beach had brought the retired Queen Mary ocean liner into its harbor and supported its conversion into a dockside hotel, as a public relations idea. Then to further promote tourism they brought

Howard Hughes' Spruce Goose, a giant wooden airplane, into the parking lot next to the Queen Mary and proceeded to erect a huge geodesic half-dome over it. The evening before the opening of the new dome, Barbara (representing Cal State Long Beach) brought Bucky to town for a formal dinner. She invited about two hundred "community leaders" to attend. Kathryn and I were included. In fact we sat at Bucky's table. Conversations over dinner were fascinating— I was captivated with stories from Bucky's colorful lifetime, and he revealed some insights into his personal search for meaning in life. Barbara stepped to the podium to introduce and honor Bucky, and he rose to add a few words. He talked about the wonders of the geodesic dome, and he told how domes emulated one of nature's miracles (also famous for its intrinsic strength)— a chicken's egg. Then he invited all of us to walk next door for a personally guided tour of the "world's largest geodesic dome ever built." We even followed him into the insides of the Spruce Goose, the largest wooden airplane ever built. The next day I attended a daylong seminar at CSULB which featured Bucky, Alan Hammond, and other interesting speakers. Bucky died less than a year later in the middle of 1983. I was fortunate to have known him.

In 1984 I discovered a movie which addressed some important questions. *The Razor's Edge,* starring Bill Murray, is a story of one man's search for meaning in life. Yes, that Bill Murray in a serious role. He was also a co-screenwriter— it was clearly a labor of love and an effort to depict something meaningful. The music and cinematography seemed brilliant to me, though the critics at the time were not impressed. The movie, based on Maugham's novel, was set in the early 1900s, but it is timeless really. It follows Larry Darrell through a number of challenging life experiences that lead him to an unexpected spiritual quest. Larry eventually finds his way high into the Himalayas. There a Buddhist Lama delivers the line about the razor's edge and the narrow path to salvation, which in the Upanishads relates to liberation from the delusions of the world. He was talking about enlightenment. I particularly relate to the ending where Larry appears to reconcile some painful personal issues, finally ready to return home to a simple life based on the spiritual consciousness which he has developed.

The idea of "Being Awake in L.A." (my title for this chapter) talks to my efforts to be spiritually conscious while earning a living, raising a family, and endlessly driving along that serpentine freeway system which to me more than anything defines the "L.A." experience. Lin Sample, a friend from Oregon, was now living in nearby Orange County. Together we created a monthly series of meetings that we dubbed "Integrity in Business." We advertised via mailed fliers and phone calls, but attendance mostly came from word of mouth— people who we ran into in our day jobs. We met at restaurants, we invited speakers, but mostly we talked informally about each other's efforts to demonstrate integrity in our business dealings. The value for everyone came primarily from those forums where we discussed our inner motivations with others of a like mind. It reinforced for each of us that we were not alone in our quests— others driving around in the belly of the serpent were also working each in his own way on remaining awake to his or her higher consciousness.

In 1984 we became aware of a larger organization called Renaissance Business Associates. They called themselves "An international association of business men and women demonstrating the power and effectiveness of integrity in business." Lin and I hopped in my car and drove nearly non-stop to one of their events in the Rockies. We found numerous business folks from a variety of organizations much like ours. There we met some very substantial people like Dr. Elaine Gagne, Bill Becker, and our old friends Bob Hollis and Alan Hammond. On our drive home we decided to start operating under the RBA banner, and we began planning an event to be held in the spring of 1985 on the grand old Queen Mary. It took about a year to plan. We booked the Grand Salon, arranged an exquisite luncheon, and organized a large slate of speakers including Dr. David Banner, Alan Hammond, Dr. Elaine Gagne, John Gray, Stan Grindstaff, and Achal Bedi. Topics included "dealing with subconscious blocks to real success in business; beyond war: a new way of thinking; and the rising tide of change in business." I was the emcee, and we drew about 100 people. Our event even earned an article with a picture of me on the cover of Business Dynamics magazine, a small but very interesting bi-monthly published by Norman Smookler in British Columbia.

A few years later, I was the keynote speaker at an RBA event at the Wawona Hotel in Yosemite. This time we added some outdoor experiential sessions, including silent morning walks through a forest of old-growth trees, and again we had excellent speakers in Dr. Elaine Gagne, Dr. David Banner, Dr. Sherrie Connelly, Steven Orsary, and Peggy Sebera. My talk, entitled "Attitudes in the Workplace," was printed as a featured article in the September 1989 Business Dynamics. Here is an excerpt. "Why has it been so difficult to work with people's emotions in the workplace? Why is work exhausting instead of exhilarating? The answer I have found lies in the qualitative content of our expression, which is called spirit. Ignore this dimension of expression and your personal world will appear to be an amalgam of unrelated accidents and happenstance. Pay attention to the qualities of spirit in your expression, and your perspective on just about everything will change. Following is my list of Seven Spirits in Business. It's easy and enjoyable to do this kind of exercise. Simply take the time to look around you and recognize some of the symptoms on this list. Above all, recognize that you are the means for bringing the associated qualities of spirit into any circumstance."

| Seven Spirits In Business | Symptoms Of Their Presence | Symptoms Of Their Absence |
|---|---|---|
| **Newness** | Fresh ideas, Fresh Methods, Innovation | Stagnation, Bureaucracy |
| **Focus** | Attention, Coherence, Stability, Balance | Scattered attention, Overstressed and frenzied, Excess |
| **Appreciation** | Thoughtfulness, Praise, Thankfulness, Respect | Criticism, Backstabbing, Voodoo |
| **Delegation** | Prioritization, Trust, Elimination | Constipation, Pollution |
| **Life** | Focus on people, Initiative, Enthusiasm | Focus on circumstances, Apathy, Despair |
| **Wisdom** | Holistic vision, Cooperation, Accuracy, Humor | Shortsightedness, Carelessness |
| **Love** | Generosity, Freedom, Joy | Greed, Slavery, Death |

Over the years we held similar events at Palm Springs, San Diego, Glen Ivy, and a resort near the Kern River where we enjoyed some river rafting. Our meetings and events may not have triggered a defining moment in anyone's life. That was not our goal. We were simply seeking to do things in the midst of all our other activities which would reinforce the finest qualities of our own personal identities. At the same time we were providing a safe space in a business setting for others to explore and express the essences of their own inner being. In fact, each of our lifetimes viewed in its wholeness is simply an amalgamation of what we do in all of the days along the way. So each day is significant. Each day is everything actually. For me this was an essential part of staying awake in L.A., and I was fortunate to have friends with similar intent walking with me. Walking the razor's edge? Yes it is difficult, but definitely easier with practice, practice, practice.

# Chapter Thirty-Five

## DID I EVER TELL YOU ABOUT THE TIME I RAN AWAY FROM HOME AND JOINED THE CIRCUS?

*"There can be no keener revelation of a society's soul than the way in which it treats its children."*
—Nelson Mandela

In Cerritos, Brian and Tracy started pre-school at Gonzalves Elementary. When we bought our own home and moved across town, they spent Kindergarten through Fourth Grade at Cerritos Elementary. In fact they attended Kindergarten for two years; we looked at it as a gift of extra time for them to mature. Kathryn was volunteering in their classroom; she was also in the PTA, even serving as PTA President for two years. This was a stable time for all of us.

*"Kathryn, Tracy, and Brian."*

I was too serious and way too busy for much of the time when the twins were growing up, though I didn't reach this conclusion until years later. I never did little league or soccer coaching, but I did enjoy taking them on bike rides though our neighborhood streets, sometimes even venturing together as far as the A&W Root Beer drive-in. Bedtime was also a precious time— I was committed to telling stories, reading, or just listening to them. I loved lightly massaging their feet and backs, and while trotting my fingers along each one's back I asked them to guess what kind of animal was walking on them. I invented a game where I told them two stories and had them guess which was true and which was made up. Once I told them of a time when I was young and I ran away to join the circus. I made up a detailed and colorful story—both of them guessed it was true. My main concern was to assist them in releasing their cares for the day so that they could enjoy a peaceful and healing sleep.

Sometimes children (and adults) find it difficult to let go of stressful experiences, and the memories and emotions may stay with us for days, weeks, or even years. Kathryn and I developed a little bedtime ritual that proved helpful. One of us would verbally guide one of our children to close his or her eyes and imagine the troubling situation— then wrap it up in a blanket and tie it to a large pink balloon. Imagine taking that package out the back door and letting it float up to drift away forever. Let it go. If that concern comes back, do the exercise again. Sometimes it works immediately. Sometimes it takes years; eventually most people will give up and let it go. Good riddance. Does this sound too simplistic to really work? Letting go actually happens in an instant, and looking back at any experience of letting go, after the fact it always seems so simple. The real question is why do we resist for so long and insist on carrying our problems inside?

As everyone learns when they have their first child, there is no manual on how to be a good parent. Sure there are lots of books and everyone you know will offer you advice, particularly those who do not have children. A lot of first-hand learning lies ahead for every new parent. Most of us start with plenty of enthusiasm; then come the doubts and self-judgments. Everyone makes some mistakes, or at least we think they are mistakes, but the spirit of love can flow easily from parent to child. That is the thing each child wants and needs most, and in the end that is what the child remembers most. Why do some parents and some children resist this natural flow? That is a complex and disturbing question, probably best left for a different book.

It can take many years, sometime into adulthood, before a child develops his or her own perspectives such that they can truly understand and appreciate the depth of their parents' (and grandparents') love for them. The amount of material things provided along the way is not what matters, although good nutrition is very important. The gift that provides the most lasting impact is simply surrounding a child with love.

A key factor in the healing of our world is how we each accept responsibility for all of the world's children. I'm thankful for teachers, particularly those who love their work; unfortunately they are all underpaid. There is always more that each of us can do. A smile goes a long way, yes even when writing the property tax check that supports the local schools. I particularly enjoy donating time and money to school lunch programs.

Yes, we can still find abused children and many estranged family relationships in the world. As with everything else, we have to start by focusing on whatever situation is right in front of us. Hugs can work miracles. Random acts of kindness with children are particularly powerful, even with grown-up children. It takes practice to welcome all of the situations that appear right in front of us. None of them happen by accident. Each morning when I wake, I give thanks first; then I remind myself to be watchful and ready for the opportunities that will soon present themselves.

# Chapter Thirty-Six

## ONE MORE PROMISE TO GOD

*"There is one God looking down on us all.*
*We are all the children of one God. The sun, the darkness,*
*the winds are all listening to what we have to say."*
—Geronimo, Apache Indian Leader (1829-1909)

Five years after I married Kathryn, I told Jennifer that I wanted to become her legal father. Kathryn and Jennifer agreed, so we filed a Stepparent Adoption petition with the Los Angeles County Department of Adoptions in February, 1982. We started gathering a lot of paperwork. Jennifer's birth father signed his approval, so we thought the rest of the process should go forward smoothly. That's when we hit a problem. When my first wife secured a Judgment of Dissolution of Marriage back in 1972, neither of us filed the judgment at a courthouse. On it was clearly stated, "This judgment does not constitute a final dissolution of marriage and the parties are still married and will be, and neither party may remarry, until a final judgment of dissolution is entered." I was able to secure a new copy of the original court papers from the Superior Court, Mary signed it, and I finally got it filed on April 22.

So this is also the story of why Kathryn and I got married to each other three times. Our first marriage was February 13, 1977 in Canada. We had been advised to get married again in the U.S. since we were American citizens, so our second marriage was in Seattle on the following weekend at the reception in the the Ghirardi's home. Ken performed the honors of signing the Washington State marriage certificate. That certificate also shows the date of February 13, since we all agreed this was the date we had actually become married.

Now we were living in California, when I discovered that I had no legal right to be remarried. We got another wedding license and decided to do it again, to make sure we were legal. Chris Jorgensen officiated. Six people joined us in the Jorgensen's living room in Torrance. It was simple and short, on June 12, 1982. Ken and Diane Ghirardi, living in Thousand Oaks at the time, were our witnesses as they had been at our first (and second) ceremony back in 1972.

Finally in October we received the written report and formal recommendation from the Department of Adoptions, and we went before a Superior Court judge in Norwalk. He swore us in, explained the proceedings, and advised Jennifer and me that we were making a very serious and legally binding commitment. Jennifer swore to become my legal daughter. I swore to become Jennifer's legal father. Even more seriously for me, I was making one more promise to God, and I knew He was listening. Her new name was now Jennifer Kathryn Oftedal. We were both happy. We did continue to have some differences and there were still times of stress between us, but beneath it all our trust, appreciation, and love for each other would continue to grow over many future years.

I also learned that I needed to be more thorough when reading legal documents.

# Chapter Thirty-Seven

## SENDING JENNIFER TO EUGENE, MEXICO, AND ARGENTINA

*"What's new Buenos Aires?*
*I'm new, I wanna say I'm just a little stuck on you*
*You'll be on me too.*
*I get out here Buenos Aires.*
*Stand back, you oughta know whatcha gonna get in me*
*Just a little touch of star quality..."*

—Tim Rice and Andrew Lloyd Webber,
"Buenos Aires" from the musical *Evita*
*(sung in the movie by Madonna)*

We knew from an early age that Jennifer cared deeply about her world and the people in it. We knew she would live an interesting and meaningful life. We knew she had more than a little touch of star quality. Here are a few of her true adventures, stories I love to tell because they touch my heart.

Little did we know that her work at Boy's Hamburgers in Cerritos would provide such a practical springboard to her future careers and travels. We would go there often to enjoy their hamburgers and outstanding freshly-made onion rings. It was just a short walk or bike ride down Carmenita Street. At the beginning of her Junior year, just after she turned 16, Jennifer began working part-time at Boy's. She worked afternoons, following her classes at Cerritos High School. It turns out the cooks at this popular fast food restaurant in the eastern part of Los Angeles County could only speak Spanish. She learned to take orders in English and then quickly turned to rattle off the order in Spanish to the cooks. She clearly had a gift.

She was studying Spanish language in high school, and the previous year she had accompanied our friends John and Pam Gray to a one week Spanish language immersion course (no speaking in any other language) at the IDEAL School in

Cuernavaca. It is in the state of Morelos about a 30 minute drive south of Mexico City. Cuernavaca has a rich history, and its nickname is the "City of Eternal Spring." http://www.ideal-school.com/index.php?idioma=2.

When Jen graduated from high school, we gave her a gift of another trip to Mexico for more immersion in the Spanish language. This time she went with her Uncle Charlie (Kathryn's brothcr) to thc Ccccmak School in Morclia, which is thc capital of the Mexican state of Michoacan. Morelia is located between Mexico City and Guadalajara. It is not very touristy, but it also has a lot of history.

After Jennifer's many moves in her younger days, she seemed to relate more to Oregon. She thought about going to a culinary arts school but decided to study Spanish at the University of Oregon in Eugene. Her grades were good and she had no problem getting accepted. She was also realistic about the expenses and the fact that we did not have much money saved for helping with her college education. She researched and found that she could regain Oregon residency status in 6 months, which would make tuition costs much more reasonable. Jen packed her bags, and one July day I drove her to the Orange County Airport where she boarded a plane to Portland by herself. She had some friends and family on the other end, but in my book she was showing a lot of initiative, courage, and good old-fashioned gumption. She started working right away as a waitress at David Orange's restaurant- The Riverway Inn. Later she worked at Maya's Taqueria. In six months she was once again an Oregon resident, and she moved down to Eugene to begin her college career in January of 1987.

She will have to give you details of those college days in her book, if she ever writes it. But one statistic I can provide was the number of football and basketball games she attended. Unlike me, who never missed a game at UCLA, her total was zero. She was simply not interested.

At the end of her Junior year she wanted to take some time away from college. She told us her idea of a longer visit to a Spanish speaking country. Eric Crocker, a family friend, had recently moved to South America and was running a lemon farm; El Pucara was its name. It was just outside the city of San Miguel de Tucuman in northern Argentina, on the lower slopes of the Andes Mountains. Due to successive years of drought the trees had been struggling; he was trying to revitalize the farm with the help of a few others. He had married an Argentine woman named Maria del Sol, who identified an allergy to citrus and could not live on the farm full-time. Eric sent an open invitation to Jennifer. Kathryn and I agreed it would be a worthy educational investment, so we covered Jennifer's airline tickets and sent a contribution to Eric to help with her living expenses.

*"Jennifer, my shining star."*

The wildly popular musical Evita, depicting recent turbulent years in Argentina, was still running on Broadway but it had yet to be made into the movie starring Madonna. Eva Peron herself had died 37 years earlier, but her memory was still fresh with the older Argentine people who deeply loved her. The country survived the Peron years of government and the coups d'etat and the revolution that followed. Carlos Menem, their newly elected President, was trying to re-privatize the nation's nationalized industries. Argentina had amassed a huge foreign debt position, and inflation was raging. Their banking system was struggling. The Argentine Peso was continuously weakening so they devalued again and converted their currency to the Austral, trying but failing to inspire confidence from foreign banks. It was trading at 1,500 Australs to the U.S. Dollar in January of 1990. Within six months it took 8,000 Australs to buy the same dollar's worth of goods. Shortly after that it went to 12,000. It was senseless to save for the future; your money would devalue before you walked out of the bank. These events were making it very difficult to operate for everyone; yet life went on.

Jennifer took a long flight by herself from LAX to Buenos Aires and was met at the airport by a beaming Eric Crocker. She was 21 years old. It was January of 1990, the middle of summer in the southern hemisphere. Hello, Buenos Aires. Jennifer got to look around a bit in the big city, known as "the Paris of South America." She admired the European-style architecture, the broad avenues, and the sidewalk cafes. It was a busy city of three million inhabitants. Then, off they went by bus for an 815 mile ride to the northern countryside. She was basically the housekeeper and cook for eight months. She met many people and experienced the simple lifestyle of the country folk. Jennifer learned to drink Yerba Mate, a caffeine-rich tea that smells very grassy— it was widely popular down there, even called the national drink of Argentina. She spoke a lot of Spanish, though she later had to clean up the up-country dialect and leave behind some of their local idioms. If approached by a panhandler there, she was taught to say "Estoy pato." It was an idiom meaning "I am broke." When she said those words years later in Mexico she was looked at in a very funny way; there it translated literally as "I am temporarily a duck." She wanted to audit a class (taught in Spanish) at the University of Tucuman, but it was an hour ride by bus to the campus downtown. When she got there, too often she found the whole school was shut down by student strikes. That didn't work.

With her American passport, she was only authorized to stay three months at a time. Then she would need to exit Argentina to qualify for another three months. Eric had been invited to a wedding in Buenos Aires, so Jennifer went with him and they stayed in the city for a few days. They took a ferry across the Rio de la Plata to Montevideo, the capital of Uruguay, where they stayed for a couple more days with a doctor friend. She enjoyed visiting with people and seeing a tiny bit of that major city. She got her passport stamped in Uruguay. Now they could retrace their path back to El Pucara.

After another three months she needed a new passport plan. She had remained in contact with her high school Spanish teacher of three years, Mr. Rolando Gutierrez. He liked to travel during his summer breaks from teaching, and he knew Jennifer was in Argentina. This year he headed south. One day he arrived at El Pucara and stayed to visit for three days. Together they hatched a plan to go to Bolivia. A civilian government had resumed control of that country just eight years earlier, following a series of military coups. Only twenty five years earlier in 1965, Ernesto Che Guevara had come down from Cuba to help organize a communist revolution. The Bolivian Army along with U.S. advisors had smashed the revolt, and on October 8, 1967 Che was killed there. Jennifer's feeling was that it was now safe, and Eric gave his blessing. So she and Señor Gutierrez headed north.

The bus this time was more dated, not at all like the modern express buses that sped down the highway to Buenos Aires. They travelled higher into the Andes on their way to the western edge of Bolivia, where the altiplano averages 12,000 feet in elevation. The travel books describe the picturesque route as winding through river valleys amidst cultivated fields of tobacco and corn. In the smaller villages it is common to see Quechuan women wearing colorful ponchos with babies strapped to their backs, while horses, goats, and cows roam and graze in the surrounding fields. At the most northern tip of Argentina, 300 miles from Tucuman, their bus reached the end of the line in the small city of Humahuaca. It sits in a narrow mountain valley in the Province of Jujuy. Jennifer got a bed in a local youth hostel with the intent to stay a couple of days. Meanwhile she was reacting to the higher altitude with dizziness and shortness of breath. She remembers thinking that a beer in a quiet tavern might help. What she found was a bar with fifty crazed Argentine soccer fans cheering their national team on television. It was July 8 and they were watching the final game of the 1990 Soccer World Cup. Argentina was going down to defeat 1-0 at the hands of West Germany. Oh, the agony.

She enjoyed walking the quaint town streets and chatting with people along the way. She was even offered a job to do some translating. She declined. Her legal status did not allow her to take a job, and of more immediate concern was a need to get more oxygen to her brain. She made her way to the border, but the officials on the Bolivian side wanted her to stay 48 hours before they would stamp her passport. She finally convinced them she had altitude sickness and desperately needed to get back to Argentina and down to a lower elevation. Jennifer must have dazzled them with her Spanish skills, because it worked. She got her passport stamp and walked back across the border. Soon she was on a bus to Tucuman, while Señor Gutierrez continued his adventure heading east to Paraguay and Brazil.

I knew nothing of this at the time. In a letter she received from me after her return, I asked if she had any plans to see other countries like Peru while in South America? In her next letter back to me she said, “Are you trying to get me killed?” She explained that the Shining Path Guerrillas were still freely roaming the Peruvian countryside (until two years later when their leader was captured).

Jen soon decided her adventure was nearing its end— she was ready to return to Oregon and finish college. After a long flight home, we met her at LAX. She returned an experienced world-traveler and a more mature young lady. With renewed energy, she completed her college work in Eugene. In August of 1991 we drove with the twins to attend her graduation. The ceremony was held outdoors at U of O’s Hayward Field, famous for its track and field meets. It was sunny and hot that day; fortunately we were seated in the shady side of the grandstands.

Over the following years Jen met a lot of Latin American people. At one point she embarked on a solo nine-week tour of cities in central Mexico so she could visit a number of these new friends in their own homes. To this day Jennifer has retained her adventurous spirit, and she continues to dream of spending time south of our borders. For her it is all about the people, and that is something I want to emulate. She definitely has more than a little touch of star quality— she inspires me.

# Chapter Thirty-Eight

## MEN ARE FROM MARS AND WOMEN ARE FROM VENUS

*"To keep your marriage brimming,*
*With love in the loving cup,*
*Whenever you are wrong, admit it;*
*Whenever you're right, shut up."*
—Ogden Nash, American Poet and Humorist

The communication styles of women are very different from those of men— it's almost as if we are from different planets. Sometimes it even seems we speak different languages. It took me a long time to figure this out. For much of my life, all I knew was that women were a great mystery. Sometimes they get upset if men do not respond in the way they expect, after they have sent signals which they think we should understand. For instance, I have noticed that women often ask a question, when it is really a gentle request in disguise. Like her saying, "Do you think it is too hot in this room?" Then she gets upset if we do not interpret correctly and jump to lower the thermostat.

I have a copy of a Boston Globe newspaper article from 1982 by Ellen Goodman. It is entitled "Men Want Decisions When Women Are Seeking Consensus." Here is how it begins. "They are going out to dinner. He turns to her and asks, 'Where do you want to eat?' From his point of view it is a simple matter for which there is a direct answer. She hears him, holds his question in the air, and looks it over. From her point of view it is the opening line of an exploration, the beginning of a process. Slowly she runs through her Rolodex of options. Three or four possibilities finally present themselves before her mind for screening purposes. She responds with her questions: 'What about Chinese food? Are you in the mood for pizza? How did you like the fish place last time?' 'I'll go anyplace you like tonight,' he repeats, 'Where do you want to go?' There is an edge of impatience now lining his voice. For her a choice as simple as the restaurant is recast as a concern about pleasing everyone. As a rule he thinks she has trouble making up her mind. As a rule she thinks he is impatient." And on it goes.

It is all about building relationship skills. And you have to want to do it. Some people never do. A lot of tips can be gained from Books like *Mars and Venus Together Forever* by the author John Gray, Ph.D. Yes, a different person from our friend (John C. Gray) with a similar name. He says that men speak Male and women speak Female. He says, "It is obvious to a woman when another woman is upset and needs to talk in order to feel better. It is obvious when her talking has been successful in releasing stress. To men, none of the above is obvious at all."

I have noticed that men usually think women are looking for an answer when they start talking, particularly when referring to problems. Men promptly offer thoughts on potential solutions and become surprised when the discussion is not then finished. The woman becomes irritated because he does not want to simply listen and be with her. The man over time may slowly start to understand this, but too often develops a bad habit of only partially listening because he thinks the discussion will continue long beyond his capacity for focused listening. The woman then decides, "He is never really listening to me."

The whole thing about "chick flicks" goes down the same path. To the man, the women in the movie just seem to talk a lot while slowly revealing their characters and personalities; there is very little action. The women viewers come away in tears because of the depths of reality that have been shared. The men prefer "action flicks," which are louder and the characters more obvious. These have much faster scene changes. They also usually include at least one car chase where a good number of cars fly through the air and are destroyed. The guy says, "Awesome." The woman says, "Can you please turn that down!"

Then both men and women wonder why it is so hard to find a little romance. Here is a quote from the magazine called "Men Are From Mars & Women Are From Venus." "For women romance still involves candlelight and roses and lots of loving attention. For men it's about being appreciated and admired-whether by candlelight or not. And that's where difficulties occur. When men and women have different expectations, they may have trouble communicating their needs and desires. Resentment rather than romance takes over too often."

Here is what I have learned. Both parties have to be ready to learn from each other. You have to talk about it together, many times. Read a book about communication together and discuss each chapter, just like back in school. Do something unexpected and kind for the other person. Say, “I love you,” if you really mean it. Many men find this difficult, but it gets easier with practice. Make concessions more frequently to the other person’s preferences. Always give thought beforehand about how your decision may affect your friend or partner. Listen more, and speak less. Give up trying to defend yourself.

I like this tip also— “Prepare a space for romance to appear.” Try some of these ideas: clear your calendar, clean up the bedroom, put on fresh sheets and turn back the bed, lay out some attractive apparel, and dim the lights; turn on some relaxing music, or perhaps even cook a nice meal and do the dishes. At some point along the way gently mention whatever might be of interest to you, and ask your partner how they are feeling and what might be of interest to them— don’t expect anyone to be a mind reader. Above all be sensitive to timing. Timing is everything! I’m still learning.

Here is a paraphrase of something my UCLA professor Dr. Carl Faber used to say about romance, “You cannot force a rose to bloom. You can provide light and warmth and patience. And when the petals do begin to unfold, move slowly and drink deeply of the experience.”

# Chapter Thirty-Nine

## THE SPIRITUAL WIND

*"... to overcome evil by good, sorrow by joy,*
*cruelty by kindness, ignorance by wisdom;*
*... to serve mankind as one's larger Self."*

—from "Aims and Ideals of the Self-Realization Fellowship,"
As set forth by founder Paramahansa Yogananda

Have you never felt yourself being pulled in a certain direction whether or not logical reasons seemed sufficient to explain it? Sometimes one's larger Self has things in mind which fit into a larger plan that is simply beyond the range of our individual minds at the time. Give that idea some time to sink in. I have felt the Spiritual Wind many times, and my family has been moved by it. Forget the theory of predetermination; you can still buck the wind if you insist. But it is wiser to pay attention.

After living in Los Angeles County for about eight years, Kathryn and I began to talk about possibilities of moving somewhere else. The air quality was one concern— Kathryn was experiencing chronic respiratory problems and a nagging cough that kept getting worse. I was getting tired of the freeways (again). Then somewhat unexpectedly Richard Stubberfield, a co-founder of Acton (one of my customers in Santa Barbara), approached me about a position. His timing was right and we liked the offer, which included covering our expenses for relocating to Santa Barbara. Yes, gorgeous Santa Barbara! I gave notice to Hitachi. We put our Cerritos house on the market with Gary Bingaman, a local agent we had befriended. It was 1987; demand in the California real estate market was improving, but for the first few weeks we received only lowball offers. Kathryn and I flew out on a prearranged trip to Japan and left a limited power of attorney with Gary. A few days later he called us with a good offer which we told him to accept. We would realize a nice capital gain on our first home sale. We planned to pay back my parents and net enough cash to buy another home on our own.

We found a four-bedroom house in a lovely older and quiet section of Santa Barbara. The backyard featured a lush vegetable garden; alongside was a marvelous treehouse in a big tree. Located just off Old San Marcos Road, I would be close enough to Acton that I could ride my bike to work. We made the deal. I started my new job and left the project of dealing with the movers back in Cerritos to Kathryn. She did not appreciate that, but she persevered. Soon enough the four of us were together again, living temporarily in a motel while waiting for escrow to close on both houses.

One morning I was called to the executive offices at Acton. Marty Horn, the CEO, informed me confidentially of an announcement planned for the next day— Acton had been acquired by Information Magnetics (another of my previous customers). We would all be moving to San Diego County. It was too late to stop the closing on my new home. We let it close. As we moved into the Santa Barbara house that week, we put it right back on the market. The movers left most of our things packed in boxes which they stacked in the garage.

We could not wait until the following weekend when all of the Acton employees would be bused down for a series of welcomes, parties, and real estate tours hosted by Infomag. Kathryn and I found a realtor based in North San Diego County, and the two of us drove down for a look. We got lucky. We found an attractive home in the city of Encinitas. It was close to El Camino Real, a major boulevard, and the I-5 Freeway. We would even have access to a community pool. We fell in love with the neighborhood, made an offer, and it was accepted. When we bused down the following weekend, the corporate tour entered our new neighborhood, which was being described by the realtors on board as very desirable. As we passed right by our new purchase I jumped out and excitedly pointed out our home to everyone in the two buses, both of which I had briefly brought to a halt.

Luckily real estate demand was quite strong in the Santa Barbara area. We lived together in that house for about a month, and then we accepted an offer. We even made $20,000 on the deal, because all of our selling and moving expenses were covered. I relocated to a motel in San Diego, while Kathryn and the children stayed behind for another month until both escrows closed. Thankfully we were soon reunited, though the twins had to change schools again. We had been moved yet again by the

Spiritual Wind. Interestingly we were now living near the headquarters of the Self-Realization Fellowship that had been founded by Yogananda; I was reminded of the wisdom in his autobiography.

We were now just minutes from some wonderful beaches, and the ocean water was warmer down in San Diego. Some days I met my family at a beach on my way home from work. They would already be playing in the waves when I arrived. I would immediately change out of my business suit and into swimming trunks. Kathryn and I mostly sat on a blanket on the sand, while we watched Brian and Tracy play, the calming waves do their dance, and the sunset.

Ross and Marcia Marks, came down from British Columbia for a visit and we were delighted to see them. I remember leisurely driving with Ross, Marcia, and Kathryn through the high desert in east San Diego County. We were simply relaxing and feasting on the unique scenery, while enjoying each other's company. I was heading to the old gold mining town of Julian— It was now more famous for apples. I wanted Ross to experience Mom's Pie House. His eyes got really big when presented with a slice of the tallest deep-dish apple pie that any of us had ever seen. Marcia and Kathryn, accomplished bakers themselves, were equally impressed. Simply delicious moments. And the pie tasted great too.

We knew about First Lady Nancy Reagan's "Just Say No" campaign. She wanted children to just say "No" whenever they were offered drugs or alcohol. We wanted our children to make that pledge, for at least their school years, and we felt that we would also have to join them for there to be any real power behind any of it. So we all did it; we wrote our own pledges and signed our names. I cleaned out our liquor shelf and gave away a box of bottles to friends at work. In fact neither of us touched a drop of alcohol for the next fifteen years, from age 40 to 55— not again until after the twins were 25 and we were empty nesters. We focused on offering Attunements, hosting spiritual discussions, and organizing RBA events. We planted a lovely rose garden at our front door and enjoyed many opportunities for relaxing work in the yard. I enjoyed frequent bicycle rides. Kathryn and I found time for some dates, and we arranged plenty of family activities. We reconnected with Carl Romaner, our friend from Ashland, who was now living nearby; we made new friends as well.

I convened a regional RBA event that year at the famous Hotel del Coronado. Our featured speaker was Dr. Ernesto Contreras, who ran the Oasis of Hope Hospital in Tijuana. There he provided alternative treatments for people with cancer, many from the U.S. and other countries. His methods were controversial, but we were impressed with his huge heart and dedication, as were all those who were experiencing improvements while in his care.

I bought my first personal computer with my relocation bonus, and began learning how to use it at work. I chose the newest Apple Macintosh with a 40 megabyte 5.25" internal hard disk drive and one 3.5" floppy disk drive; it only covered a small corner of my desk. The screen was tiny (by current standards), but I liked the mouse and the Apple operating system was so intuitive. I even bought a carrying case so I could lug it home. I needed both hands to lug it (lightweight laptop computers didn't exist yet). I learned Microsoft Word and Excel. Spreadsheets—wow!

At Infomag I was responsible for sales in Southern California, Colorado, Korea, and Japan. I enjoyed the travel, especially my first trip into the Japanese Alps to Seiko Epson's disk drive factory. But the traffic got worse as North San Diego County continued its rapid growth. My commute became increasingly stressful. At work, I ended up with a new boss and the merger process was a mess. We had too many people in the merged company, even though volumes in our market were growing and we were a prominent player. Headcount reductions were inevitable. I had a suspicion that my days might be numbered.

The four of us (my immediate family) were living together in Encinitas; it had also been the four of us in Santa Barbara. At our Ashworth Street house in Cerritos there were five of us, including Jen. Before that it had been different. In the previous leased house two friends lived with us, and prior to that we lived communally in South Gate, South Park, Mountlake Terrace, Ravenna, and Ashland. We were quite surprised when one day John and Pam Gray invited us to move "for a season" to a larger intentional community at Glen Ivy. We were familiar with it from previous visits, and they told us the community would benefit from added residents with our particular skills. Timing is everything, as I still enjoy saying. I gave two weeks notice at Infomag but was told I could leave that same day. They were indeed looking for ways to downsize. I felt many pounds lighter as I strolled out the door. We easily sold the house in San Diego County (at a profit), and when the check arrived we put the liberated equity into an online savings account with Discover Bank.

We had recently purchased a new gold-colored Volvo station wagon. We loaded the back of the car and rented a truck. Amazingly, my old friend James Danks was now living just around the corner from us; the Spiritual Wind yet again. He helped us load the truck. Then, the Oftedal family headed north for the one hour drive to our new home in Riverside County. I didn't feel disoriented by all the changes of the previous years—everything had flowed from one thing to another, and there was a purpose for each step along the way. It all seemed to be part of some larger plan. Still, I knew these next years would be very different from anything we had experienced so far. We were ready.

# Chapter Forty

## FOUR YEARS LIVING IN AN INTENTIONAL COMMUNITY

*"Reach up to the stars,*
*Feel God touching creation,*
*And breathe His spirit."*
—A Haiku by Terry Oftedal

Taking a timeout was one reason for our move into an intentional community in 1989. We wanted to withdraw a bit from the hustle of city life, hoping perhaps for an experience of realignment with a more natural life rhythm. We also wanted our twins to have a chance to play in the dirt. Brian and Tracy were in the 5th grade; Jennifer was at the University of Oregon. After a bit of refurbishing we moved into an old 3-bedroom prefab house in the midst of a recently acquired orchard, which sat adjacent to the original Glen Ivy property. Both properties were owned by one non-profit entity, of which I had been serving on the Board of Directors for a number of years. We were just off Old Temescal Canyon Road, tucked along the base of the Santa Ana Mountains on the Riverside County side. The larger property had its own rights to pump water from Coldwater Creek, which was mostly running underground these days. During rare days of strong rain, however, it swelled and rushed above ground, once even rendering Glen Ivy Road impassable. We extended the system of water pipes from the well near the creek into the orchard and connected it to the system on the new property. We now had a plentiful supply of water for the 1,000 fruit trees, avocado and grapefruit, on this rustic 10 acre plot which had historically been called Warm Springs Ranch. Our commute down the dirt and gravel ranch road to the main community took only a few minutes, even when walking or riding a bike. We still drove the car a bit, but the dust stirred up en route would cover it like a blanket, making it always appear in need of a wash. It was a big change from the freeway commutes I had left behind.

Technically I was leasing and operating the ranch, with no intention of personal profit. Actually there were no profits usually for small landowners, after averaging the losses in the lean years with small profits in the good ones. It all depended on market prices, which fluctuated annually based on the size of the total California avocado crop. If not for the internal water supply, I would have had no hope of even breaking even. It was all worth it to havc our own supply of this marvelous fruit. The 600 avocado trees were generous in their yields, though avocados tend to "rest" with a leaner crop on alternate years. They enjoyed our soil and the gentle slope on which we were situated. I intended to become the first organic certified avocado ranch in Riverside County, which would allow for a modest premium in selling price. I hired a ranch hand— Salvador had been an employee of a much larger fruit ranching company, and he was working the Warm Springs plot before it was carved off of the larger ranch and traded to us. He worked five days a week, trimming and caring for the trees. I joined him one day most weeks for picking and distributing the avocados, in addition to my other part-time ranching chores of planning, selling, and general care-taking.

An amazing thing about avocados is that you can pick them any time during their several months long maturity season, and then each one ripens about a week or two after its stem is clipped. We had a system for roaming a few rows each week, picking only the largest fruits from each tree. This was done by means of a long pole with a rope which operated scissors on the far end. When I snipped one stem, that fruit fell into a little bag on the end of my pole. After collecting two or three avocados in the bag, I would hand over hand bring the pole down and manually transfer fruits from the little bag into a bigger bag worn over my shoulder. When the big bag got heavy, I emptied it into boxes on the racks of a sturdy four-wheeled Honda ATV (All Terrain Vehicle) which I had purchased from a Hollywood movie technician. In a few weeks, we would return to the same rows to find more fruits had grown to good size and were ready for picking. Over a few months each tree would be fully picked. Pinkertons matured first and we picked them from February to April. Then the popular Haas trees, planted in the next section, were ready to pick April to August. Finally the larger Reed avocado trees, planted nearer to our house, were picked later in the year. For our own consumption, we always left some fruit on a few trees all the way to the end of the year. January was the only month we (and the other residents up the road) did not have ripened avocados available for our meals every day.

When my parents visited, both Dad and Mom eagerly threw on picking bags, grabbed poles, and roamed in the shady rows of trees with us. It was cooler and more enjoyable than working the hot acreage that Grandpa Doc had planted with fruit trees in Clovis when I was young. Kathryn, the children, and other volunteers joined in the picking some weeks.

*"Jennifer, Brian, Tracy, Terry, and Kathryn in the orchard."*

The other 400 trees at Warm Springs Ranch were Ruby Red Grapefruits. That crop came ripe all at the same time and it was so bulky we hired out the picking each year to someone with several large trucks and adequate manpower. They sent me a check for the net, which was usually pretty minor, even after getting the organic certification.

We all loved the magical avocado, including our black labrador who we named Sunshine but usually called Sunny. Kathryn and the kids brought her home as a young puppy; the whole litter was being given away in front of a supermarket. Sunny was a female and the runt of the litter. She would be our one and only family dog and we loved her. Sunny and the local wild critters would eat avocados that had fallen onto the ground, and the oils in the fruit made their coats extra shiny. As Sunny grew, she had the run of the ranch and she would frequently dash full speed through the trees. She did her best to protect us at night from the coyotes, raccoons, weasels, possums, and even larger animals which ventured down the mountainside in the evenings for a snack. We could hear her barking at them from around the property, until she finally came back home and retired for the night onto her rug in our laundry room, just inside the back door. We also adopted a cat that Tracy named Cross-eyed Molasses; she was living on the roof of our carport when we moved in. Molasses mostly kept to herself and lived off of mice and other small creatures, which she was very adept at catching. From our vantage on the ground, Tracy enjoyed looking up at Molasses and meowing with her.

Our non-profit entity also leased a downhill part of the primary property to Glen Ivy Hot Springs, a for-profit business. GIHS was the largest day-spa in Southern California. Operating since 1860, it was quite well known in the region. The spa utilized hot mineral-water wells to fill "healthful" soaking tubs (while also filling the air with a distinctive sulfur smell). In previous centuries, local Indians gathered at this site to enjoy the waters and share in healing and social events. Recently the facilities had been significantly upgraded. John Gray had a passion for the spa business and he actively participated in the leadership team there as well. We offered professional massage and salon services. At times we had as many as 100 massage practitioners on board. Our guests also enjoyed sun bathing, saunas, swimming, aqua aerobics, and the popular mud baths, while surrounded by lush walls of landscaping. I invented our PR motto— "Club Mud" (a play on the very popular Club Med of that day)— which we plastered on t-shirts and other items that we sold in our little boutique.

People drove to our facilities daily from the Los Angeles Basin and surrounding areas. As we were much closer than other day-spas situated further out in Palm Springs, we were an easy get-away. Sometimes we saw famous Hollywood people. I worked at GIHS for a few years as the CFO and served on the Board of Directors. Cash flow planning was important because of the seasonality of that business. I developed some spreadsheet models on my little Macintosh computer to help us conserve cash appropriately for the leaner cold months. For a time I was also the CEO. I always smiled on my five minute commute, remembering ugly freeway traffic of the past, as I walked down our little road through the fruit trees. I would be wearing a Hawaiian shirt, from a broad selection I had accumulated, plus shorts and sandals— the uniform for all of our employees. How many people get to wear shorts and sandals to work and have a walking commute of five minutes? I loved it. As a side benefit, my family received free passes to enjoy the facilities. I suggest you check out their web site and enjoy a visit some time- http://www.glenivy.com/tag/glen-ivy-hot-springs/.

The Glen Ivy intentional community was led by John and Pam Gray, with the assistance of Achal Bedi and a coordinating team. John and Pam were two of the founders, and it was the clarity of their expression that drew many of the others who came. They were following their dreams. No one was there for personal gain. Some lived there for numerous years; some were visitors staying for weeks or a few months. Through each year the population fluctuated from about sixty people up to nearly one hundred. Most shared meals together in the large historic old Lodge, where we expanded and modernized the kitchen and added a spacious dining room. Our kitchen staff focused on the importance of healthy diet, including provisions for special dietary needs. Residents and guests shared in chores which ranged from cooking, dishwashing, housekeeping, and office work, to tending of the grounds, another orchard, and a large organic vegetable garden.

Spiritually oriented discussion hours were central elements in the rhythm of each week. Special events and seminars which attracted non-residents also filled our calendar. Attunement was a core part of daily life at Glen Ivy— Kathryn and I participated in a larger team which offered over a hundred Attunements each week to residents and guests. She and I spent many hours in the little Sanctuary that sat next to the Lodge.

We learned about CranioSacral Therapy at Glen Ivy from Dr. Bill Plikerd, a dentist visiting from Ohio. He demonstrated his CST process on Brian, and we observed beneficial effects with Brian's learning skills after just one treatment. Kathryn soon started training in CST with the Upledger Institute, which had been founded by Dr. John Upledger (an osteopathic physician). In fact, one of her classes in San Diego was taught by Dr. Upledger himself. This therapy utilizes a very gentle touching of the body to stimulate the flow of the fluid which naturally pulses through the core of the spinal column from the sacrum up into the cranium and then back down. Here is further commentary from an Upledger Institute brochure. "CST is a gentle method of detection and correction that encourages your own natural healing mechanisms. The practitioner monitors the rhythm of the craniosacral system to detect potential restrictions and imbalances. The therapist then uses delicate manual techniques to release those problem areas and relieve undue pressure on the brain and spinal cord. CranioSacral Therapy strengthens your body's ability to take better care of you." Our community recognized CST as a valuable adjunct for Attunement, and Kathryn offered her services during posted office hours. She practiced for hundreds of hours at no charge. I have personally experienced beneficial results from CST treatments more times than I could possibly count. She has a marvelous intuitive feel for it. In her, CST and Attunement methods have blended quite naturally.

We met a lot of interesting people while living in the community, people from around the world, all on their own spiritual quests. Steve Tashiro, one of our fellow residents, became a good friend. At the time he had an outside job as a sales representative for Standard Process Labs. He has since moved to Colorado where he is now a practicing chiropractor. Steve has a very quiet manner and he always thought for a few moments before he spoke. When he did speak, I listened. He could also be quite funny. He loved a little saying which I still remember and try to practice- "He who speaks little may be thought a fool; he who speaks too much can remove all doubt."

Diane and David Pasikov moved into the community one season. They were Canadian. She had a rapidly progressing case of cancer which she decided to treat with alternative methods, while being monitored by a doctor in Los Angeles. As part of her efforts to let her body be made new again, she took on the new name Annie. Three times each day at home, Annie was injecting 714-X into her lymph system through the groin area. 714-X is a botanical mixture containing camphor extract (from camphor tree bark), ammonium salts, nitrogen, sodium chloride, and ethanol. Developed in the 1960's by Gaston Naessens, a French biologist who had relocated to Quebec, this therapy is controversial and still not approved by the U.S. FDA. She brought it herself from Canada. 714-X reportedly supports the body's abilities to flush toxins, stimulates the immune system through increased flow of lymph, and prevents cancer cells from robbing nitrogen from the healthy cells. Kathryn and I provided general daily support and a caring surround for Annie and David, including frequent Attunements for several months. She had lost a lot of weight, yet she retained an irrepressible strength of character and a persistent positive attitude. She unwaveringly expressed an attitude of thankfulness. Annie was quite an example. Over a period of months she advanced from extreme weakness to modest strength. Eventually she regained her appetite, returned to full strength, and was declared free of cancer. The last we heard they are living in Colorado and she is in strong health.

Our community hosted a constant stream of visitors and guests from Russia, Europe, the Far East, South Africa, West Africa, Australia, Mexico, and South America, as well as all parts of North America. They spoke many languages and came from many backgrounds, but they all were eager to experience the positive energy of our community and learn about the spiritual principles that we were practicing. The Europeans told us first-hand about how they felt the world was experiencing a rebirth; everything now seemed possible after the opening of the Berlin Wall. Destruction of that monstrous symbol of the Iron Curtain and the Cold War began in November of 1989 and took years to finish. The two Germanys were reunited in 1990, and in 1991 the Soviet Union was broken into smaller parts. We shared renewed hopes for possibilities of world peace. Some Russians who visited were filmmakers; they told us that we were much more successful in applying Lenin's principles at our community than they had ever been in Russia. Black people from South Africa told us their personal stories of surviving apartheid, then about their resurgence of hope with the release of Nelson Mandela. Finally in 1993 they would see negotiations for transfer of power and the beginning of an end to the brutality.

Popular speakers of the day came; we listened to them and they listened to us. We experienced a variety of New Age workshops, some of which I related to more than others. We held many drumming sessions, which the men particularly enjoyed; but they gave me a headache. We hosted retreats and meetings with old friends like Martin Cecil, Michael Cecil, Bill Bahan, Alan Hammond, and Jim Wellemeyer. With so much external activity, it was important to find time for quiet walks and contemplation. I loved exploring up the Coldwater Creek Canyon and even practiced water divining there with some steel rods. We built a narrow trail up into the hills, in the rear of the property, which led to a quiet spot with a peaceful view of undeveloped hillsides. Below, silent winds would often blow through seas of native grasses and dry scrub—it was a perfect site for meditation.

I continued my work with Renaissance Business Associates. One year we hosted a regional RBA event at Glen Ivy. The event attracted a quite interesting assortment of guests and speakers, as usual. We joined in silent walks, explorations, and experiential exercises. We convened one session up the

Coldwater Creek Canyon and another under a huge oak tree in the middle of the avocado orchard. I conducted a tour of the Hot Springs business and we took afternoon breaks to relax at the Hot Springs Spa. The meals were superb.

We felt ours was a healthy lifestyle— though seen from the outside, many of my old friends would have judged it to be "quite unusual." I must admit a few of the residents were not my favorite people, and of course our income was quite modest. I began thinking that if I wanted to help the twins go to college and if I wanted to fund a retirement someday, I needed to start looking once again for higher paying employment. Kathryn was ready for a change; actually even more ready than I. I made some calls to prior associates and quickly found a solid lead. Ray Saunders, a co-worker from my previous job at Infomag, had been hired as CEO for a high-tech company that was waning and in need of a turn-around. If I was ready for an adventure, he would hire me as VP of Sales and Marketing and pay to relocate my family to Omaha, Nebraska. After Kathryn and I flew out for introductions and a tour of the city, we gave formal notice back home. Even though the twins would have to move to yet another high school, they agreed. Tracy would be parting from her best friend Melissa Gray. Brian really enjoyed working at the Spa— he would miss friends as well. I had developed a very close working relationship with Achal Bedi; I would miss him most.

It was 1993, and our "season" at Glen Ivy was drawing to an end. It had been four years exactly. We had changed and, as we reached up to the stars in our daily living, our world had changed. I didn't feel we had been disconnected from the "outside world"— I felt more connected than ever.

We packed, and movers soon arrived to load our belongings into a large van. After many hugs and a farewell party, four of us set off in our Volvo for the drive eastward. Sunny went with us. Traveling with a dog and two teenagers had its challenges, but we stopped for numerous breaks. I encouraged everyone to try different regional foods along the way. The scenery changed as we moved from Arizona to New Mexico and then into Colorado. The high deserts of the Southwest were filled mostly with hardy plants like cacti. When we reached the Rockies we enjoyed a majestic contrast. The roads became flat as we rolled into Nebraska, just prior to our first experience of winters with plenty of snow. Our lifestyle was going to be different— of greater importance this next cycle would become a time for even more significant internal changes. I was filled with hope, and I trusted the Spiritual Wind.

# Chapter Forty-One

## OMAHA, JAPAN, THAILAND, AND BEYOND

*"Infuse your life with action. Don't wait for it to happen. Make it happen. Make your own future. Make your own hope. Make your own love. And whatever your beliefs, honor your creator, not by passively waiting for grace to come down from upon high, but by doing what you can to make grace happen...yourself, right now, right down here on Earth."*
—Bradley Whitford, American Film and Television Actor

Is there such a thing as God's Grace? I believe it is carried on the Spiritual Wind. I have felt it many times, and even when I am not aware of it that subtle guidance has been there. Can we as individuals make grace happen? For most, that would require a shift in consciousness and a profound acceptance of responsibility. It would require active engagement with the Spiritual Wind and seeing everything that is brought to us as an opportunity. Does that include things I don't enjoy doing? Yes, everything. Long car drives and quiet walks are good times to contemplate such things.

We checked into a Homewood Suites in Omaha and started looking at the housing market on the west end of the city. Because downtown Omaha's eastern edge abuts the Missouri River, which is also the state border, the city's growth is focused in the other direction. We quickly learned that in this region people liked having a lot of rooms in their homes. Most good-sized houses had a small room at the front door for receiving guests, mud rooms at the back door, a formal dining room, a piano room, and possible other unique rooms in addition to the usual main ones. Every house had a full basement where the family could retreat during tornado alerts. Husbands would often create a male retreat in the basement, or at least add a wet bar. We were more accustomed to California style open floor plans where living areas flowed into each other. We got lucky and found a spec home built in a newer development called

Cambridge Oaks, just west of Father Flannigan's Boys Town. This house was actually discounted because none of the local buyers liked its open floor plan. It was brand new and had never been occupied so we made a deal, closed quickly, and moved in.

The twins signed up for Millard North High School. Kathryn made friends with new neighbors Jim Neff and Julie Bridge, both doctors, and Kathryn became a nanny for their baby daughter Rachel. We found new favorite restaurants like the Garden Cafe— their Key Lime Pie was irresistible. We went to the Nebraska State Fair and enjoyed the many animals and craft exhibits, just like the county fairs back home. One year at the fair we saw the rock group America, who sang all of their old hits, sounding as good as ever. We became fans of the Omaha Royals and took our kids to several of their AAA league baseball games, which were surprisingly affordable. I attended some of the College World Series baseball games also held downtown at the old Rosenblatt Stadium. We drove past Warren Buffett's modest home and his Berkshire Hathaway offices in Omaha, just to see them.

My new employer, Brumko Magnetics, was located in the tiny town of Elkhorn, just west of Omaha's suburban sprawl. I would commute in the opposite direction of traffic flow, as most folks drove to and from Omaha jobs. Brumko had once been a cash cow division for the leading recording heads maker- Applied Magnetics. We were now a spin-off, and still quite good at refurbishing internal parts of older disk drives. But a major change was sweeping our industry— the rapid emergence of smaller 3.5" disk drives, which sold at much lower prices. This was making the value proposition for repairing 5.25" (and larger) disk drives increasingly obsolete. Businesses and consumers could now simply replace their old larger HDD with a faster and lower cost new drive (which also had more storage capacity) and send the old dog out for recycle. We could see Brumko's traditional business shrinking each quarter. We searched for new business niches in the Midwest and California, but the American disk drive manufacturing was rapidly migrating to Asia— Ray and I knew we had to focus our efforts there. When I was with Indiana General, over 100 companies were assembling disk drives in the U.S.; now only five operations remained. We offered our services to all five, even though we knew they would inevitably move off shore as well, lured by lower labor and overhead costs.

Peter Lorince, our Director of Engineering, was chasing opportunities in Thailand. He was working with some professional acquaintances whose jobs had recently transitioned from California to Asia. I embarked on my first trip to Bangkok; Peter would meet me there at the airport. Getting to Bangkok was an experience. Northwest Airlines flew me from Omaha (which was blanketed in snow and sub-zero temperature) to Minneapolis (which was even colder) and then to rainy Seattle, where I waited for the even longer flight to Tokyo. At Tokyo's Narita Airport, I paced the terminal as I watched through the large windows workers outside scurrying about in even heavier rain; it would be another few hours before boarding my plane to Bangkok. I was thankful I didn't have my heavy winter coat, which I had left with Kathryn at the first plane's boarding ramp in Omaha. Bangkok would be over 80 degrees and humid, and I didn't want to lug that coat around for two weeks. Arriving at the old Don Mueang Airport (Bangkok's main international airport at the time) was an unforgettable experience. First the heat and humidity hit me, even though the sun had set hours before, and I was surrounded with an improbable concoction of noise from the dense crowds. Mostly I was struck by the visual differences—bright colors everywhere, radically different architectural and decorative styles, and traditional clothing made with beautiful fabrics. As I threaded my way through the terminal I saw six Buddhist monks, all with shaved heads, dressed in saffron robes and sandals. Each had his eyes closed and was holding the shoulder of the monk walking in front of him. At the front of the line was a young novice monk, walking with his eyes open. He was leading the way so the older monks could avoid seeing any of the women, particularly ones in scandalous western attire.

Peter emerged from the crowd and led me through an equally chaotic luggage area. Outside, we stepped into a brightly decorated taxi cab for a short drive into the city, but due to the ever present traffic jams at all hours the ride took over an hour. Peter had booked us into a hotel he liked, the Royal President, on Sukhumvit Road Soi 15. It was quiet, cool, and he had arranged to have fresh fruit and chilled bottled water waiting for us in our rooms. The rooms were spacious and pleasantly decorated. Exhausted from the long trip and already feeling 12 time zones worth of jet lag, I took a quick shower, ate half of the pineapple, and crashed hard into a large western style bed.

What a trip! Not the airplane flight. Over breakfast I was recalling the amazing chain of events that had led me to this exotic country. It started with the job at Tek-Electric in Seattle. After moving to Los Angeles, I worked for a similar electronics distributor- The Hundley Company in Glendale. This led to John

Breickner and Indiana General, during which time I traveled the western eleven states and flew regularly to their New Jersey factory. Next came five years with Hitachi, where I began traveling to Japan. Acton hired me away from Hitachi and moved me to Santa Barbara. Infomag acquired Acton and moved us to San Diego. Now I was working for Brumko in the midwestern flatlands of Elkhorn, Nebraska. That's it, the short story of how I got to Thailand.

Peter and I returned from that trip with a proposal to establish a new Brumko operation in Thailand. Over the following year I would make several more treks to Thailand, and my experiences in that beautiful country were unforgettable. It is called the "Land of a Thousand Smiles." The people were friendly and I loved the food. We established our operation in Korat, near the Cambodian border, under the leadership of an American expat who we found already living there. This city, Thailand's second largest, was known by the locals as Nakhon Ratchasima, but its alternate name of Korat was easier for us. Our major customer was Read Rite. They were producing HGA's utilizing the newest thin-film style recording heads. Located just north of Bangkok in Ayutthaya, they made the complete heads themselves in highly capital intensive semiconductor-like fabs.

To make a long and very colorful story short, Ray Saunders was recruited to another company back in California. Read Rite ramped us up to significant volumes of business salvaging sliders for them, and then just as fast figured out how to live without us. Our Thailand Division turned from cash flow positive to negative, and Brumko's bottom line weakened further. I was passed over in the search for a replacement CEO, and Bob Woods was promoted. He and Brumko's owner moved to quickly shut down the Thai operations, and they decided to downsize me along with a few others. It was rumored that our owner had bought Brumko and another larger AMC subsidiary named Magnetic Data for one dollar, allowing AMC to shed some potentially onerous liabilities related to the Magnetic Data European division in Belgium. The money man would milk cash from these operations for a few more years and perform a few more cost cutting rounds, until finally he reportedly walked away. I heard that the operations reverted back to an unhappy AMC.

I looked for a new job in Omaha but could not find many high-tech companies. I didn't have the kinds of experience that would readily qualify me for a management job in any of the other industries thriving in Omaha, though I did have a promising interview with FirstData Corp. I negotiated a package with Brumko that would carry me a few months, and I refocused my job search back on California. Kathryn and Tracy wanted to stay. Brian wanted to leave, though he had enjoyed after-school cooking jobs at Tony Roma's and Applebee's and volunteer work in the emergency rooms at our local hospital. We had survived two winters of snow and icy roads, which we would not miss; but we would miss new friends, and most of all we would miss our dog. Sunny was now older and had some health problems; she would live out her remaining days with a nearby loving family.

We enjoyed our peaceful time of transition from the large communal experience at Glen Ivy back to a home life based once again on our smaller nuclear family. We sensed that communal living and participation in more structured spiritual activities were now behind us; I had even let go of RBA. We were discovering new ways of learning and new forms for our creative expression. Much of our spiritual work was now focused in the vast inner spaces that we call consciousness. We knew others who were sensing the same trend. The Spiritual Wind was shifting.

# Chapter Forty-Two

## BACK TO CALIFORNIA, AGAIN

*" Patience and perseverance have a magical effect before which difficulties disappear and obstacles vanish."*
—John Quincy Adams, Sixth President of the United States

This transition took some patience and perseverance. After a few flights to California (at my own expense) to do some networking, I finally identified an opportunity for which I was well qualified. Digital Equipment Corp. (DEC) had a thin-film recording heads business based in Shrewsbury, Massachusetts and Hong Kong. They maintained a sales office in the Bay Area, and a position there had recently opened for selling to one of their most important California customers- a major HDD manufacturer named Quantum. After a phone interview, Mike Hanley flew me to Massachusetts for interviews and then the following week to California for informal meetings with key engineering managers at Quantum. I thought all had gone well and was expecting an offer, but Mike became very hard to reach for several weeks. Eventually I learned that he had been required to go silent while Quantum was finalizing an acquisition of DEC's recording heads and data storage businesses. Upon completion of the acquisition, I was immediately the first hire as a Quantum employee into their "new" internal Recording Heads Group. I would not formally be a salesman— I was more a technical liaison based on the Quantum campus to coordinate between the Quantum HDD Engineers in Milpitas and the Recording Heads Group (RHG) still headquartered back in Shrewsbury. The title on my business card was Account Executive. We had a 401(k) plan, and I rolled over my small Brumko 401(k) account. Even more exciting was an employee stock purchase plan which allowed us to buy company stock at a discount twice a year. I received a signing bonus and a stock option package. My salary was the highest I had ever seen. Welcome to Silicon Valley, baby!

Quantum paid for our move to the Bay Area and paid for the temporary housing we found in Pleasanton— a two-bedroom unit in the Stoneridge Apartments. It was a large complex, just a short walk from the Stoneridge Mall and a reasonable 30 minute commute to Milpitas. Quantum would also pay the expenses for selling our Omaha house, but that proved to be somewhat difficult. Open floor plan homes were still out of favor, and the inventory of competing new houses was sizable as Omaha continued its never ending westerly expansion. Meanwhile the twins enrolled in Foothill High School, the main reason we had picked Pleasanton, and Kathryn began searching for a new home with realtor Louise Davis. The Bay Area market was booming and houses quickly drew multiple offers as soon as they went on the market. Prices in Pleasanton, though lower than many areas surrounding the San Francisco Bay, were steeper than in Omaha; so we were looking at smaller houses. Plus, we still had our home equity tied up in the Omaha house, further complicating our search. Meanwhile hormones were raging with our teenage twins and they did not appreciate sharing a small bedroom. This was not good for Kathryn's health, as I was already working long hours and she had to be the main manager at the home front. We slowly reduced our asking price in Omaha. Finally we received an offer which allowed us to break even on our investment.

Kathryn looked at over 100 houses with an incredibly patient Louise Davis, who by then had become a personal friend. When they finally found a house that fit our needs, just a few doors up from Louise's house on Knollbrook Drive, I left work early to take a look. We liked the area and we liked the house— a single story with three bedrooms, two bathrooms, and a nice fenced backyard with a few mature trees and a hot tub. We immediately submitted an offer. The house had gone on the market that same day and there were already two other offers. Our's turned out to be the cleanest, plus we offered a little over their asking price. We got it! After six months in a small apartment we joyously moved into our new home. Brian and Tracy had separate bedrooms once again. We were also only a two and a half hour drive from my family in Fresno.

Kathryn joined the Newcomers Club and made many new friends. We loved exploring the Bay Area in addition to partaking in events held right downtown in Old Town Pleasanton. We soon discovered a new favorite breakfast restaurant- Dave's Country Kitchen. We were within walking distance of the Stoneridge Mall, which included a Nordstrom. On the other side of the Mall, barely into the next town of Dublin, was our new favorite Mexican restaurant- Casa Orosco. Whenever I ordered their Chili Verde everyone would watch to see how long it took for beads of sweat to pop out on my forehead; it only took seconds. I loved their verde sauce and the noticeable kick it had. Up the freeway in Walnut Creek we discovered The Hickory Pit, our new favorite BBQ restaurant. We could watch them work the smoking pit inside the restaurant, while enjoying their ribs and pork tenderloin— the best I had ever tasted. The drive to Santa Cruz now took just over an hour, so we could easily go there on a day trip. We left early so we could enjoy breakfast at the Beach Street Cafe; I loved their shrimp and avocado omelette and their amazing orange cranberry muffins. Sometimes we had lunch at the Miramar, on the Santa Cruz Wharf, where my parents had enjoyed so many seafood meals over the years. When we went there I always had to call my mother and say, "Guess where I am?" She always knew I was calling from the Miramar just to tease her. It was now also easy for us to rejoin the Oftedal family gatherings each summer when all of them made their trek from Fresno to Santa Cruz.

The bay area offered a lot of attractions. We saw B.B. King again, this time outdoors. At a beautiful winery we enjoyed the smooth jazz of Dave Koz and David Benoit with our friends Ken and Marsha Nakamura. My father and mother drove up to visit, and we enjoyed touring some of the local wineries, in the days before Dad stopped drinking. We became Golden State Warriors fans and took the BART (light rail) to the Oakland Coliseum many times to cheer them on, back in the days when they unfortunately were not very competitive.

We signed up for a couple of student exchanges. Two young girls from Fukuoka, Japan, Miki and Nao, spent time with us. We also enjoyed sharing our home with Maelenn LeGall from Brest, France. In the year 2000, when Kathryn and I went to Europe on vacation, we spent time in Paris and then took the high speed TGV train out to Brest, on the Northwest tip of the country. We were hosted graciously by Maelenn's family. At her grandmother's home we enjoyed a second floor bedroom, with a beautiful view of the North Sea (which came right up to the edge of her backyard). We toured her father's business, some very old local churches, and beautiful countryside— at one point we walked into a corn field to touch a VERY tall and mysterious rock that had been planted many centuries earlier by the Druids. The history of the area was fascinating, and it was so very different from Paris.

Back in Paris we stayed at a quaint old hotel on Ille de la Cite, an island in the middle of the Seine River. It had been recommended to us by Sanat Dave, who stayed there during his honeymoon. It had "old world charm," which we suspected was code for "there is no elevator, the plumbing has difficulties, and when you sit on the toilet you will not be able to close the bathroom door." We lingered over famous paintings in the Musee d'Orsay, including some by Jean-Francoise Millet, an ancestor of Kathryn's. We watched the Bastille Day parade. For me, the highlight of our time in Paris was the Tour de France. Strolling on King George V Street while looking for a spot to watch the Tour, we found ourselves at the Woola Moola Restaurant. It was a warm July afternoon, and this Australian restaurant had sidewalk tables in the shade of some mature trees. We stood to cheer for Lance Armstrong and everyone in the peloton as they bicycled by us for several laps. Each time, we returned to our seats to resume our leisurely sidewalk luncheon and the always enjoyable "people watching." Lance won that Tour, but later his victory was vacated after it became known that he had doped and covered it up for many years. What a stunning disappointment. I was inspired by Lance's recovery from cancer and his amazing leadership in the fight against cancer. Then I was crushed when he finally admitted to one of the biggest hoaxes ever carried out in the history of sports. He tried to explain his actions, but he would become a textbook example of what inevitably results when anyone chooses to jettison their integrity and ignore the qualities of their behavior.

Earlier that morning we had awakened before dawn for another special event. Along empty Paris streets, in the early morning hours before the traffic appeared, we rode two rented bicycles toward the Eiffel Tower. Along the way, as the sun started to show itself, we were joined by others riding in the same direction. At a large park called the Champ-de-Mars, we became part of a pack of 2,000 amateur riders all eager for a guest ride over the Tour course in Paris. The Tour organizers had dreamed up this once-only event to celebrate the Millennium. I had learned about it on the internet months before and reserved two spots for us. In the front row we were led by some famous prior Tour champions- Miguel Indurain, Laurent Fignon, and five-time winner Bernard Hinault. Miles of barricades had already closed off the streets along the Tour route for the day and gendarmes were posted along the way, so there would be no cars. What a thrill! We reached the Champs Elysees and took pictures of each of us pedaling in front of the Arc de Triomphe. Though we were amongst the last to finish, we declared it a huge personal triumph.

Our route had covered many miles and we had enjoyed many sights along the picturesque streets of Paris that morning. We were tired, but we were also filled with waves of happiness. As we returned our bikes, I thought about our ride through the cleared streets; it reminded me of how protected our journey had felt over the recent years. Patience and perseverance had been required of us, and indeed difficulties and obstacles had vanished. At last, I was also getting better at patience.

# Chapter Forty-Three

## HAPPINESS AND HOPE IN SILICON VALLEY

*"Plant seeds of happiness, hope, success, and love; it will all come back to you in abundance. This is the law of nature."*
—Steve Maraboli, American Author and Psychologist

I learned a lot while working at Quantum— I really enjoyed that job. Their campus included a gym, and all employees were encouraged to take advantage of it with exercise breaks. To minimize my morning commute time, I developed a routine for getting to the gym early. The night before I would place my business clothes in my car, which was now a Volvo sedan with an unusual deep purple color. I also prepped my next day's breakfast and lunch the night before and put them in the refrigerator. When the alarm rang at 5:15AM, I pulled on my sweat clothes, transferred my food bags into a little cooler, and drove out of the garage at 5:30. This allowed me to beat the morning freeway crush, which only got worse each year, and arrive at the gym at 6:00 when it opened. I went through the same exercise sequence every day, ending on the elliptical trainer. I would shower at 7:00 and be at my desk fully invigorated before 7:30. That is, if I wasn't traveling.

I made numerous trips to Quantum's Japanese manufacturing partner- Matsushita Kotobuki Electronics. Their main manufacturing, procurement, and engineering sites were at the far western end of Shikoku Island. I would love to mention many names from those days— some I counted as close friends— but the list would be too long. I still have numerous boxes of their business cards.

I will however mention a few personal friends. On some of my Japan business trips, whenever I had time, I enjoyed seeing Casey Henderson, an old friend from Seattle. He was living in Tokyo as an ex-pat, working first for Credit Suisse Bank and then for the software giant SAP. I could meet up with him just about anywhere in the city, as I had become quite familiar with Tokyo's extensive and convenient subway system. One visit I met him at a local restaurant which was offering unlimited shabu-shabu. We took advantage of their generosity, boiling numerous rounds of vegetables and thinly sliced beef at our table, while enjoying a few beers. The Japanese beers tasted fresher than those back home, probably because they actually were. My favorite was Asahi Super Dry. Years later, Kathryn and I had the pleasure of staying a couple of nights at Casey's apartment.

Alison Clark and David Stubbs also moved to Tokyo for jobs. David was connected with several interesting groups in Japan, including the Institute for Cultural Affairs (ICA Japan). Some of their members, which included a variety of ex-pats and Japanese business people, met monthly at an ICA Breakfast Club. These meetings— larger and fancier than our RBA breakfasts of previous years— were held in the ornate Palace Hotel (located in Tokyo's Otemachi business district). It was a hot and humid July in 1987; the Yen was strong and Japan's export driven economy was the envy of the world. My topic was "Working for Japan in America." I spoke in English (interspersed with Japanese translation) about how I felt as an American who chose to work for a Japanese company. I called California "the last bastion of individual expression" and contrasted it to Japan as "the epitome of collective thinking." As reported in a subsequent article in Business Dynamics magazine, I used a gardening analogy and emphasized the importance of respecting natural cycles as part of bringing a nurturing attitude into our business dealings. Here is a portion of my talk, which David taped. "It is all too common, in the East or the West, to seek reasons to justify the inadequacies in our experiences. 'My boss is ineffective, my wife is grouchy, my long commute makes me very tired, the weather is terrible.' What is missing in these attitudes is the willingness to take the tiger by the tail. The tendency everywhere is to blame the lacks in our lives on external factors rather than seeing the powerful opportunity that each one of us has to balance ourselves internally and take responsibility for the quality of our own expression." The attendees were very attentive and it was an enjoyable experience.

On that same trip I was interviewed for the feature article in "Business English for Millions," a Japanese business magazine. It was printed in English and Japanese, side by side on each page. Businessmen of the younger generation were eager to learn proper business English, and they found this magazine interesting and helpful. My four page interview appeared in the October edition. At one point, the interviewer referred to my talk at the ICA and asked me to elaborate. Here is part of my answer. "Tending a garden and business have many similarities. The seed sprouts, the tree grows, then it blossoms, and the fruit appears after all of the other things happen. If we approach a business relationship in the same way, we can allow cycles to develop quite naturally and easily. But, if we expect the fruit to appear immediately we'll experience frustration, because there is no way for the seed to give you fruit. Similarly, we are shortsighted when we look at the calendar or defined business goals rigidly, without allowing them to be alive and flexible and changing. We may actually damage something with great potential. When we remain aware of the natural flow of the developing cycles, like the seasons in our garden, our experience can be much easier and less filled with tension. We begin to see business cycles developing more naturally, seemingly almost without having to work."

*"Terry speaking at ICA in Tokyo."*

I loved that gardening analogy; it reminded me of all those farmers in the generations before mine. Yes, dreams and understandings do flow to the next generations— to me and on to those after me. And, yes, I enjoyed actively participating in the natural cycles of the garden that is my world— passing on the abundance of love and nurturing that I was experiencing inside— season after season. It felt good to be awake, with a greater purpose to my days.

# Chapter Forty-Four

## THE TWINS GROW UP

*"Remember there's no such thing as a small act of kindness. Every act creates a ripple with no logical end."*
—Scott Adams, American Cartoonist and creator of Dilbert

Brian is one of the few people I know who knew what career he wanted before he was five years old. "I want to be a Fireman or a Paramedic," he repeatedly told us in his early years. He loved the television programs Rescue Eight and Emergency, and he would watch old episodes again and again. John Gage was his favorite actor; years later Brian would meet him at a Las Vegas conference and get his autographed picture. Many times when Brian was young, we would hear a siren off in the distance and he would stop and cock one of his ears in the direction of the siren trying to discern if it was ambulance, fire, or police. If it was an ambulance or fire engine and it came into view, he would beg us to get in our car and follow it so we could see where it was going.

While we were living at Glen Ivy, he worked at the Hot Springs Spa part-time. He started as a lifeguard at the big pool. He became famous for volunteering to do just about anything that needed to be done. Soon he had a major collection of minor responsibilities that were actually essential to keeping the place running but unknown to almost everyone else that worked there. I suggested we give him the title of "Vice President of Miscellaneous." He loved it and it suited him perfectly. In later years I told the story many times of his youthful spirit of willingness, and numerous young people have told me that they wanted the title of Vice President of Miscellaneous.

Brian got his first taste of hospital work in Omaha, where he pursued an opportunity as an ER volunteer at Clarkson Hospital. He liked it a lot and he was gaining valuable training. Brian did not enjoy school; he had learning difficulties with the way classes were traditionally taught. Something special happened when we moved to Pleasanton, California. At Foothill High when he met his new counselor, Ms. Judy Fisher, she asked him if he had a goal in life. He told her his dream, and she really listened. She recommended that he join the local Explorers Post. Explorers got to ride as volunteers with the American Medical Response (AMR) ambulance Paramedics while training to become an Emergency Medical Technician (EMT). Brian was soon riding along several times a week in the evenings— sometimes as late as Midnight on the weekends. He loved his Paramedic trainers, Camille Barino and Luis Abaunza, and they were great with him. Though he was challenged with book-based teaching and testing, with verbal instruction and real-time demonstrations he rapidly absorbed a broad array of information and techniques. He ended up volunteering thousands of hours.

While still in high school he began classes weekends and nights at Las Positas JC, and in 1996 he received his EMT certification. He became the triage expert at his high school. Whenever he heard over the intercom system, "Brian Oftedal to the office please," he would hustle over and advise whether an accident or illness was serious enough for a hospital visit or simply warranted a rest with a damp cloth on the forehead. Brian delivered his first baby in the back of an ambulance when he was a Senior in high school. That evening we asked him what he thought about it all. He said, "It was very messy and took a long time to clean up." In the future he intended to tell each pregnant woman to squeeze her knees together tightly until they arrived at the hospital.

After high school, he took more courses at Los Medanos and Chabot Junior Colleges. He graduated with Paramedic training at Samaritan Training Center in Vacaville and then received his Paramedic certification in 1998. He was soon hired as a Firefighter-Paramedic at Bethel Island (40 miles northeast of Pleasanton), where it was more feasible to start. Then in the year 2000, with some experience now on his resume, he was hired by the Oakland Fire Department. He, along with about 20 others, had survived the cuts from thousands of applicants. My parents drove up from Fresno and joined us for his swearing-in ceremony; Grandpa Bill had the honor of pinning on his badge. Brian became an officer in 2005. In 2015 he qualified for promotion to Captain. He will no doubt work with them until he has earned full retirement benefits. Who knows what will come next; he has many ideas.

Brian has a sensitive and caring manner and he loves to perform random acts of kindness. He has touched thousands of people and he has literally saved many lives. Check this web site for ideas- http://www.randomactsofkindness.org.

Tracy was the gentle and sensitive one. She was affected more by our numerous moves, which meant new schools and making new friends. After Cerritos, she attended four schools in three years at Foothill Elementary, Flora Vista, El Cerrito, and Lincoln as we went to Santa Barbara, Encinitas, and Corona. This was followed by the normal changes to Corona Intermediate School for seventh and eight grades and then Centennial High School for ninth grade. We moved to Omaha and both twins changed to Millard North High School. Then back to California and they finally finished at Foothill High in Pleasanton. Yes, I know- that was a lot of moving.

While the move back to California was positive for Brian, this last change was tough on Tracy. She was smart but increasingly less interested in school— she started skipping a lot of classes. We nicknamed her "instant oatmeal" because when she did do her assignments it was always at the last minute. Tracy and Brian went to their Senior Prom. They both graduated; the ceremony commenced on a hot and sunny day. Grandparents drove from Fresno to attend, and longtime friend Francine Ladd flew up to honor them as well. Tracy had no desire for college. Succumbing to parental pressure, she did try a brief stint in Ashland at Southern Oregon University (where her mother had attended), but that didn't work. She moved into a tiny apartment with friends in San Francisco and took some classes at City College of S.F. Later she thought she might be interested in Accounting and took classes at Fresno City College, earning an AA degree.

She did have memorable and interesting experiences back along the way. She made a lifelong best friend in Melissa Gray. Their relationship began developing in our four years at the Glen Ivy Community. One summer, just after Tracy finished the fifth grade, she went with Melissa, Brian, and some other friends to British Columbia for Educo, an outdoor adventure school similar to Outward Bound. We knew the Educo organizers and trusted them. We thought it would be a valuable experience for our kids. They spent 10 days in the mountains with lots of hiking; they cooked their own so-called "yucky" food, which they had carried in their own packs. They slept under the stars. They experienced obstacle courses, real mountain rappelling with long ropes, and other challenges designed to expand their perceived limits. Sound exciting? We thought so. But at the time they all asked each other, “What did we do so awful that our parents sent us away to this craziness?”

Tracy must have liked it at some level because the following summer she went to Colorado for Educo. She was even motivated enough to raise money washing cars and cleaning apartments. This time in the Rockies for ten days, she enjoyed it even more. The next two summers she engaged in performing arts retreats and received training in singing, drama, and dance. I forgot to mention that Tracy was known for constantly humming and softly singing to herself, that is until one of her teachers forced her to stop it. Too bad.

It took years longer for Tracy to discover her own special gifts and dreams and to find her true calling, just as it had with Kelley, my sister. I'll say more later. I can say this now— Tracy has touched many people with acts of kindness in her own special way.

Kathryn and I were 40somethings when Brian and Tracy went through their teenage years. The process of puberty presents challenges for teenagers and for their parents. As young adults experience hormones at higher levels, their physical changes are the most apparent. However, changes on the mental and emotional levels are where the biggest challenges present themselves, as those faculties are also beginning to function in new ways. Just like learning to ride a bike, it takes time. We felt challenged, because we had to move beyond the parenting skills that had worked previously. We could no longer tell our children what to do and expect them to simply obey. While they were exercising new decision making skills, we were being compelled to relinquish some of our authority in that area. How do we accomplish this while still providing protection for our child's well-being? Great question. Whole books are written on that topic.

We had been through this once before with Jennifer (as well as our own teenage years); that helped. Frequent communication between the adults (Kathryn and me) helped us maintain a balanced perspective. We reminded ourselves that the most significant changes affecting our teenagers were those working at the level of spirit. Their Essential Beings were emerging in a natural progression, activating their bio-energetic bodies at new vibrational levels. Just as we celebrated their birth, we reminded ourselves to celebrate these next phases. Maintaining an atmosphere of harmony and balance in my own life, and consequently in our home, was the primary gift that I could bring to this party. My experiences with the Attunement process came in handy over and over again— find a place of stillness, lightly touch the patterns of disturbed energy, allow the power of the Divine to flow into the physical forms, and give thanks for innate balance as it reveals itself (however long it takes).

# Chapter Forty-Five

## MORE SILICON VALLEY YEARS

*"For the past 33 years, I have looked in the mirror every morning and asked myself: 'If today were the last day of my life, would I want to do what I am about to do today?' And whenever the answer has been 'No' for too many days in a row, I know I need to change something."*
—Steve Jobs, Founder of Apple Computer and Pixar Studios

I flew back to Massachusetts at least once each quarter, for training and meetings within our Recording Heads Group. The Boston Airport sits on an island. I always dreaded renting a car there and then joining the mess at the tunnel where impatient Boston drivers would test my nerves in their aggressive efforts to get off the island. Next I negotiated the winding old Boston streets to reach the Turnpike. Then it was simply a matter of enduring the trek west to Shrewsbury. My flight always arrived late in the evening, because we lost three hours in time zone changes along the way. I felt as if I had run the Boston Marathon by the time I reached my hotel room.

I interacted with hundreds of people at Quantum. I particularly enjoyed many in the strategic section of procurement, called the Commodity Management Department. That's where I met Colleen Cayes, who became a wonderful friend to Kathryn and me. After two years in my RHG role, Wes Worth (Commodity Manager for Hard Disk Media) recommended me for a new position- Commodity Director for Heads and Media. I knew a lot about heads, not so much about media; but I knew Wes would play a solid lead role under me on the media side. I got the job, and I brought Sanat Dave, a Program Manager at RHG, from Shrewsbury to Milpitas to be my Commodity Manager for Recording Heads. His presence meant that RHG could discontinue my previous liaison position. Two other Directors, one for Electronics and one for Mechanical parts, sat in offices next to mine. Commodities had personnel in Shrewsbury as well;

Stepan Piligian, the head of Commodities, was based there. Our VP of Materials, Andre Neumann-Loreck, who had overall responsibility for Commodities, Purchasing, and Logistics, was based in an office just across from mine. Andre was an adept executive who happened to be multi-lingual, including Japanese; he was quite a visionary as well.

The disk drive industry was undergoing a major consolidation cycle and the compctition was brutal. Every company had to repeatedly reinvent itself and commit to cost reductions as a way of life, or it would soon find itself absorbed by a competitor or spun-off, as DEC had done. Once leading brand names like Conner Peripherals, Hewlett Packard, Miniscribe, Micropolis, Hitachi, IBM, Quantum, and Maxtor have now all disappeared from the HDD business. In an effort to keep us competitive, Michael Brown (Quantum's CEO) challenged our three Commodities teams to reduce component acquisition costs by one billion dollars per year. Together we reached that goal. In my group we actually achieved six hundred million dollars per year in cost reductions, after extensive meetings and many projects with our key suppliers. We all had a lot of money on the line— huge investments were being made annually by our big name suppliers including TDK, Alps Electric, Read Rite, Yamaha, Fuji Electric, Mitsubishi Chemical, and Komag, in addition to our own RHG. Working together, we redefined the specifications of our components to make them more easily manufacturable with higher yields. We even got involved with sub-components like disk substrates for the media and the flexure assemblies that went into the heads. I travelled regularly to headquarters, research centers, and factories in Japan, Singapore, Malaysia, Indonesia, Thailand, China, and the Philippines. Along the way, I had the pleasure of seeing beautiful foreign cities and countryside; I met a lot of interesting people and experienced some amazing food. There was also a lot of sake, hot and cold sake, filtered and unfiltered sake. A lot of sake. That's how the Japanese liked to do business— a lot of sake.

I met a brilliant young manager named Ted Deffenbaugh, when he was in the strategic planning side of our HDD business. I was learning a lot in Commodities, but I told Ted that I would love to move into a different kind of strategic work with him. Quantum also owned a very successful Tape Drive Division (based on DLT technology)— another part of the data storage business package acquired from DEC. When Ted moved to the DLT Division, he recruited me to come with him. Ted had come into the data storage industry through IBM and while there he knew Mike Cannon, a highly respected top manager in IBM's engineering and research groups. Stick with me, because this got interesting. Mike had just been hired as the new CEO at Maxtor, another leading hard drive company based nearby in Milpitas. Mike recruited Ted to join Maxtor and fill a new VP-level role. Ted's parting words to me were, "I won't forget you; keep a low profile and be patient." Weeks later I got his offer to join his strategic planning group in Maxtor. I received matching pay, new stock options, and even a signing bonus. Ted was the best boss I ever had. He was a great people person, and he understood and appreciated my specific talents. We worked well together.

I'm going to skip a lot of details and go straight to Maxtor's big strategic maneuver. Ted was on the hush-hush team involved in research and negotiations that led to Maxtor's 2001 acquisition of Quantum's HDD business. He brought me onto the team to develop some modeling of the Enterprise side of the business, which would become a new market segment for Maxtor. Completion of the merger brought good news and bad news. Along with the other Maxtor personnel, I moved back over to Quantum's much nicer campus with the gym (which now had the Maxtor name out front). The bad news was that Ted got a generous package to go away in the first round of headcount reductions.

I was assigned a new boss- Tex Schenken. Tex was part of the new executive management team, but he came from the Quantum side and was "not one of Mike's boys." Tex would head up a newly established Consumer Electronics Group, and I was his strategic specialist. We were directly involved with providing key technology in the emergence of the Digital Video Recorder, while working closely with Tivo, Dish Network, and others. I was on a team developing a tiny one-inch disk drive for the consumer electronics market; our engineers created a lot of innovative technology for it, but the project was cancelled before going into production due to forecasts that its market would never reach "acceptable" volumes. Defining market opportunities for a new "ultra-low-cost disk drive," to be used in the video game market, was another favorite project. I made several flights to Sea-Tac to meet with Microsoft in Redmond, Washington and worked to get us into their secret X-box program while it was in development. I took a lot of airplane flights in those days, and it got pretty routine.

I was at the Maxtor gym, going through my usual workout the morning of September 11, 2001. This would not be a routine day. I was watching CNBC on a television mounted to the wall in front of my elliptical exercise machine. Then it happened— the broadcast was interrupted to announce a tragedy unfolding in New York City. Everyone and everything around me came to a sudden stop. We were seeing live news coverage of people running in panic, as commentators struggled to understand what was happening. Slowly we learned of preplanned terrorist attacks, including other incidents unfolding beyond NYC. Along with millions of people watching these broadcasts around the world, I didn't know what to say or think. When I watched an airplane being deliberately flown into the second twin tower, I was stunned and speechless. It would get even worse. The second tower collapsed before my eyes. I didn't want to hear reports of the NYC firemen racing up the stairs of that building. In their heroic efforts to help those trapped in the fires on floors high above, they themselves also became victims. My son was a firefighter, and my thoughts rushed to him. I was now in shock. Somehow I showered, dressed, and went to my office; but I couldn't begin to think about business. I called my wife and confirmed she was struggling with her feelings. She was also thinking about Brian and praying for his safety, even though he was thousands of miles from NYC. I told Tex that I needed to go home. We later learned that 343 firefighters died, amongst a total of 2,996 dead from all of the attacks that day. As bad as I was feeling, I couldn't imagine the pain of those actually involved in the incidents and their friends or family. It would take a long time for an entire nation of people to put this behind us. Even as I write these words, thirteen years later, tears come to my eyes.

While I survived several rounds of head count reduction at Maxtor, they just kept coming. The combined company still had too many people. On about the sixth round, my name came up— Tex broke the news and offered a severance package with six months pay. I wasn't surprised. In fact, I had been thinking about an exit strategy for months during my evening commutes, which now lasted over an hour. Kathryn and I had been talking about next steps, including eventual retirement possibilities in the Northwest. Interestingly, we were already packed for a flight the next morning to Portland to take some specific steps. Our "some day" timeline was now being accelerated. It would be difficult to move farther from Brian and Tracy and farther from family in Fresno. Tracy was living in a small San Francisco apartment. Brian was living in an apartment nearby with a girlfriend. We saw the severance package as a sign and a gift. We made our decision.

# Chapter Forty-Six

## BACK TO THE NORTHWEST- THE CAMAS YEARS

*"My grandmother started walking five miles a day when she was sixty. She's ninety seven now and we don't know where the hell she is."*
—Ellen DeGeneres, American Comedienne and Actress

We moved around a lot, but at least our family knows where we are. I believe we have found our final home. Upon deciding we would retire in a state other than California, we developed a list of attributes that we were seeking. When we found a spot with everything on the list, we would know our destination. I had financial objectives like finding a smaller house in the best neighborhood and no state income tax. Nevada had no state income tax but it was too hot, so Washington became our primary candidate. Kathryn's relatives were in Washington, and our daughter Jennifer was in Portland, just across the Columbia River from southwestern Washington. We would definitely enjoy more time with her. We wanted physical things like an abundance of mature trees, a water view, hiking trail nearby, quiet neighborhood, and a feeling of country seclusion. At the same time we wanted to live only a short drive from city amenities like good hospitals and a major airport.

I was still at least ten years away from being able to afford retirement; I thought maybe we could buy property somewhere and then build on it later. A few months earlier, we found ourselves standing on a lot in Camas, Washington in a beautiful community of custom homes where about 25 scattered empty lots remained unsold. This one had a wonderful view of Lacamas Lake, and the price had just been discounted, partly because the land was steeply inclined down toward the lake. There would be no typical backyard for any home on this property, so no families were interested— for empty-nesters like us it appeared perfect. We literally checked off everything on our list as a deer came down the hill and started to eat some blackberries while giving us a casual look just a few yards away. Surely it was another sign. The next morning we were introduced to Bob and Karen Pearce, who lived up the street. As a side job to his sales position with Kraft Foods, he had built several homes in the neighborhood. Bob inspected our lot and deemed it buildable. We bought the lot for $100,000, drawing on the HELOC account we had with our Pleasanton home, and we flew back to California.

One month later we flew north again to spend a holiday with Jennifer, and we visited our lot on the lake. The location felt so very peaceful; we decided to begin designing the house. We started with bubble charts on a big piece of paper, laying out different areas in general. Then we sketched in details and features we liked from all of our previous houses. We put numerous windows along the back of the house to enjoy the views of the trees and lake. After several iterations of sending our ideas to a draftsman in Camas, and then marking up the drawings he returned to us, our house was taking shape. It would be our dream home, and we grew eager to build it as quickly as possible. We qualified for a construction loan with Wells Fargo Bank. We signed a contract with Bob and Karen via mail. We were ready to fly north for signing loan papers and to participate in a ground breaking ceremony. That was when I was given notice at Maxtor. Coincidence or the Spiritual Wind at work again?

We put our house on the market, and Louise Davis soon brought us a buyer. We were sad about leaving Pleasanton, but we made a substantial capital gain on that nine year investment. Actually we sold near a market peak, just a few years before the next California housing market down-cycle.

I didn't have a job, but I would be getting paychecks for six months while we built our new house. For the first time we would be moving without children. We would pay for the expenses of this move, so we attempted a major thinning of everything in our garage. After weeks of packing, hired laborers arrived to help load our belongings into a moving van. The house was empty by late afternoon and Kathryn and I were quite tired, but we decided to drive north for a few hours, just to get out of town. I drove our Mazda Tribute SUV and Kathryn followed me in her blue Volvo 850 Sedan. It was the Spring of 2002. When we reached the I-5 Freeway and stopped at a motel near Sacramento, I had memories of driving north along that same freeway in my VW Van in the Spring of 1972. That first time I was still single and thirty years younger.

The next day we stopped in Ashland, to rest overnight and

reminisce about the days when we first met. The following morning we discovered a restaurant-bakery named Munchie's; new to us, it was located downstairs at the end of Lithia Square. They served great breakfasts and incredible freshly baked pie. After one more stroll, we drove straight to the construction site, arriving just in time to see Bob finishing a pour of our concrete foundation. I was impressed with the massive amounts of concrete, and all of it was securely attached to a series of huge boulders sitting underneath. Our house would not be moving. We were very excited and I felt liberated.

We quickly found an apartment in nearby Vancouver, Washington. When our van arrived, some local hired helpers moved us into part of the apartment and stacked most of our boxes and excess furniture into the second bedroom and half of the two-car garage. We drove to the construction site every day to watch the progress and learn what decisions needed to be made next. It was a memorable experience, one day shopping for fixtures and another day deciding colors and locations for switches. Construction moved forward at a good pace. Bob Pearce had a flair for building and loved adding "drama" into his houses. We ended up with a Great Room with an eighteen foot ceiling at its peak and large windows looking out to the trees, lake, and mountains beyond. Bob finished in exactly six months, and we were eager to move. We loaded all our things from the apartment into a rental truck, again with the help of some hired hands, and staged the truck in our driveway for the night. We thought we had arranged for the same men to meet us at the house to unload the next morning, but there was a misunderstanding and they never came. We started without them and never stopped. I can't believe Kathryn and I did the whole thing by ourselves, at age 55. Needless to say, we were sore for days. We swore, "Never again; this is the last house." We were so happy to sleep in our own bed that first night. An extra bonus was the quiet and serenity of the location, which was beyond our expectations. Ours was the last house on the street and surrounded by trees on three sides.

The search had already started for our new favorite restaurants. The only breakfast restaurant worth mentioning on our side of the river was the Starlight Diner— I loved their pork chops, eggs scrambled, and hash browns (skip the toast). We found a couple of decent Mexican restaurants. One nearby called Los Dos Compadres had tasty chili verde, but we soon discovered what became "my favorite chili verde and rice on the whole west coast" at El Sombrero on Sandy Boulevard in Portland. We still return regularly, and I reconfirm that yes it is still my favorite, even though it lacks the peppery kick I enjoyed at Casa Orosco. In downtown Camas we found Camas Thai Cuisine— I loved their shrimp Pad Thai. For barbecue, I have to go across the river into Portland to Podnah's; they produce amazing smoked ribs and brisket. I found out about them on television, thanks to Guy Fieri and his Diners, Drive-ins, and Dives program.

I could now reconnect with some old friends. Craig Bleeker and Ken Jablonski, UCLA rowing buddies, were living in Seattle. Jim Sims was still in Ashland. We see him sometimes when we are driving to California. He comes our way for an annual crew regatta on Lake Vancouver. We enjoy watching his races, and he seems to have even more endurance than decades earlier. He got serious about Triathlons in his 60s, and at age 70 he qualified for the Iron Man World Championships in Kona, Hawaii; he can tell you amazing stories about that experience. We see Larry Smith whenever we are in Seattle, and he comes down once a year to attend a Portland Trailblazers basketball game with me.

I felt relaxed and rejuvenated. Now all I needed was a job. I knew the Spiritual Wind would surprise me yet again. Meanwhile, every day I gave thanks for our journey.

*"Back on my bike."*

# Chapter Forty-Seven

## IT'S ALL ABOUT THE JOURNEY

*"Do the difficult things while they are easy and do the great things while they are small. A journey of a thousand miles must begin with a single step."*
—Lao Tsu, Chinese Philosopher and
Author of *The Tao Te Ching*

Here is something I learned along the way. Seemingly difficult things can be made easy by looking at them in a different way. Great things can be made small in a similar way. I like to say that great journeys are nothing more than the next step you are about to take. I'm not philosophizing here— I want to give you a tip. Take the time to look at things differently and all kinds of possibilities will appear. I accomplished many things in my business career, and in my daily living, because I took the time to see processes and people differently.

Not yet ready for retirement, I was job hunting one more time. I interviewed at some high-tech companies. The commutes all looked unappealing. Few jobs were being created at the time, and the competition was stiff. Eventually I reconnected with my old friends in the yogurt business, the ones I had worked for in Seattle twenty five years earlier. They had closed their retail shops and were now operating a factory, where they produced frozen yogurt mix for sale to other retail operators. Near the Portland Airport, it was only a 16 minute drive from my new home. They renamed their company YoCream International and had grown it to nearly ten million dollars in annual sales. Their biggest customer was Costco. Costco had opened food courts in all of their clubs, and their customers were now enjoying YoCream's yogurt (sold under the Kirkland brand) while they shopped. Credit for the development of that exclusive recipe goes to Frances Hanna, Dave's wife, who was now heading up R&D. YoCream had earned a 100 percent share of Costco's business in the U.S. and Mexico, and the volumes were growing steadily as more clubs opened every year. YoCream's two biggest challenges were developing sales on the non-Costco side of the business and getting costs under control. I interviewed with John and Dave Hanna, the two founding brothers who were now actively managing the company. They remembered me fondly and were eager to hear about my recent experiences. When I talked about my Commodity Management years in Silicon Valley where I had contributed to cost reductions on the scale of several hundred million dollars per year, their eyes lit up. They needed me, but due to their always tight budgets, they could only offer a starting salary that was about one third of what I had been earning in California. However they promised I would have opportunities for pay increases, advancement, bonuses, 401(k) matching, and possibly company stock. They were a public company, and their stock was listed on NASDAQ as YOCM. I had a good feeling about the opportunity, and I still loved their yogurt— I decided to join in the cause.

My California friends were amazed when I left Silicon Valley without a job lined up, but they were happy for us— particularly when they learned I was back in the frozen yogurt business, which was quite trendy at the time. Colleen Cayes, our friend from Quantum, came up to visit. She marveled at how wonderfully everything had come together. She created a painting as a gift; it contained the words, "Kathryn, Quilts, Terry, Yogurt, Faith, Home, Lacamas." It sits on the desk in my office, where I am sitting now while enjoying the view of our lake and writing this book. I have discovered that Faith is not something passive— I can't sit back and wait for great things to fall into my lap. Faith is something that has to be actively demonstrated, and patience is a necessary ingredient. Timing is essential as well, and I always expect the unexpected. It all takes practice.

I started at YoCream as Manager of Purchasing and Logistics. Expenses in these two departments absorbed over 50 percent of every revenue dollar— they were ripe for innovation and cost reduction. I wanted to understand their existing operating processes (all undocumented), so I spent time every day roaming the production floor, the warehouses, and the drive-in freezers; I asked a lot of questions. Instead of developing a series of logical arguments in a Powerpoint presentation, as I did in the big corporations, I set about to develop one number. That one number would be the amount of dollars we could save every year by making one specified change in our practices. Few people take the time to quantify the value of potential changes, but I enjoyed the challenge. I would continue to repeat that one number in meetings and conversations until I got everyone's attention. When each change was approved and implemented, I was expected to measure and report on the actual savings achieved. Each time I delivered on my original claims, it got easier for the next proposals. Within my first twelve months we were implementing cost reduction programs that would amount to millions of dollars per year. This was huge for a company that size.

My trick was to simply look at things differently. Instead of looking at processes the way they had always been done, I took the time to imagine them being done in a simpler way. The hardest part was convincing everyone involved that benefits would indeed follow. Resistance to change is all too common. In some cases people pointed out actual obstructions; so I wrote new procedures to work around them. In later years I would develop a list of ten to twenty change projects every year and work them as part of my daily routine. We never ran out of new possibilities.

Why did this seem so easy? Because I had already practiced these skills in my personal life, where the process is even more difficult because my own mind is the primary objector— where my own preconceptions and preferences sometimes clouded my ability to perceive new possibilities. On the personal level the stakes are even greater, because successes are truly life changing. If you want to be successful in business, pay attention to your personal work first.

Meanwhile, my NBA allegiances shifted from the Warriors to the Portland Trailblazers. I was attending 10-15 of their home games a year and watching the rest on television. I became a true Blazermaniac. Since YoCream was a corporate sponsor of the Blazers, I had a VIP pass which admitted me and my guests to The Sphere, inside the Rose Garden Arena, for free food and drinks before the games. There we could mingle and chat with team executives, former players, and VIP guests like team founder Harry Glickman and Bill Shonley, the well-known original Blazers' announcer. Twice Gordon Brazington, our banker at Wells Fargo, arranged for me to participate in a Blazers Fantasy Camp. I joined in drills and shooting competitions on the floor of the Rose Garden. I was playing alongside famous NBA players like Wesley Matthews, Andre Miller, Rudy Fernandez, and Damian Lillard. Up close you realized how very young they all were, yet they were all millionaires. I stood on my toes for a picture next to Rudy, so we would appear the same height. He noticed, and not to be outdone, he stood on his toes also. They were just kids! And they were younger than my own children. It made me think about how we have developed such a bizarre system for over-rewarding people with certain talents— at least jobs are created along the way, and many NBA celebrities are extremely generous in giving back with their time and money. After showering, Kathryn joined me for dinner at a restaurant (on the ground floor of the arena) with the coach and other players. Coach Nate McMillan was the prime speaker at one dinner, Coach Terry Stotts was at the other. I sat up front and asked plenty of questions. They were very nice people; they just happened to have a high-profile job.

During my ten years at YoCream I had opportunities to participate in other facets of the food service industry; I was encouraged by my boss to give some of my time freely. I participated in committees at the Northwest Food Processors Association, and in January of 2008 I was awarded their Eagle Award for my contributions. For four years starting in 2005 I had served, as an appointee by then Governor Kulongowski, on the Oregon Innovation Council; I was the sole representative from the food processing industry. I became Chairman of one of three OIC Committees and immensely enjoyed the development of our Council's recommendations to the Governor and the Legislature. We basically developed the investment strategy for stimulating business innovation and jobs creation in Oregon. David Chen, a local venture capitalist, was the Chairman of the OIC. It also included four members of the Legislature, State Treasurer Randall Edwards, head administrators of the state's major research universities, top management from some of the largest employers, and research specialists from high-tech companies in the area like Intel. We were involved at the ground floor in some exciting emerging technologies like Nanotechnology, Wave Energy, and new high-speed drug screening technologies.

Over the years I also developed personal friendships with several people who supplied materials and services to YoCream. I'll mention just one. Dave Kurtz was the sales representative for a global supplier of food commodities. YoCream purchased a few of their products in significant quantities. He was one of several suppliers that reliably supported us through many growth challenges and played a contributing role in our successes. I learned a lot from him, and indeed we became personal friends. Dave is an honest and genuine person. He is also humble. Over lunch or dinner it was easy and natural for us to share personal stories and to talk about our challenges as well as our dreams. His biggest concern was getting overly preoccupied with the many details of the day and losing site of the bigger picture. He recognized that he was creating undue pressure on himself; it was like a bad habit. He often reminded himself, "It's all about the journey." This is as true in business as it is in our personal lives. It seems all too easy to become preoccupied with objectives, destinations, or little details; and we forget to enjoy the present moment. Dave and I still call each other, and I always enjoy saying to him, "It's all about the journey, Dave." Sometimes when he answers the phone, I start with the words, "It's all about the journey." He immediately knows who is calling. He always says, "Yes. Thanks for reminding me."

# Chapter Forty-Eight

## THE BEST PRICE IS FREE

*"When you come to a fork in the road, take it."*
—Yogi Berra, Baseball Legend and Accidental Philosopher

Have you ever received advice that didn't quite make sense? Have you ever tried something in business that defied conventional wisdom— like offering your most valuable product for free? I want to tell you about some amazing experiences along these lines, but first I have to digress a bit. I was promoted to Director and given added leadership responsibilities for R&D, Quality Assurance, and Retail Operations. Because I had experience with managing our Yogurt Stand retail operations back in the 1970s, I was also assigned the lead on a new project. We decided to build and operate one retail frozen yogurt shop near our factory. We were aware of the self-serve concept that was developing in California. We also knew that the average self-serve shop was selling several times the yogurt volume of most traditional full-serve shops.

When our YoCream Frozen Yogurt shop opened in Cascade Station near the Portland Airport it was the first self-serve FroYo shop in the Northwest. It was a new concept that would require explaining to our local consumers— fortunately weather would be a significant ally. That first summer was a long and hot one. We soon became incredibly busy with lines stretching out the door on many days for most of the afternoon and evening hours; within months we achieved profitability. However we didn't see this as just a profit center. We saw it as a place to test new flavors and new product concepts. We learned more about the challenges facing our retail operators; this led to ideas about how our manufacturing business could better satisfy the needs of our customer base— which now had grown into an international network of retail operators.

Then a truly novel idea began to develop. We would train other people in how to open and operate their own retail yogurt shops, and we would make our money by selling them our yogurt mix to run in their machines. It would be much simpler than franchising. We named our idea YoCream University. Several of us added to the original concept, and it evolved along the way. It took the form of a two day seminar held in a nearby hotel conference room. We offered a variety of presentations, guest speakers, and outings for behind-the-scene tours of our retail shop and factory. I did a lot of the talking over those two days, so we recruited more speakers to help. Some machine and equipment suppliers came in to help demonstrate the primary hardware used in the shops. The participants particularly loved tasting different flavors of our frozen yogurt. Our R&D staff told them how our yogurt products were developed and manufactured. We brought in successful retail operators to tell about their experiences. We started in Portland and soon found even greater demand in the Eastern U.S., so I organized Yo.U East. We staged the first ones in New York; then we moved to Orlando, where the weather and logistics were better. We averaged about one class per month; usually 20 to 30 people attended. We could actually see retail shops opening in every region as a direct result of our seminars. We offered Yo.U for free, and it paid for itself.

To be honest, I dreaded the first Yo.U's. I was always busy with operational projects. I had to get used to stepping away from the day to day and changing into a different mode. The attendees were interesting and enthusiastic, and they loved hearing my stories, so I became "the professor." I had a lot to talk about because of my retail operating experiences, plus I really did understand the dynamics and finances of the frozen yogurt industry. I collected some stories from the early days (in the 1970s) that I enjoyed telling. After the first few, I started looking forward to each Yo.U.

As a member of YoCream's Senior Management team I played my part in growing our company dramatically. Eight years after my return we capped it off with selling all of the stock in YoCream to Danone Yogurt of France for over $100 million. I was offered a "transition" employment agreement, which required my commitment to stay through two additional years. I signed it, and I calculated my retirement date. I participated in 50 YoCream Universities before I retired. At the end of my time I handed Yo.U off to Jackie Nelson, our retail shop manager, who had become my primary partner in delivering the seminars. It turned out to be a lot of fun, and I have many memories.

Applying "free" in our personal lives may also seem counter-intuitive. It raises questions and fears like, “What if I run out?” Practicing generosity is actually the best way of dealing with that one. Here is my simple exercise— when I tip, I round up. Then I round up a little more, and smile. That extra money can mean a lot to workers in our service industries. At the same time, I am also benefitting; I am experiencing the joy of giving. Remember the spiritual expression approach to living? I experience what I express, and abundance surrounds me— it’s the nature of the universe.

My intention with this book is to give it away. Yes, you may have paid to cover the costs of printing and distribution. If I net anything over my expenses, I’ll donate it to my favorite charity. I want this book to be my gift to you. Am I lessened by this? No. Will I receive any benefit in this? Of course I will. Some might even say that in giving I get to touch God. The best price is free.

# Chapter Forty-Nine

## NOW I AM THE GRANDPA

*"A zest for life is one of the most important examples a grandparent can pass on to their grandchildren."*
—author unknown

We have never had a single regret about moving to the Northwest. Kathryn loves spending more time with her mother Helen, her brother Charles, and other relatives. We spend a lot more time with our oldest daughter Jennifer. She married David Gonnella in September of 2003— the ceremony was held in his hometown of Wakefield, Massachusetts. I enjoyed walking Jennifer, dressed in her beautiful white wedding gown, down the aisle. They took a memorable honeymoon trip to Amsterdam, Netherlands and Florence, Italy. Jennifer has been working with non-profit organizations coordinating healthcare services, provided by volunteer professionals, for the uninsured in the Portland area. Many of her clients and coworkers are Spanish speaking and they all marvel at her fluent speaking ability. She remains dedicated to helping those most in need.

Jennifer told me that her travels to other parts of the world contributed to long-held feelings of guilt because of the abundance that we enjoy in the U.S. This is not unusual. Yes, there may be many who are suffering; we can be kind and help others as opportunities present themselves. We may have more than many; we can be thankful and take responsibility for stewarding what we have been given.

I want to share something from my heart. Here is the blessing that I wrote and was privileged to deliver at Jennifer's wedding reception:

"O Lord, we pause in these moments of joy
and celebration to give thanks to thee.
We are thankful for this food which nourishes our bodies
and we are thankful for this gathering of family
and loved ones which nourishes our soul.
We give thanks to thee O Lord for the
blessings that fill our days.
May we always have the patience and wisdom
to recognize and receive thy blessings,
and may we pass them along in our words and deeds.

Now let us add our own blessings to this marriage
of David and Jennifer Gonnella.
May they experience joy in their days together.
May they seek to understand each other and
readily overcome any differences,
thereby growing as individuals and as a couple.
May they both continue with acts of
charitable work in their community,
and may we be inspired to generosity of
spirit by their example.
And every day may the world be
blessed by their presence.
In thy name, Amen."

—Terry Oftedal, Father of the Bride

Lindy Pearl Gonnella, our first grandchild was born June 21, 2005. Her middle name was picked to honor her great-great-grandmother Pearl Oftedal, who Jennifer remembers as being "particularly spunky." Lindy turned ten years old in 2015, and she started the fifth grade. She has hazel brown eyes, long brown hair, and she is one of the tallest in her class. We are guessing she may grow to six feet. Of course we think she is quite special. She is crazy about cats and loves music— she enjoys drumming and practices often. She likes to read; *The Familiars* is one of her favorite books. She loves to cook and she is the biggest fan of my gluten-free and dairy-free waffles, which she helps me prepare. She has a lot of friends in school. Though not very interested in sports, she loves recess, running around, and climbing on bars. She is also very brave— in Cancun she jumped off a cliff into a river about 20 feet below; she also enjoyed the zip lines, letting go at the end and dropping into the water. She likes to draw pictures; she thinks she might be an architect someday. I think she might find a career in the world of healthcare, like her parents have done. Lindy is also sensitive to energy work. I help her practice Attunements; she can feel the rainbow of energy that exists inside everyone's body. And while she is beginning to wrestle with hormones in her body, and her mind is beginning to come of age, she also spends time cultivating a still space in her consciousness. I do know this— she will make an impact on the world in her own special way.

Tracy, our younger daughter, moved up to Portland. She bought a house in North Portland, near her sister. We enjoy seeing her quite often and hearing from her on the phone almost every day. She established an elder care and housekeeping business, and she also enjoys visiting and helping with her grandmother. She married her longtime friend Kelli Snetzinger in a small family ceremony at our house in Camas on Nov. 9, 2013. Tracy looked lovely in her simple white dress. The ceremony was short and sweet, exactly the way they wanted it. She raises chickens, enjoys growing vegetables in the raised beds that we helped build in her backyard, and loves her dogs and cat. She represents the spirit of the Earth Mother, and in her gentle ways she inspires me.

Our son Brian married Nicole Rangel in 2006, but I am saving the story of that event for a later chapter. In February, 2015 they delivered a baby girl- our grandchild number two. Her name is Bailey Renee Oftedal, and she is a real charmer. She is as beautiful as she is sweet.

Karla Gervais, a friend from California days, moved into our area. We meet Karla almost every week; we visit and share Attunements. She brought news that the Glen Ivy community had disbanded and the property was for sale. Many of the residents from our time there had already moved along to their next ventures. Years earlier John and Pam Gray moved into a suburban neighborhood in Lake Elsinore, near their married daughter Melissa and her children. We still have friends from those days and we learned a lot. The people are what really mattered. Properties come and go.

Many of the spiritual elders who inspired me have now passed on. Jim Wellemeyer, George Shears, Roger DeWinton, George Emery, Grace Van Duzen, and Martin Cecil are gone. I heard that Michael Cecil declared the organizational structures which had developed in Martin's lifetime were no longer needed. Michael and others moved into more individualized phases of their own spiritual quests, as had I. The Spiritual Wind continues to work its magic, and we still find ourselves crossing paths. During this time I came to realize that I am now a spiritual elder.

I also love being the Grandpa. This role provides me specific opportunities to reveal Sunseed's spirit and zest for life. I look forward to family meals and getting to pay the bill. When anyone else offers, I say, "I am the Grandpa now and I get to pay." I remember those family times when I was a child and my grandfathers brought the food or paid the bill. I have been blessed with a wonderful family, and I love being able to pass along blessings to them. Based on my experience, I believe that my whole purpose for living is so that I can express the spirits of God's nature in each moment.

# Chapter Fifty

## OUR TWENTY-YEAR PLAN

*"Plans are useless, but planning is indispensable."*
—Dwight D. Eisenhower, 34th U.S. President
and WW II 5-Star General

Some people hate planning. I have come to love it. I had some good jobs in the 1980s, but raising children and paying down debt prevented us from being able to save very much. Kathryn was able to work, but after paying for her commute, extra taxes, and childcare, it made more sense for her to stay focused at home most years. Many young families find themselves in this same bind; the first priorities are paying the bills on time and making house and car repairs. Donating to favorite causes, helping others in need, and being generous with gifts are things we try to fit in if we can. We strive to pay down debt, because credit card interest rates are a killer— and the college loans and doctors bills don't just go away by themselves. For years, saving toward college for our children and preparing for our own future retirement may seem like impossible tasks. In addition to all of these challenges, I lived four years in an intentional community, where my income covered only the basics. Others may have done stints as volunteers in a community service organization like AmeriCorp or the Peace Corps.

Nevertheless, at age 45, when we moved from Glen Ivy to Omaha, Kathryn and I were determined to focus on some longer range goals. We would both be 65 years in 20 years, and we hoped we would not have to work beyond that age. We also wanted to help our three children and their children in the future. We knew that college training would become an increasingly important step for the next generations. A degree will be even more important to grandchildren, so they can earn a suitable living while also following their dreams. We formulated a 20 year plan and dedicated ourselves to its accomplishment. Our experience with living on a monthly budget for all of our preceding married years provided solid groundwork. We had paid off all of our debts and credit cards. Thanks to a good California housing market we had made money off of the sales of our houses in Cerritos, Santa Barbara, and Encinitas. Hopefully the equity in our next homes would appreciate and contribute to our asset base. Home ownership is a terrific tax advantaged investment in thc U.S.

Our plan had several parts. Start participating in the 401(k) plans at work and maximize all of the possible employer matching contributions. Find a way to increase my 401(k) contributions each year and get IRA's started for both of us. Look for future jobs which had stock options, generous compensation, and programs to pay for our relocation if needed. Develop an emergency reserve savings account. Then live within our means on whatever was left. We made some agreements that may have appeared to be of minor help, but they held great significance to us. Kathryn and I pledged to set our retirement-at-65 plan as a higher goal than any personal spending, except when the two of us agreed in advance. I pledged to make my own breakfasts and lunches the night before and brown bag them to work so I could avoid the higher cost of buying lunches. Kathryn volunteered to learn how to give me haircuts so we could save barbershop money for at least the next 20 years.

How did we stay focused on our big goals? We broke them into little goals that we could then focus on every day. We watched our progress by writing down everything, reconfirmed agreements regularly, and celebrated achievements of milestones along the way. Sustained agreement between two people multiplies the power of such focused intent— this is a powerful tool, and it has been a foundational element of our marriage. It was also key to achieving our rctirement goal in exactly 20 years. We hit our asset goal in 2012. I was 65, and I qualified for Medicare Health Insurance. I had given one year's notice on my job the previous January, so I retired at the end of the year and the next day I walked onto a plane to Cancun with family members who were happy to help me celebrate.

Did this sound simple? Well it was a simple plan, because we broke it down into manageable chunks. I learned that trick in business, it's called "chunking." We invested a lot of work and a lot of living into those 20 years. We did make some mistakes, like being too speculative and borrowing on margin. We learned, after licking our wounds. We agreed to avoid leverage and never again invest with borrowed money. We sought to invest with a long term diversified strategy, avoid speculation, and ride out any downturns while remaining fully invested. We avoided bonds, until retirement when we purchased a portfolio of Municipal Bonds (not bond funds). Like Peter Lynch, the famous Fidelity investment manager, we otherwise focused totally on equity investments. Many pundits on Wall Street hate that approach, but we took the responsibility to find our own path. We didn't try to time the market; we simply slept soundly through the ups and downs and continued to "average in."

I can't promise that the same approach will work for anyone else, but we did prove that it is possible. Don't let all the uncertainties stop you from starting. Most people should begin well before their twenty-years-to-go mark. Also, you should never be ashamed of achieving your goals; too often those who have saved diligently are collectively branded as greedy. All of us (100 percent) share the responsibility of generously helping others, and we each decide how to do that in our own way. Some may say that Kathryn and I had a lot of luck along the way. Do you know how the Indy Car racers define "luck?" They say luck is a lot of preparation, combined with the ability to recognize opportunities and the resolve to act decisively. Yes, that was definitely a big part of it.

# Chapter Fifty-One

## THE INVENTION OF RETIREMENT, AND MY RE-INVENTION

*"America, I love this country!"*
—Yakov Smirnoff, Russian-American Comedian

Yes, I do love this country. My ancestors immigrated here to find opportunities, and I was blessed to be born here. My parents (and their's) started with very little, yet I was able to partake in a wonderful education system. In my first 20 years after college, I had the freedom to pursue personal interests and start a family, instead of focusing on long term goals. Twenty years later I was able to retire and re-invent myself again. Permit me to share some of the perspectives I gained in this process. Retirement, as I am experiencing it, is a very recently developed concept for the common person. Royalty and those born into wealth do not have to worry about working in old age. The rest of us do. For centuries it was common for people to work right up to the day they died. In prior generations lifetimes were also much shorter. With an amazing 100 years of medical advances, by 2010 our expected lifetime at birth had reached 67 years. Now in the U.S. over 14 percent of our population is at least 65 years old, and that percentage will keep increasing. Half of those who are 65 today are expected to live to at least 85. Most people would love to be able to stop working, but many are not taking the steps required to achieve that goal. A reported 36 percent of workers have zero money saved for retirement, and 60 percent have less than $25,000 put away. It seems to be a conundrum—America is truly a land of opportunity, but at the same time many are disadvantaged.

Another report reveals that only 10 percent of the working population are on track in saving for an adequate retirement and a much larger percentage have no hope of ever achieving any type of retirement. Some are simply not trying. Some face more challenges than others. Some people have no confidence in the future of the international monetary system and believe it is doomed to collapse; that theory has been around for a very long time. Others do not want to stop working— there's nothing wrong with that. In the middle are the rest who will have to continue working (at least part time) into their elder years or will struggle to make ends meet after they do stop working.

To be honest, when we were younger Kathryn and I had little confidence in the future of the Social Security system. We knew we were part of a big Baby Boomer bubble that would someday reach retirement age and change the dynamics of the system. If Social Security still existed when we wanted to retire, we expected our benefits would be reduced. So far it has performed as designed, and the expected population ratio changes are having the expected impact. Now, the system needs some restructuring. Members of Congress will eventually be forced to make tough decisions on which adjustments to make and which parts of the populace will be impacted most. The American people have embraced Social Security. Members of Congress like to get reelected. They will figure it out.

Social Security was designed to be supplemental only, it is very difficult for anyone to live on that income alone. Employer pension plans helped fill the gap for some fortunate people in recent generations, but those programs are quickly disappearing. In 1950 almost 10 million workers were covered by 13,000 private pension plans. By 1975, 43 percent of corporate workers were offered a private pension plan (enticing workers to stay with the same company for decades so as to qualify for actually receiving full benefits). By 2012 that percentage has dropped to 12 percent and it continues to decline rapidly. Spending ones whole career with the same company is no longer the norm, and maintaining liquidity in the programs has become increasingly difficult for the employers. For more details on understanding the hidden risks in pension plans and other retirement options, I recommend a book by my friend Jim Jorgensen- *Retire Tax Free*. It is available as an ebook for only $4.99.

Congress recognized the need to provide new vehicles and tax incentives to assist individuals in developing their own privately owned nest eggs for funding retirement. They came up with three terrific inventions.

1. In 1975 Congress created Traditional IRAs. The original tax-deductible contribution amount was limited to $1,500 or 15 percent of earnings. Now it is up to $5,500. It needs to go higher. Individuals can take tax deductions in the contributing year, compound the earning on a tax-

deferred basis for years, then pay taxes later (at the time of withdrawals) when many will hopefully be in a lower tax bracket. Do not forget to discount your fund balance when you read your statement; part of that money will disappear as tax payments eventually.

2. In 1978 Congress passed the Revenue Act of 1978, which allows any employee to treat a portion of their earned income as deferred compensation. This provision is in Internal Revenue Code Section 401(k). By 1983, nearly half of all large employers either offered a 401(k) plan or were considering one. By 1996 assets in all 401(k) plans surpassed $1 trillion, with more than 30 million participants. By 2014 it has increased to $4.4 trillion. Again earnings compound on a tax-deferred basis, and income tax is paid on withdrawals. The best thing about 401(k)'s is that most employers will match part of your contributions; this is free money— the best return on investment you will find anywhere.
3. In 1997 Senator William Roth presented to Congress his idea for a Roth IRA. This offered yet another great alternative. There would be no tax deduction at the time of contribution— instead all of the earnings would be totally tax-free. Zero taxes at the time of withdrawal! Later Congress adapted this concept to the 401(k) plans and created the Roth 401(k).

In recent decades other savings and investment tools became available to more than just the wealthy, giving everyone an affordable way to invest in new alternatives to low-interest bank savings accounts and government savings bonds.

1. Congress passed the Investment Company Act of 1940 and mutual funds were invented. Individuals could now invest in a package of stocks or bonds and enjoy the benefits of diversification. This reduced some of the risks inherent in owning individual stocks. In 1975, John Bogle founded The Vanguard Group and introduced the concept of <u>index</u> mutual funds. Now you could avoid paying a portfolio manager and invest in an index such the S&P 500; you would own a part of all 500 companies, rather than a collection of stocks picked by some "expert." Equally as radical, these index funds had very low operating expenses and no sales fees. Many companies soon began offering similar fund packages.
2. In May of 1975 Charles Schwab began offering discount

brokerage accounts, with access to the stock and bond markets through a simple phone call. In September he opened his first branch office in Sacramento, the city of his birth. In time he provided the consumer access to his account through the internet, real time quotes, and the ability to place buy and sell orders directly. In 1978 Schwab had 45,000 client accounts, by 1982 it was up to 374,000, and by 2014 it was 9.3 million. At the time, the idea of discount brokerage services was considered radical. It was a major departure from the big full-service investment houses which catered to the most wealthy, but it was the right idea and soon there were many competitors. This only served to further quicken the pace of innovation and further reduce investing costs.

3. ETF's were invented in 1989. They rolled the diversification of a mutual fund into a package you could buy or sell like a stock. ETF's also provided increased liquidity and transparency along with even lower operating costs (which allowed investors to retain more of their investment gains). By 2001 many companies were packaging and selling ETF's, and they were rapidly gaining in popularity as an investment vehicle. In 2012, I sold my last mutual fund and moved forward with an array of ETF's as my investment strategy. There are now over 1,700 different ETF's available, holding over $2.7 trillion in assets.

That is the technical part, and I enjoyed reading and educating myself about all of it. In fact it became my primary hobby. I read articles online and financial magazines almost every day. I traded ideas with friends and sought professional inputs, though I didn't agree with everything I heard or read. I know some people do not enjoy or do not trust themselves with this kind of work on their own. That is allowed; there are plenty of honest advisors around. Some people feel all of these gyrations are just devious means for avoiding taxes. Everyone can have their opinion. The government wants each of us to avoid becoming dependent on them for support, and I have been following their rules just as they have been asking me to do.

In school I read that "All roads lead to Rome." Now everything I read was leading me to one very important question that everyone should be trying to answer. "Given all the uncertainties around my longevity, the unknowable costs for my future healthcare needs, and the unpredictability of future events like inflation rate cycles and stock market fluctuations, how do I determine how much money I need to save before I make my big decision to retire?"

I'm going to boil down my answer into three steps and share them with you, in the most simple words possible. Please keep reading. This is important, and it will only take a few minutes. First of all, no one can ever eliminate uncertainty. I decided to plan for what I call the best-case scenario, which assumes that Kathryn and I will both live 100 years or more. Then I worked backwards to perform a short series of calculations. Here they are:

1. *Decide how much money you need for annual income in retirement.* It helps if you have been keeping budget records and have learned from your monthly spending patterns along the way. Budgeting, which all companies and governments must do, also gives you the confidence that you will know how to live in the latter days on a budget, be it seemingly meager or abundant.
2. *Determine how much you expect to receive annually in retirement from any pensions and Social Security.* The Social Security web site helps you estimate what your benefit stream will look like, or you can call and talk to them. You also need to make a strategic decision on what age you and your spouse will file for these benefits. After reading a lot of articles, I learned that the most important strategy for anyone to maximize his or her lifetime benefits is for the highest earner to wait as long as possible before taking benefits. Ideally wait to your 70th birthday, IF you believe there is a good chance that you will live to at least age 80 and you can afford to wait.
3. *Then subtract your pension and Social Security income number (step #2) from your desired living expense number (step #1), and the difference is the annual gap amount that has to be funded from savings and investments.* Now all you have to do is decide how much of a nest egg you need to have invested to generate that annual gap number so you won't run out of money before you die. This is actually a bit tricky because of all the unknowns, so it is wise for everyone to seek assistance in this task from a professional. Ask potential advisors if they know how to do Monte Carlo Modeling, which projects your data through thousands of different potential future economic scenarios. If you are lucky maybe an inheritance will

help. This third step will take the longest to answer, but that's it. My explanation is finished.

I am loving retirement. I don't miss commuting, and I certainly never derived my sense of identity from my position. I am proud of some of the business contributions I was able to make in my career. I do miss some of the friends I knew along the way, although it appears many of them have scattered and moved on to other things.

Retirement is a time for possibilities. There are many ways to continue learning, enjoy social interactions, and contribute to society. The most immediate change for me was time-freedom. Time to read a book, time to spend with family, and more time for recreation and vacations. Time to write this book. And more time to focus on personal health. I could now take more time for sleep and carry less tension. At first I took some golf lessons and played a few rounds— but I didn't find the same enjoyment as I had when playing with my father. I now had time to enjoy music concerts more frequently. My generation never gets too old for rock and roll. I remember being in the third row at the Chinook Winds Casino to see Leann Rimes; what a great singer and such a beautiful woman. I have enjoyed quite a variety of artists— Michael McDonald, Paul McCartney, Fleetwood Mac, James Taylor, Jackson Brown, Tom Petty, Kenny Chesney, Dave Mason, the Steve Miller Band, the Neville Brothers, Taj Mahal, Keb Mo, Peter Frampton, Huey Lewis and the News, and Richie Furay. We saw a reunion of Sting and The Police. In a dirt field well outside of Portland, someone built a stage where Bonnie Raitt did her thing. Best of all is our favorite club band Cousin It, which features our son-in-law Dave Gonnella on bass guitar; I have them booked to play at my birthday party.

Instead of flying to California and having to rush right back home for work, we now had time to drive and enjoy the scenery. We developed a list of our favorite restaurants along I-5, some of which I already mentioned. I recommend breakfast at the Hot Rod Diner in Turlock, California. Their portions are so generous that I can rarely finish. I order the Big Daddy breakfast which has a sausage patty "as big as a catcher's mitt." I always take a picture of the plate when it arrives and email the picture to my Amigos. Yes, as big as a catcher's mitt!

I developed a "bucket list" of things I would like to do before I die, and I am already doing some of them. I feel no urgency to complete all of them— some may never be done. I also have more time to exercise and regularly visit my healthcare team. We love

Diane Wintzer, our acupuncturist, and we took Tai Chi lessons with her friend Andrew Schlabach. I have my favorite doctor, dentist, and dermatologists. We are blessed with a caring and capable support network.

I started doing a lot of the cooking at home and most importantly I am now paying more attention to signals from my body as to which foods I should not be eating. One of the gifts of retirement is that a lot of the business details that had been taking up space in my consciousness simply dissolved. This leaves me more space to observe my body and my world with increased clarity. I soon recognized a greater need for internal healing than I had expected.

# Chapter Fifty-Two

## DEALING WITH FOOD ALLERGIES

*"Be careful about reading health books.*
*You may die of a misprint."*
—Mark Twain, American Author and Humorist

When I was young I could eat anything. At the same time I seemingly enjoyed robust health. I consumed great quantities of milk, white bread, eggs, peanut butter, sugar, soy sauce, fruit juice and everything else under the sun while growing up. At different points along the way, that has all changed. Every year the consequences of ignoring my body's messages become more visible and more immediate. In my thirties I became aware of increasing reactions to gluten and dairy. I didn't stop eating these foods. I simply endured the consequences. Taking antihistamines usually helped. Then, at about age 50, I had a severe attack one evening at work after eating two slices of pizza on a really empty stomach. Antihistamines did not help. I experienced problems with breathing, a severe headache, and I couldn't sleep— it was agony. I would have to get more serious about food choices.

It didn't help when, a few years later, I returned to the dairy business. At least I was eating cultured yogurt, a more digestible form of dairy. But the reactions progressively got worse and more immediate over the next 10 years. I finally had to swear for myself, "No more dairy, no more gluten." That helped, but some of my symptoms continued; I suspected there were other problem food groups.

I perused books and articles on anti-inflammation diets. We found *The Virgin Diet,* by J. J. Virgin. Her approach seemed simple, and her points all resonated with my experiences. In her 21-day plan, all you have to do is temporarily eliminate 7 food groups from your diet. Not only did I lose 10 pounds quickly, but according to the notes in my journal, "I'm feeling lighter, sense of well-being, sleeping better, definitely breathing better, no itchy eyes, no wheezing, esophagus and trachea are not irritated." Kathryn eliminated her nagging skin eczema and joint pain. When she pays attention to her eating she can also get to sleep more easily, otherwise the sometimes unnoticed agitations to her nervous system make it hard to doze off. I continued on this diet another 35 days for the challenge period. By day 60 I was down 15 pounds, with only a modest amount of exercise, and I didn't even feel like I was dieting. Later I did the whole thing again and dropped another 12 pounds. I admit that some of that weight has come back, but I do continue to enjoy breathing more clearly.

Here are her seven food groups to avoid- dairy, gluten, soy, eggs, peanuts, corn, and sugar & artificial sweeteners. I had already given up dairy and gluten. In the challenge period I reconfirmed two suspicions- I did indeed need to give up peanuts and soy. Then came my big surprise- I was also sensitive to eggs, which I now mostly avoid but haven't completely eliminated. These changes in eating habits simply require diligence, particularly at restaurants where the inflammatory foods hide in all kinds of dishes, including sauces and gravy. Sometimes cooks soak fried chicken or fish in milk— a good reason to order "grilled." In one Mexican restaurant we discovered the hard way that they added sour cream into their guacamole. Fortunately there are many alternatives. Cooking at home I use almond beverage (for milk), gluten-free flours, and almond butter (for peanut butter). I just skip soy sauce, soy beans, and tofu. Skipping eggs was hard at first, but there are baking substitutes- I can use crushed banana, apple sauce, and flax seed meal in my waffles. Kathryn and I developed some great recipes in my personal recipe box, and we found a lot of tips on the internet.

This may sound like a lot of work, but what is more important along the way than maintaining personal health? Actually it is not even extra work after a little relearning and stocking up on the right foods. I do have to read a lot of labels. I feel like my body is continuing to heal, after so many years of ignoring the symptoms and allowing the inflammations to fester. I hope that sharing these thoughts and experiences may be an inspiration for you to take some next steps in caring for your health, now. Why do so many of us resist changes in our dietary habits? Basically we find comfort in foods, and food behaviors become anchored deeply in our psyches. Here are some tips— recruit everyone in your household to make changes together, clean the inflammatory foods out of the house, and make sure new tasty alternatives are readily available. Don't feel deprived.

Sadly, there is gluten in most beers— no more Coronas for me. But I did confirm that I have no problem with corn; so I can still enjoy corn chips, salsa fresca, and margaritas during Happy Hour.

# Chapter Fifty-Three

## WHY I LOVE CANCUN

*"A true friend freely, advises justly, assists readily, adventures boldly, takes all patiently, defends courageously, and continues a friend unchangeably."*
—William Penn, American Pioneer and Visionary Leader

I have met many warm-hearted people in Mexico, and I find their country to be a special place for friendships. We found our second home in Cancun in a roundabout way, maybe some would say by accident. I don't believe in accidents.

In August of 2003, on my first vacation from YoCream, Kathryn and I took a one-week trip to the Yucatan. I wanted to see the Mayan pyramids, which I studied with great interest in my Anthropology classes at UCLA, and we had read about the spectacular beaches in Cancun. Why not Cancun? We found a good deal on a beach-front condo at the Royal Mayan for one week. It was located in the Hotel Zone right on the edge of the Caribbean Sea, facing east toward the morning's rising sun. Yes, the sands were as white as advertised, and the sea water was even clearer and bluer than we could have imagined. We enjoyed the sunny beach and the warm waves, lots of excellent food, and a pool with a swim-up bar. Happy Hour started at 3 PM and continued for hours. Everyone was friendly and relaxed. We enjoyed excellent margaritas, cold beer (before I quit drinking beer), and endless corn chips with salsa fresca. The only drawback was the heat and the humidity, which became even more intense when I took my bus trip to Chichen Itza, in the interior of the Yucatan Peninsula. The Mayan ruins were spectacular. I climbed to the top of the main pyramid and looked out in all directions to jungle as far as the eye could see. Awesome! The whole time I was dripping wet.

Kathryn opted out of the jungle trip and chose instead some pampering in the air conditioned spa at a sister resort, the Royal Sands, just a short bus ride up Kukulcan Boulevard. Upon my return she told me the Royal Sands was incredible, and for breakfast the next morning we had a date with someone named Pancho, who would give us a tour. She was right, I loved it as soon as I walked in the front door and gazed out through huge windows to a very large pool, beautiful landscaping, and the Caribbean Sea. The facilities were well maintained. All of the units were two bedroom villas with full kitchens, plus a spacious living room fully furnished and a balcony with an amazing view straight out to the sea. We decided that we wanted to return in May when it would be cooler, after the crazy Spring Break weeks were over, but still in time for Cinco de Mayo. We bought the fractional rights to one villa that we would own in the first week of every May until 2050, probably beyond my lifetime.

When we returned in 2004, the beach and the sea were even more beautiful than we had remembered. And, the May weather was indeed more enjoyable. It was sunny, but the afternoon temperatures peaked at 90 degrees F with low humidity and a cool tropical breeze. Cinco de Mayo was great fun but we learned it was not a big holiday for Mexicans; mostly it was celebrated by those of us from El Norte. I de-stressed from my job right away and quickly decided we needed to stay for two weeks every year. Pancho was only too happy to help us buy the rights for a second week (to begin the following year). He became a good friend actually, and we looked forward to seeing him every year. We found him to be well educated, and he gave us a view into the thinking and perspectives of a Mexican citizen. We also formed friendships with the bartenders and endeavored to never miss a Happy Hour, unless it was for some swimming or sightseeing excursion. The Mexican economy was improving. We considered our money spent there as an investment in jobs for people who would much rather live near their families than move to the U.S. in search of employment. That year our son Brian also came with his girlfriend Nicole. In the middle of that week I met Syska and took her scuba diving course. In two and a half days I received my PADI certification and experienced my first two dives in the warm waters off Cancun. The wait until our next May visit would be agonizing, but I looked forward to enjoying TWO weeks in paradise.

In 2005 Brian and Nicole came again. In fact he also bought rights for the first week in May at the Royal Sands. We went swimming down the Yucatan coast in the calm bay of Akumal, where we shared the waters with sea turtles of different sizes. Nearby we visited the smaller Mayan ruins on the coast in Tulum. I went diving with Syska. Having the second week was definitely an excellent idea.

Our visit in 2006 followed the destruction of Hurricane Wilma. She was a Category 5 storm that hit in the previous October, extending damage along the entire Riviera Maya coast and then actually sitting on Cancun for almost two full days. Many people lost their homes, and many of the hotels were still closed while undergoing extensive repairs. We were happy to arrive to a fully restored Royal Sands, which had reopened after only 10 days. Our developers had done an outstanding design job in anticipation of such storms. I went diving in Akumal, where Syska was now living. This year we had traded our week and delayed our trip until June, so that more people could join us for the big event— Brian's wedding to Nicole Rangel on the beach at the Royal Sands. It was hot that afternoon. I was sweating in a blazing sun, standing on the beach while dressed in a tuxedo. The ceremony was colorful, with hundreds of extra guests in swimsuits applauding from the edge of the pool as the bride marched with her father down to the beach. For their wedding reception we strolled to the Hacienda Sisal restaurant, right in front of our resort. The Sisal management provided a special table for our honored wedding group on the edge of their dance floor. We all enjoyed the extensive and tasty buffet dinner and margaritas right along with other resort guests. The entertainment was fabulous; our host was unforgettable- "The Fabulous Johnny Ross." He sang popular songs in the style of Elvis and Tom Jones. He also bilingually introduced the other entertainers— a Mariachi band, Caribbean Dancers, and then a dance band resembling Gloria Estefan and the Miami Sound Machine. The newlyweds were honored with a spotlight dance, and we all swooned over a mouth watering Tres Leches wedding cake. It was the best party ever, and the easiest of no-planning-required weddings. The bridc had simply conveyed her wishes at a brief meeting a few days earlier.

In May of 2007, besides diving with Syska (this time in Cozumel), she brought her massage table to our villa. While we were away, Syska had taken massage training. She was really quite good. Brian and Nicole were with us again, and we enjoyed our usual lunch meeting with Pancho. This was also the first year for Terry's Tunes. I started to peruse Latino pop music through iTunes on my computer back home, and even though I didn't understand the Spanish lyrics I did love the rhythm and sound of Latin artists such as Marc Anthony, Maná, Reik, Draco, Shakira, Miguel Bose, Ricky Martin, and Julieta Venegas. They all reminded me of happy times in Cancun. So when I collected

20 songs I liked, I would burn them onto a CD and make at least 12 copies to take with me on my next trip. I named them each year— like "Terry's Tunes: Cancun 2007 Mayo"— and gave copies as tips to the bartenders, drivers, maids, and people I met at the swim-up bar.

By 2008 we knew more of the staff at the Sands; our favorite bartenders were Miguel Manzaneiro and Manuel Jiminez. Manuel developed a special "Terry's Margarita" using Hornitos tequila and adding orange juice; it became my favorite indulgence. Kathryn brought baby quilts for their children, we gave extra tips, and every year we continue to share pictures and stories of each other's families. One evening after the swim-up bars closed, we boarded a bus with Manuel to El Centro (downtown). He led us to a soccer park where the Royal Sands Bartenders soccer team was playing in a city league. Miguel was a forward and Gerardo was the goalie. Unfortunately they were crushed by a brutal opponent— it seemed the referees were pretty lax and the game got rough. The bartenders were thrilled that we had come, and Miguel drove us back to the Sands in his little car. We discovered the Thai Lounge restaurant that year; great Thai food and an awesome location right on the Lagoon. If we reserve in advance we can eat in one of their private huts right on the water, with a great view of the sun setting over the lagoon. The Thai Lounge has also become an annual tradition.

In 2009 Kathryn decided that one week in May was enough for her. She wanted to get home to enjoy prime blooming time with her flowers; also she wanted to visit her mother on Mother's Day. So I invited some guy friends to join me for the second week. "Amigos Week" was born. My UCLA buddy Larry Smith has made all of them. Bob Smith, a friend from Orlando, has made most of them. These weeks are so relaxed. We follow the same "boring" routine almost every day- sleep late, beach in the morning, play in the waves, read a book under the thatched roof of a little palapa, and walk on the beach. Then it's back to our room to cook breakfast, go to the gym, siesta, read, and prepare for Happy Hour at one of the swim-up bars. If we are hungry in the evening and have the energy we might go out to dinner. More likely we stay in the room watching a movie or NBA basketball play-offs on television. For an entire week we vacation from consulting or negotiating with any women.

By 2010 Amigos Week was already a resolute tradition, and a much needed time for unwinding from the tensions of our jobs back home. This was also the year of the Bird Flu epidemic. It would not deter the Amigos. My boss thought I was crazy for going to a foreign country at such a risky time. I found only a handful of people on the plane with me. We were tested for our temperatures upon arrival at the airport and anyone with a fever would be refused entry. Attendance at the resort was so sparse that the employees were moaning about their tips, and some of the larger bars and restaurants were ordered closed by the government. We loved the peace and quiet. There was not a single reported case of Bird Flu in all of the Yucatan states that month.

*"Three Amigos, in deep contemplation."*

I particularly love our swim-up bar, which adjoins the Char Hut mini-restaurant. They serve delicious food like fish tacos, shrimp ceviche, Hamburguesa Mexicana, loaded potato skins, nacho grande, and grilled grouper. The drinks are half price during Happy Hour, so Grandes are only $5 each. The freshly made chips and salsa fresca are always free. I began a tradition of collecting the straws from my previous Margaritas into each of the next ones. This way I could keep track of how many I had consumed by the end of Happy Hour (which really lasts at least 4 hours)— I just count the straws. The first year the Amigos had left it up to me to determine the schedule each day, and we had gone to Happy Hour every day without fail at 4 PM. This year the

Amigos were looking forward to our first Happy Hour when they heard a conch shell sounding loudly somewhere below our villa deck at exactly 3 PM. They asked and I told them that this marked the start of Happy Hour. Larry and Bob looked at each other and then at me and said, "You mean we missed one full hour of Happy Hour every day last year?" Apparently it was important to start on time, so for every succeeding day and every succeeding year during Amigos Weeks we have been promptly in the pool by 3 PM. I must say that the Chocolate Banana Monkeys are also an excellent drink and a particular favorite of Amigo Larry.

In January 2011, we decided to visit the Royal Sands during the winter season, in addition to our May trip. Kathryn loved the cooler weather in January; it is usually in the low 80's and sunny. Family came along- my sister Kelly and her husband Doug, Brian and Nicole, plus Jennifer and Dave, with granddaughter Lindy. Lindy absolutely loved the swimming pools; you could find her there for hours every day. My brother Randy also joined us. The following year his wife Judy began to attend. Others come some Januaries, but now it is an annual tradition and I go twice every year. What a life! We use our credit card and airlines points to get free tickets some years. In fact our family now meets there more frequently (and for less expense) than in Santa Cruz. Jennifer and her family like going for day trips to the small nearby island of Isla Mujeres; it is much quieter and slower paced. One year we all stayed there for three nights in addition to our time at the Royal Sands. We swooned over a great dinner at Lola Valentina's, one of many restaurants along the narrow pedestrian Hidalgo Street.

These are only a few of the stories about how Cancun and the Royal Sands became our second home. I have not gone scuba diving in recent trips, since my diving partner Syska moved back to her native Hungary. But diving was a major source of enjoyment for me for several years. Here is a poem I wrote after a day of diving with Syska in Cozumel, one of the most beautiful diving spots in the world. It is an island in the state of Quintana Roo, just off the Yucatan peninsula.

***THE MOMENT***

*"I love the sea in Quintana Roo*
*I love to dive beneath its waves*
*There the little fish swim so joyfully*
*The lobster hides so stoically*
*The corals wave so happily*

*I breathe so rhythmically*
*In and out, in and out repeatedly*
*Peace emerges and focus appears*
*The moment slows, time disappears*
*There is only the moment*

*I love the sea in Quintana Roo*
*I love to dive beneath its waves*
*There the little fish swim so joyfully*
*The lobster hides so stoically*
*The corals wave so happily"*

*—Terry Oftedal (June 2, 2006)*

# Chapter Fifty-Four

## EIGHTEEN UNFORGETTABLE MEALS

*"A book of verses underneath the bough,*
*a jug of wine, a loaf of bread, and thou*
*beside me singing in the Wilderness..."*
—Omar Khayyam: *The Rubaiyat*

While on the topic of food, please indulge me as I reach back over the years to share special memories of some exceptional meals that I have enjoyed. I know, I could have folded some of these stories into other chapters. Consider this a bonus tour of short stories. Remember my Psych class at UCLA, when I first read *Zorba the Greek*? The lead character, Zorba, was always in the moment— loving life intensely in each moment, particularly if food and wine were involved. Here are some moments that vividly stuck with me, because of the exceptional or unusual food, the special friends I was with, or the unique ambience.

18. MOMMA'S FISH HOUSE (in Kahului on Maui's north shore): It sits right on the beach with a large thatched roof overhead and open sides. Their menu not only describes how each item is cooked, but it adds details on what time the fish was caught that morning plus the name of the boat and the captain's name. Fresh! We could feel the cool tropical onshore breezes. Jennifer and Dave were with us. Dave does not usually like fish, but he still raves about Momma's. The mahi-mahi encrusted with hazelnuts and the Ono were unforgettable. http://mamasfishhouse.com/

17. THE PANCAKE BAKERY (Amsterdam, Netherlands): It is just a few blocks from our favorite Amsterdam hotel, The Estherea, in the old section of Amsterdam on the Prinsengracht Canal. It operates in a 17th century warehouse formerly owned by the Dutch East India Company. Dutch pancakes, YUM! Theirs are the best— since 1973.

You get one large pancake, cooked the old fashioned way in an iron frying pan over a gas flame, with your choice of either sweet or savory mix-ins. On every table you'll find a pot of molasses. We like to sit upstairs. They are open until 9:30 PM so sometimes we have gone back twice in one day (once for sweet and then for savory). You must go to this web link and view the video clip. Then click on the icon for their menu to be totally amazed. Now they have a gluten-free flour option. Did I already say, "YUM?"
http://www.pancake.nl/en/

16. THE FISH MARKET (Bergen, Norway): It's not a restaurant. It's an open air market at the foot of the beautiful Bergen Fjord, situated right on the dock next to our favorite hotel, The Admiral. The scenic old Hanseatic League Warehouses sit directly across the harbor. Pretty little houses planted up the sides of the fjord are all brightly decorated with window boxes of fresh colorful flowers. I was in heaven sitting on the dock while eating delicious hot-smoked herring with some rye crackers. All the while I was thinking about my Norwegian family and how my great-grandfather had braved the journey across the Atlantic to America at the age of 15, setting out from this very spot. My first visit here was our unforgettable 1996 trip with my parents. We returned in 1998. Memories of a lifetime.
http://www.visitbergen.com/en/Product/?TLp=179000

15. GALLAGHER'S STEAK HOUSE (inside the New York, New York Hotel in Las Vegas): I recommend the thick aged rib-eye steaks or prime rib, which must be enjoyed with Atomic brand horseradish. Our waiter is always Sam. Their beef dinners compare to the best anywhere. I don't have the same yearning for Las Vegas that I once had, but I could enjoy another dinner at Gallagher's. I do recall enjoying some talented entertainers over the years in Vegas, including Celine Dion, Cirque du Soleil (many times), Donnie and Marie (who put on an amazing show), and even Juice Newton. I never saw Elvis, who passed in 1977, but once outside the NY-NY we met a very short Thai Elvis impersonator, who for a few dollars was happy to pose for a picture with us.
http://www.nynyhotelcasino.com/restaurants/gallaghers-steakhouse.aspx

14. PHIL LEHR'S GREENHOUSE (Sutter St., San Francisco): Famous as a steakhouse, they also produced "San Francisco's most popular Sunday Brunch." On a date with my parents in The City, my father suggested we go there one Sunday morning. I was so glad that we did. We walked together from our hotel, the St. Francis, and then took a trolley car. Talk about a greenhouse— every table was surrounded by plants. On that same trip we saw Tony Bennett perform one evening at the Fairmont Hotel, which was a huge event-of-a-lifetime for my father. Tony was still in fine voice and he clearly loved to entertain. Father could hardly stand waiting until his favorite song, "I Left My Heart in San Francisco." Unfortunately, according to the internet, Lehr's is now closed.

13. KYUBEY SUSHI BAR AT THE NEW OTANI HOTEL (Tokyo): It was my first business trip to Japan. We landed at Narita, took a cab into Tokyo (faster than the less expensive local train), and checked in to one of the most elegant hotels in the world. I literally gaped at their incredible outside gardens visible through the immense lobby windows— their gardens are a very popular and pricey site for many formal Japanese weddings; I caught glimpses of several over the years. My first trans-Pacific flight across several time zones had been quite tiring, but my new boss at Hitachi Magnetics, Joe Betts, suggested we try some sushi and a beer right away. It was not cheap, but our expenses were covered (he was a V.P.). We sat at the counter in front of a master sushi chef who had been working there for decades. I was advised to not add soy sauce; instead trust his mastery and eat each piece exactly as it was presented. I experienced a variety of raw dishes, along with a few Japanese beers. Incredible! On my twenty-four subsequent trips to Japan I made many visits to sushi bars all over the islands of Honshu and Shikoku. Many of them were memorable, but this one was the first. http://www.newotani.co.jp/en/tokyo/restaurant/kyubei_tower/index.html

12. SOME LOCAL RESTAURANT IN TOTTORI, JAPAN: I was visiting Nippon Ferrite, a subsidiary of Hitachi Metals, on a later trip to Japan. They were located on the other side of Honshu Island, facing the Sea of Japan. I was selling Nippon Ferrite products in the Western U.S., in addition to the ceramic products from Hitachi Metals. Matthew Kogano, who was stationed in Michigan as NF's U.S. Sales Manager, was

with me. We were guests of the factory General Manager, who met us at a simple old building perched right on the edge of the Sea. Inside, the restaurant was very clean and very traditional in style. We sat on the floor in a private room upstairs. Whenever we were ready for another round of food or drinks, our host would pick up a phone at his side, talk directly to the kitchen, and it would soon appear. Local fish from the chilly waters of the Sea of Japan are particularly tasty, and being so fresh, their texture was firm yet quite delicate. The cooking was exquisite, and presentation was made with utmost care by ladies in traditional clothing. The local sakes were memorable. None of us wanted that party to end.

11. A SMALL RESTAURANT ON SHIKOKU ISLAND, JAPAN: MKE, short for Matsushita Kotobuki Electronics (now called Panasonic Shikoku Electronics), assembled hard disk drives for Quantum. Their main factories were on the far western side of Shikoku, the fourth largest island in Japan, in a small town called Uwajima. Getting there was always quite a trip— after a long flight from SFO into Osaka's Kansai Airport, I took a smaller plane to Shikoku Island, then a taxi, a train to the end of the line, then another taxi. The few ryokan's (small town hotels) had very small rooms, short beds, and always smelled of tobacco smoke. However, their communal Japanese-style hot tub and steam showers were superb for relaxing before bedtime. After a day of meetings at MKE we were hosted that evening by Alps Electric, a major Japanese electronics company which was supplying us recording heads. We went by taxi to a nearby small fishing village, right on the edge of the water. About 14 of us sat on the floor around a large table in a quaint local restaurant which had been reserved exclusively for us. First came many toasts with Japanese beer and incredible arrays of fresh sushi and sashimi, followed by lots of sake and more local specialty dishes. After I was completely stuffed, the main course arrived. It was the largest fish I had ever seen— caught early that morning in nearby waters, it had been slowly baking with hot coals in the ground all day. I couldn't refuse. I wished that I had saved more room; it was so incredibly tasty. We barely made a dent in that huge fish, but the staff and many neighbors later finished it for us.

10. KITA NO MARU LODGE at the KATSURAGI GOLF CLUB (Shizuoka, Japan): Golfing is very expensive in Japan and those who play are passionate about it. For very special guests, Yamaha Corporation hosts golfing, drinking, and private dinners at their exquisite Katsuragi Golf Club. One evening after meetings at their Thin Film Heads factory in Hamamatsu City, Yamaha executives drove us to the Kita No Maru Lodge. Upon arrival we removed our shoes and received traditional jackets to wear. It was an old and beautiful building, built and meticulously finished with gorgeous hard woods in a 14th century architectural style. It had been maintained over many years with boundless care and attention. Its intent was to impress, and it did. Admiring the fine woodworking details, I could have forgotten which century I was in. Gazing out the windows I saw camellias, cherry and cucumber trees, crape myrtle, evergreen magnolias, sasanqua, chrysanthemums, and much more. I had never seen landscaping so lush. Their carefully manicured course rivals our Augusta National (site of the Master's PGA Tournament). Dinner was served traditional style, with us seated on the floor of a private room. The food was elegant and absolutely delicious. http://www.katsuragi-kitanomaru.net

9. YOSHIIKE RYOKAN (Hakone, Japan): On the slopes of Mt. Fuji lies a serene Lake Ashi, and on its shores sits a beautiful and peaceful village named Hakone (Ha-ko-nee), which retains much of its old-time ambience. When Kathryn accompanied me to Japan in 1987, we were invited to stay at the family-owned ryokan managed by my friend Soji Suzuki. Suzuki-san was also Head Coach for Crew at the prestigious Keiyo University and for the National Crew of Japan. After a picturesque train ride from Tokyo, where we had been staying at the ultra-modern Akasaka Prince Hotel, we arrived at the end of the line for the Dreamliner. We were met by a little and old lady from our hotel who recognized us somehow. She insisted on carrying both of our large pieces of luggage (which had no wheels in those days) as we walked the narrow cobblestone streets to Yoshiike. She was the perfect hostess. We later saw her in the bar providing company for some male guests. She was listening intently, nodding her head, filling their glasses, and regularly raising her glass of beer to her mouth, though we noticed that she never actually sipped and her glass always remained full. After registering, we were led

to an impressive multi-room traditional-style suite. Our Oftedal name had been calligraphy written in Kanji on a beautiful sheet of rice paper which was hanging on our door. From one of the rooms, bamboo doors opened onto a sprawling and lush garden. A small stream flowed lazily past our doorway; it supposedly contained "1,000 carp." We slept on the tatami floors in traditional futons, which ladies came each evening to prepare for us. Yoshiike had traditional public hot bathing pools in the common area, and we had a private modern hot tub in our bathroom. It was so very peaceful. Up the street was a famous training school for geishas, and one day we had pictures taken of us with two of their young ladies, who just happened to be strolling nearby. They were so shy, and so very lovely in their full makeup with ornate combs in their hair. We took some day trips around the countryside. During one outing we wandered into a shop which sold hand-carved and hand-painted wooden kokeshi dolls. Kathryn bought one, and I continued the tradition by bringing her a kokeshi from a different city on each of my later trips to Japan. One evening at Yoshiike we were honored with a private Japanese-style dinner served as we sat on the floor in our suite. Suzuki-san and Kohtaro Okazaki-san, who was the head of the Japanese Rowing Association, were our hosts. We shared stories of the visit I had helped to arrange when the Keio Varsity Crew flew to Los Angeles the previous year to race against UCLA and Oxford in our UCLA Crew Classic. I announced that race from the top of our boathouse, joined by Mayor Tom Bradley and actor Dudley Moore, an Oxford grad. This event brought great honor to Keio, and I had been declared an Honorary Keio Old Boy (Alumnus). The high point of that dinner at Yoshiike was a live fish sashimi sliced in such a way that it looked like a ship with a large main sail. Okazaki-san presented Kathryn a gift— an exquisite silver broach set with pearls. The next day we were honored with an invitation to meet Suzuki-san's family at his home in Odawara, a historic city situated at the edge of the Pacific Ocean.
http://www.japanican.com/en/hotel/detail/4306015/

8. MRS. TAKEMOTO'S HOME (the Shibuya district of Tokyo): When I worked for Hitachi Metals, I was privileged to develop a warm relationship with Mr. Shotaro Takemoto. When we first met he was General Manager of their Ferrite Recording Heads factory located in the town of Mooka in Tochigi

Prefecture. Kathryn was with me in 1987; we took the train to Mooka, and Kathryn was invited to suit up in clean room garb for a rare "outsiders" tour. We next were driven to nearby Mashiko to see a very old style ceramics factory. Our Japanese friends went out of their way numerous times to honor us. Usually the after-work gatherings in Japan are hosted in restaurants and hotels. It is rare to be invited to a Japanese home because they are usually so small, due to the extremely high cost of land. Also, with the old custom of arranged marriages, family relationships and the home atmosphere are not always so warm. However, Mr. Takemoto had married his wife for love, and he proudly invited us to meet her for dinner one night at their home in Tokyo. We travelled from our hotel by subway to the Shibuya Station, used by over 370,000 people per day, where we were met by Arnie Namba and Mr. Suzuki. They also interfaced with me at Hitachi Metals and both were Keio University Old Boys, as was Mr. Takemoto. They led us through some winding narrow roads lined on both sides by ancient homes, small shops, and local restaurants. We think this was the first time Mrs. Takemoto had ever received American business guests in her home. She was so excited. She had heard that this was the evening of Kathryn's 40th birthday, so instead of serving a Japanese style meal, she had taken great care to shop for western style food with which we might be more accustomed. With great respect we were served peanut butter and jelly sandwiches on white bread with potato chips. She also bought a small birthday cake with one candle that played an electronic Happy Birthday tune. We were deeply honored and touched. We enjoyed conversation, about each of our families mostly. Mr. Takemoto patiently translated for us with her. Of course she wanted to hear about our travels in Japan. After a lovely evening we departed for the Shibuya train station. Retracing our way along the narrow streets on our own, we turned several times to see Mrs. Takemoto still following us from a distance and bowing deeply to show us her respect each time we turned. She wanted to make sure we made it safely to the station, and I am sure she did not want that special evening to end. In following years I often exchanged letters and faxes with Mr. Takemoto, with each of us always concluding the note by sending love and affectionate greetings along for our wives.

*"Terry and Mr. Takemoto, outside the Hitachi Metals Factory in Tochigi Prefecture."*

7. THE PEKING GARDEN RESTAURANT (Hong Kong): Following Kathryn's visit in Japan, I had enough frequent flyer miles to add on a few days for us in Hong Kong. We arrived during a hot July— 90 degrees plus 90 percent humidity. Walking the streets, everyone's clothing was dripping wet, including ours. We loved every minute of exploring exotic Hong Kong together, and we bought some beautiful dresses for Kathryn. Niki Kopenhaver, the Purchasing Manager at Sunward, had advised me to make a reservation at the Peking Garden at least 24 hours in advance and to order Beggar's Chicken for both of us. One evening near the Star Ferry Terminal, we found the Peking Garden; we were immediately relieved that their air conditioning system was working. We had pre-

ordered, so our food came quickly. The waiter rolled a cart to our table and handed me a mallet; I used it to break open a football-sized baked clay ball which had hardened in an underground oven overnight. We had the attention of everyone seated around us. Inside the clay was the most savory whole chicken stuffed with rice and aromatic herbs. It had been slow cooking for 24 hours. The waiter sliced the chicken and served us. Unforgettably delicious and so falling-apart tender. Nana Shackelford (famous for zealously cooking chicken well-done) would have loved it. If you Google the words "beggar's chicken hong kong" you will find You Tube clips of what that entertaining experience was like. Here is one of those clips:
https://www.youtube.com/watch?v=hIo9wW2EhQ0

6. THE SEAFOOD MARKET RESTAURANT (Bangkok, Thailand): A truly unique experience. On one side is a seafood market with a very large assortment of fresh seafoods. Their motto painted on the wall reads, "If it swims, we have it." When I entered, a young lady employee appeared and insisted on pushing my cart. If I pointed, it ended up in my cart- lobster, crab, oysters, giant prawns, eels, and fish of many varieties. Some patrons paid and took their selections home, but my cart was wheeled to the other side of the large building, to a restaurant with a big open kitchen containing many cooks. Fortunately our host Dale Shadel, who had married a local woman, was now fluent in the Thai language. He spoke at length with our waiter, choosing a variety of styles and spices (and degrees of heat) for cooking all of our purchases. Vegetables, rice, and noodles were also included in different ways. For dessert we would have a variety of sliced fresh tropical fruits with hot sticky rice. Of course we started with beer. Singha was the most popular Thai beer, but we usually drank Carlsberg. It was also brewed in Bangkok at a Danish-owned brewery. We were told that if we overindulged, Carlsberg would leave us with a much lighter headache the next morning. I also preferred its flavor. I carefully ate lightly from the dishes that were extra spicy. The food was divine, the show of it all was unforgettable. Though I tried to pace myself, I soon became stuffed and could only sample the final courses. Afterward, when we went outside onto Sukhumvit Road, we saw an elephant in the parking lot. It was not unusual to see elephants walking on the streets of Bangkok. We purchased bundles of sugar cane and bananas from the

owner to feed the elephant, who eagerly snatched the bundles from our hands using his trunk. The bundles quickly disappeared into his mouth. I actually got to ride an elephant in Chiang Mai in Northern Thailand on a different trip. http://www.seafood.co.th

5. THE WATERFRONT RESTAURANT (Seattle, Washington): My friend Larry Smith decided to throw a big party for his own 60th Birthday. He booked a private room in a nice restaurant right on Elliott Bay at the tip of Pier 70, just a couple of blocks downhill from his home. He invited a variety of friends from different periods in his life. We had fascinating conversations with a number of them. Craig Bleeker was there, so we decided that we needed to order a round of Westcott Bay Oysters that were supplied to this restaurant from Craig's Westcott Bay Sea Farm. They were quite delicious. We enjoyed excellent wine and great food. The best part was that Larry picked up the tab for everything. Thank you, Amigo. The restaurant has since changed it name to Aqua, and it is still operating. We returned there for a dinner with Larry and Sandra on another later birthday. This time I picked up the tab, with pleasure. http://www.elgaucho.com/aqua-by-el-gaucho.html

4. ANTHONY'S PIER 66 RESTAURANT (Seattle, Washington): Seattle is Kathryn's home town and when we travel there we look forward to a nice seafood dinner with views of Elliott Bay. We have eaten at Anthony's many times. One particularly memorable visit included my sister Kelley and her son Andrew in August, 2013— we enjoyed a road trip with them to Vancouver and Victoria, and now we were on our way back south. They loved the food, the view, and the conversation as much as we did. The crab was tender, juicy, and delicious. We enjoyed some very nice white wine while we were at it. Kathryn and I have also dined there with Larry and Sandra Smith, who live nearby. http://www.anthonys.com/restaurants/detail/anthonys-pier-66

3. TIDAL RAVES SEAFOOD GRILL (Depoe Bay, Oregon): Kathryn's favorite restaurant in the world. When we drive to Depoe Bay every February to celebrate our wedding anniversary, we stay at the Worldmark condos. The Tidal Raves is a short walk up the street. This is a premier

restaurant surprisingly located in a small beach town. We love the gorgeous view, through their large windows, of this rough section of the Oregon coast with powerful Pacific Ocean waves crashing against the cliffs. We always have a hard time choosing from the standard menu and the specials written on the chalkboard, because everything is so good. They have a wonderful selection of wines— last time we enjoyed a bottle of Domaine Carneros, our favorite California sparkling brut, while simply relaxing and enjoying each other's company. Always an adventure, never disappointing, we go for lunch and/or dinner. Kathryn says she could eat there every day and never get tired of it. http://tidalraves.com

2. THE ROYAL SANDS' SWIM-UP BAR (Cancun, Mexico): My favorite spot in the world for a simple meal while chatting with friends and bartenders in the shade— the whole time sipping a margarita grande (made with Hornitos tequila of course). I love reminding everyone that "Life is too short to drink small margaritas." The cool waters of the pool and the gentle tropical breezes coming off the Caribbean are so relaxing. The rhythmic sounds of nearby waves provide a sweet serenade in the background. I love to order a simple meal of fresh-caught grouper fillet, grilled with garlic and lime, served with Mexican rice plus a salad with oil and vinegar and sliced avocado. I can eat the same thing day after day; but I always have their Ceviche Mixto at least once each trip. A long as I am able to travel, I want to go there and enjoy this simple meal over and over again. I am blessed.

1. MY GRANDMOTHER'S HOME ON BACKER AVENUE (Fresno): Fried chicken, mashed potatoes and gravy, green beans with bacon, fresh baked biscuits with homemade strawberry jam, and some of Grandpa's home cured green olives. Old fashioned apple dumplings or peach cobbler for dessert. I would love to repeat any birthday dinner prepared by my Nana with all my family crowded around the table in her cozy little kitchen. I can still hear her pressure cooker whistle as the potatoes were cooking. Sounds of Grandpa Leroy and Uncle Dale, watching sports on the television, float in from the next room. When I was older she always invited me to say the blessing before dinner— I loved that. I would give up all the others for one more of those precious family meals.

# Chapter Fifty-Five

## MY BEST FRIEND, FOREVER AND FOR ALWAYS

*"Bare Trees in Winter,*
*Dancing with the gentle wind,*
*Beckon us to join."*
—A Haiku by Terry & Kathryn Oftedal (December, 2012)

Retirement has also given me the gift of more time with my wife, my best friend. Some people know her as a grandmother who is crazy about quilting. She appears to be a quiet homebody. But I know she is magic. Deeper down inside lies the core of her passion for life. She has a remarkable healing touch and a natural gift for CranioSacral Therapy. Even deeper lies her love of Attunement and the opportunities to let heaven's life energy pass through her to bless others. Sometimes in her CST process, she lightly places one of her fingers into each of my ears. I asked her why she was doing that and she said, "I'm listening with my fingers; they will tell me what to do next."

More than ever I enjoy doing things for her, to show my love. I even learned how to make morning coffee for her. I rarely drink it myself and for many years had never learned how to work those simple little machines. Our evolving relationship and experience of marriage has been like a dance. In earlier days there were many times of stress. There were more things that would tend to make one or both of us frustrated or even angry. Sometimes we had difficulties finding the words to talk with each other. There is nothing worse than living under the same roof, walking right past each other, and not being able to talk, particularly if we were not able to clear it by bedtime.

What are some of the things that have helped? I had to become a lot more willing to accept differences, and even better, get to the place where I truly appreciate the differences. Learning to look at the world through the eyes of the opposite sex allows one to see, touch, and feel more of the world than we can on our own. This means we have to learn the other person's language.

We talked about this in a previous chapter. Part of this simply comes with age and experience. Taking some classes or workshops together can also be beneficial. Yes, we can learn from the wisdom of others and don't have to go through the pain of learning everything the hard way by ourselves.

When the time was approaching for my retirement, a lot of Kathryn's friends asked her quite seriously whether she would be able to maintain her sanity with a husband at home full time. If anything, having more time together has been a wonderful experience for both of us. I think it is the result of all the personal work we accomplished together. It's also helpful that our children have grown up and are successfully pursuing their own dreams. We are blessed with more space and stillness in our home. We do like to invite in the hurricane— that unbridled energy and youthful spirit of a grandchild. Of course the best part of being a grandparent, we now know, is that we get to love that youthful interaction and also get to return to the stillness between visits.

When we received money from the sale of our YoCream stock, Kathryn was able to fulfill one of her longtime dreams and establish the Kathryn Oftedal Charity Fund. Technically it is a donor advised charity fund, which resides in the care of Fidelity Investments. Such funds can be opened with relatively modest amounts of money, and they are a much simpler entity than a foundation. Still they provide a means for giving with associated tax advantages. Kathryn only donates the investment earnings, and she is committed to keeping the principal amount intact so our children can enjoy directing the fund after her. She researches potential donees extensively and will only recommend donations to causes with minimal overhead expenses, and they must be registered U.S. 501(c)(3) charities. If any non-profit has highly-paid management or pays for outside fundraising, she skips them. Her favorite charities have almost zero administrative overhead, so the donations flow through intact to those in need. Check out this one- http://www.missionoflove.org

I am now much more conscious of Kathryn's special gifts and her sense of life purpose. *The Quiltmaker's Gift* is the name of a wonderful little book. It also describes my best friend. She absolutely loves making quilts and she loves to give them away. This is her favorite hobby, and I am wise to give her all the space she desires to pursue her passion. In turn she generously invites me to join in with the design of some of her projects. Kathryn plays many roles as a daughter, sister, mother, grandmother, and wife. She said that I could reveal one thing about her— she still HATES to lose at playing cards. She is an angel at heart, and she maintains her own sense of purpose. I thank God for bringing us together and I enjoy frequently telling her, "I love you."

# Chapter Fifty-Six

## STILL CHOPPING WOOD AND CARRYING WATER

*"May God bless and keep you always*
*May your wishes all come true*
*May you always do for others*
*And let others do for you*
*May you build a ladder to the stars*
*And climb on every rung*
*May you stay forever young."*
—Bob Dylan, "Forever Young"

Forever young inside, yes. Outside is another story. My hairline is receding— it is now cut short and balding in the back. The vibrant red color of my hair is gone. I can no longer run fast or far, and my balance is not as good. Working in the yard, I get tired sooner. My skin and teeth need repair work more frequently. It seems like we are visiting doctors a lot more often. My mother used to tell me that getting old was hard work. She was right. But inside I still feel like the same young man that experienced all of the adventures I have been writing about, and I still enjoy celebrating every birthday. In fact I even celebrate my half-birthdays, which happen on Cinco de Mayo day in Cancun.

In the Beatle's movie "Yellow Submarine," George Harrison said, "It's all in your mind you know." Yes, feeling old or feeling youthful is all in our minds. Every day we choose to feel young or feel old. Here is my tip— choose to feel young. Continue to read and explore. Exercise the mind and the body. Cook a meal to share with others. Wash the dishes, regardless of whether you made them dirty or someone else did. Do something for others in your world every day. Bless the Earth by your presence, and give Thanks in all things. It is pretty simple really.

I continue to learn and grow. The spiritual quest never ends. After so many adventures it all comes back around to life's basic functions- "chopping wood and carrying water." I do love how it is put so simply in the book *All I Really Need To Know I Learned in Kindergarten* by Robert Fulghum. Share everything, play fair, don't hit people, put things back where you found them, clean up your own mess, say you are sorry when you hurt somebody, etc.

It may be that I am now in the third act of my life. Perhaps the first act went from physical birth through the years of education and into those years of exploration that led to the appearance of Sunseed. The second act would have included raising my family and touching the world primarily through my business career. The third act is this one— the so-called retirement years— and perhaps it is the one with the greatest possibilities. Every day, I have the opportunity to fill my world with spirit. This book can be a part of all that; hopefully it will come across as a simple and honest sharing of who I am and what I have come to learn. Perhaps it will be an inspiration to your greatness. I hope so.

After years of consideration, I think the personal life philosophy I have developed can be boiled down to these three reminders. I do like my lists to be short. Otherwise it is hard to remember.

1. Be Thankful.
2. Be Kind.
3. Be Responsible.

BE THANKFUL. I can still hear my old friend George Shears saying in his deep and slow voice, "Give thanks in all things." He did not say we should be thankful FOR all things that happen. He was saying we should always be thankful. In this lies a powerful remedy for the ailment of "wanting things to be different than they are." Yes, it would be great to see an end to all injustice and suffering. However, trying to right all of the wrongs in the world is an endless task. Even trying to get everyone to agree on how things "should be" is an impossible task. In fact, such arguments between the churches and the governments of the world have been contributory if not primary causes for most of the wars that have been fought. Sometimes not-doing is the best course of action. It all comes back to attitude— be thankful. Be willing to frequently give thanks to God in your own way. In this is the fulfilling of the first great commandment.

BE KIND. Appreciate others. Practice the spirits of generosity and compassion. Kathryn frequently reminds me, "You can afford to be generous." Regardless of the size of the tip or the gift, of greatest importance is the quality of spirit moving through your heart when you take the action, when you give the tip. My old friend Bob Hollis taught me that before I ever write a check, I should first pause and make sure I have a smile on my face. Yes, even when writing the tax check to the IRS. Try it some time. The act of smiling can be a powerful mechanism. I found it to be a simple exercise that works, and it is a practical application of the spiritual expression approach to living. I enjoy recalling the philosophy that guided my Great-Grandpa Martin Oftedal and his Odd Fellow Lodge friends — "To improve and elevate the character of mankind by promoting the principles of friendship, love, truth, faith, hope, charity and universal justice." In this is the fulfilling of the second great commandment.

BE RESPONSIBLE. Take care of whatever we have been given, whether we think it is a little or a lot. Spend less than has been earned, and take joy in the act of saving. Act wisely, avoid waste and pollution. We were designed to care for and tend all of God's creation. ALL of God's creation? That may sound like a big job, but there are a lot of us to share in doing it together. The opportunities to do it are always right in front of us in every moment. Pay attention and take simple actions. Lead by example. And in this is the key to how the world is truly changed, ... but first it must change in me.

# Chapter Fifty-Seven

## DEVELOPING A PERSONAL SENSE OF PURPOSE

*"You must be the change you wish to see in the world."*
—Mahatma Gandhi, The Father of India

How can one person change the world? In my lifetime there have been some powerful examples. I mentioned Gandhi, Mandela, and Dr. King. Let's add the Dalai Lama to that list. World changes resulting from his leadership may not be as visible as they have been with the others, but that's the way it is for most of us who are living with a personal sense of purpose. Can you see yourself in that group? We all should. Go ahead; pause for a moment and give it a try— say your name along with theirs. We can all make a difference, most often in the seemingly ordinary moments of our lives.

Another person who made a difference was Jesus. I am fascinated by how he conveyed his lessons to others. Clearly the world would be different if more people, including his followers, had really listened to him rather than fixating on debates about their beliefs. One of my favorite stories is told in Chapter 5 of the Book of John, about the man who was waiting beside the waters to be healed. He had been waiting a long time. Finally someone got through to him, but first came the all important question— "Wilt thou be made whole?" Whatever my issue— psychological, emotional, or physical— I have to be willing to let go of it or else change (call it healing if you like) can never happen. Some even claim that all illnesses are psychosomatic, that all physical ailments are a manifestation of constrictions further upstream. Fixating on the constrictions is part of the problem. In this case the man's attention was successfully redirected in the moment, and Jesus was quite compelling. His words were beautifully simple and they were no doubt spoken with power— "Rise, take up thy bed, and walk." I suspect that much more was moving between them than just the words.

I previously mentioned Diane Wintzer, my acupuncturist. I

see her making a difference as well. We have been meeting for treatments in her Camas office twice a month. On my first visit I asked her how she finds the exact spot to place her needles. She said that she learned about all the meridian lines and acupoints in the body during her training, but now her process is more intuitive— her hands seem to guide themselves. I asked how her process affects change in the body, and she talked about each organ having an energetic function as well as a physical function. She was singing my song; I knew I was in the right place. Another thing I appreciate about Diane, besides her beautiful spirit, is that she always starts with listening— she listens intently with her whole being. Jesus used the same technique whenever he first asked, "Wilt thou be made whole?" The answer requires more than words. Some people like to complain about their problems and actually resist change. I like to remind myself of my responsibilities as a partner in the process. I do tell Diane my latest stories, but my issue of the moment is never my primary concern. I focus on cultivating my readiness for change. Healing happens in an instant— as the spirit of Life is released, through any modality, the opportunity to "rise up" (to change) can open even to the physical level. Be ready. Lindy, our granddaughter, was with me one time and I invited her into the room to see me lying down with needles sticking out of different parts of my head and body. I assured her the needles didn't hurt. She asked some good questions; more importantly I wanted her to feel the currents of healing, whether or not she could yet comprehend the process of returning to wholeness.

Andrew Schlabach, Diane's partner, is the founder of the Acupuncture Relief Project. You can read amazing stories about ARP's ongoing efforts to provide health care for people in rural Nepal at the website http://acupuncturereliefproject.org or https://www.facebook.com/AcupunctureReliefProject. They are now in the process of establishing a permanent clinic in the mountains south of Katmandu. Many of the Nepalese people had never seen a health practitioner of any kind before the volunteers of this project arrived. I told Andrew that one of the trips on my bucket list was a trek to the base camp on Mount Everest. Instead I decided to donate that money to ARP, to help them build a clinic. For me this is an example of think globally, act locally.

"Think globally, act locally" is a popular expression that gives a powerful clue as to how each of us can make an impact in the world. Small actions taken by individuals or groups can have impact reaching further and continuing longer in time than any of us can see. Usually we never even try to envision how far our actions, our thoughts, or our expressions of spirit can reach. Every human being is connected to every other being and to the whole planet in more powerful ways than we understand.

Sometimes we never see the results. We say words, we create thoughts, and we express different spirits with every breath we take. There is always an impact. We change the world all of the time, hopefully even for the better. Some people recognize this and want to understand the dynamics of change. I applaud those who do. The quality of spirit being expressed is where the real power lies.

Some suggestions— things that have enabled me to see larger possibilities:

1. Watch the movie "Pay It Forward". He never got to see the powerful results, but at the end of the movie we do.

2. Read the story of the 100th Monkey: http://en.wikipedia.org/wiki/Hundredth_monkey_effect

3. Read "Bill and Melinda Gates' Annual Letter." It is always an amazingly clear statement on how to better understand the potential for combining innovation and cooperation in addressing some of the world's most visible imbalances. http://www.gatesfoundation.org

4. Watch my favorite music video- "World On Fire" by Sarah McLachlan. Find out why she spent only $15 to produce this video. Watch it again and again, ... and feel how far her spirit is extending. https://www.youtube.com/watch?v=FDmPcSWE0WU Join in by buying a copy.

5. Practice recognizing the spirits or essences that can be revealed through each of us in our living. This requires working with the invisible. Be still for a time and contemplate these spirits one at a time: Love, Truth, Life, Purification, Blessing, Focused Intention, and Creation. Do something or say something, and then think internally about which spirit was revealed in that word or deed. How fully was that spirit revealed? It takes practice to learn about the invisible. Practice, practice, practice.

# Chapter Fifty-Eight

## WORKING WITH THE INVISIBLE

*"And when he was entered into a ship,*
*his disciples followed him.*
*And, behold, there arose a great*
*tempest in the sea, insomuch that the ship*
*was covered with the waves; but he was asleep.*
*And his disciples came to him... Then he arose, and rebuked*
*the wind and the sea; and there was a great calm."*
—Matthew 8:23-26

A great calm extended into the energetic fields of everyone on that ship. This little vignette carries a powerful lesson. Have you ever been in a situation where you were conscious enough to perceive turbulence like "great winds and stormy seas" in the troubled energies of yourself or others around you? Have you ever been the one who caused a great calm simply through your presence or words? Maybe you have had this experience by reason of someone else's calming presence. Calming the mind and our energetic fields is a first step in consciously reconnecting with the Divine. It can allow deep healing and lead to a greater clarity of purpose. This can happen every day until it becomes a way of life— but it requires intention.

We have considered the marvelous field of substance that surrounds each physical body— our bio-energetic field. It is invisible (at least it is to me) but everyone can feel it, like we can feel the wind. Within this field are focus points, and through the practice of Attunement I learned how these points connect into the earth of each human body. This process assists in opening a portal for the order and harmony of the Divine to flow into the minds, bodies, and hearts of each of us. I have learned that this happens to the degree I turn in response to the source of the Divine, which is always present. This part may be a little difficult for the mind to grasp. To me, the "turning" is like relaxing into a yoga pose. At first I focus on tensions emphasized by the pose, and I focus on my breathing. Then as if by magic, muscles in that part of the body simply relax. I perceive a similar process of relaxing in the energetic body during the Attunement process. This should not be a surprise, because the physical body is dynamically connected with the energetic body, and the reverse is true as well.

If you have had an experience like this, then you can begin to understand where that "great calm" comes from, as it was described in the story about Jesus. He understood and mastered this process, and each of us has that potential. Once these connections and processes are recognized, the mind can increasingly realize its own potential for participation. Creative opportunities for working with the invisible will become more apparent. We can intentionally loosen the energies of creation to flow forth into the world— the world that we think is personal but in fact is one world we all share.

With a little time and maturity, the Essential Self can have greater opportunity to shine through. This emergence carries with it a greater experience of participation in a grand design, the seeds of which are imprinted within each of us. Sometimes those seeds burn inside us like the fire of a Sun. The name Sunseed reminds me of that reality.

Remember Sunseed's vision of a giant fiery bird pulling the Earth steadily around its orbit of the Sun? Even outer space is not empty. It is full of the Spiritual Wind, and that wind can blow with exceptional power. When we relax into that wind and actually hone our perceptions of it, our experience of living can become totally new. Perhaps we might even have a vision of pulling the whole world along with us as we are taking simple steps in each moment of our lives.

This is why I sought more training in Attunement and why I have quietly spent thousands of hours in my lifetime participating in Attunements with hundreds of different people. And out of all this, my investment of many hours focused and working with the invisible aspects of my faculties, has come an increasing recognition and identification with my Essential Self.

This is a natural process, often described as the process of incarnation. Remember when I said that we primarily touch other people in our consciousness? That is where our personal acts of creation actually take place. That is where we perceive our connection with the Divine. In Chapter 8 of Andrew Shier's book *Attunement, A Way Of Life,* he clearly describes this. He says, "The word incarnation means: to be endowed with a physical body. The debate about when we actually incarnate is currently a charged topic around the issue of a woman's right to choose. Putting politics aside, however, the general perception is that we incarnate once and it is sometime in the first nine months of pregnancy. What I would like to propose is that the process of incarnation actually goes on throughout our entire lives. It is a sequential process that has a very specific timing and rhythm."

Back in Chapter 1 of this book, I started by telling the Story of Sunseed's Dream and the beginning of my spiritual quest. I said, "Over the following decades I actually did find everything I was seeking." Well, I have finally now told you as best I know how "what I really did find." Through my telling of all these stories about my ongoing process of incarnation— about my increasing understanding of my spiritual purpose and why I chose to come into this earth— perhaps you have gained some greater perspective about yourself as well. So, what comes next?

# Chapter Fifty-Nine

## GRANDPA'S LAST GREAT ADVENTURE

*"Here is the test to find out whether your mission on earth is finished: if you're alive, it isn't."*
—Richard Bach, American Author
*(Jonathan Livingston Seagull)*

As I write this last chapter it is late 2014 and I am 67 years old. I hope to live another 25-35 years, but only if I can still get on my bicycle (while keeping my wits and bodily functions under control). I hope to continue this life for as long as rightfully possible, because I have more to do and more to give. That is why I came in the first place. Each day is a gift, and I give thanks to God for this gift as if each day might be the last. I do not fear death because I know that life is eternal and that passing over to the other side from this life will simply be my "last great adventure." Like my mother always said, and it still rings true about my eternal being as well, "I'm fine."

I hope that after I am gone there will be some lively parties as well as some sacred times of remembrance with friends old and new. You can all celebrate the words and works of creation that we have released together into this world along the way.

Did you ever hear the story of the man who dreamt he was a butterfly? The problem was he was never sure whether he might really be a butterfly dreaming sometimes that he was a man. That's how I feel about Sunseed. I believe Sunseed is one name for my real eternal identity, as revealed through my Essential Self, and that Terry Oftedal has been one of his lifetimes on this planet. If I am right, I will see you on the other side. Perhaps we can have another great adventure together then.

THE END ... FOR NOW

# Acknowledgements and Explanations

Writing this book was a magical journey for me. It all started with another dream. I am not talking about Sunseed's dream, which really did happen just the way I described it. This one happened in California, a week after the funeral celebration for my mother, in April of 2014. In the middle of the night I woke from this dream with an idea to start a book by writing stories about my ancestors, and I scribbled notes for about an hour filling both sides of one sheet of paper. When we reached home I pulled out that sheet and I opened a document on my computer; I had created this document months earlier, but it contained only a title— *The Story of Sunseed.*

I wrote a number of the first chapters, then I wrote some of the last chapters. Filling in all of those middle chapters was the harder part, and possibly the most enjoyable. The real magic was how clearly some of those earlier years became when I focused my attention on them one at a time. Sometimes it took a few days— more often it happened quickly. It was like taking a compressed electronic document and then decompressing it; all of a sudden I was filled with people's faces and names and details that I had not thought about for years. Touching in consciousness so many old friends was a real treat. Thank you, each and every one, for your friendships and inspiration along the way, including those of you whose names were not mentioned in this book due to space limitations. I woke up in the night many times, remembering one more detail that I just had to get out of bed and immediately type into the text. For months I had to write; I didn't want to stop. The whole process felt alive, as if it had a life of its own. The first draft took nine months.

Kathryn was with me that whole time, figuratively holding my hand and providing me grounding, just as I had done for her during those months leading to the birth of our twins. Thank you again, My Love. You were the first to read my original draft and help with some editing. How many times did you laugh out loud or say from the next room, "I didn't know that."

Thanks also to Andrew Shier for his encouragement along the way and for his permission to include pieces from his inspiring book. It was Andrew and John Gray who convinced me that I did indeed have a book that others would want to read. You can order Andrew's book and learn more about Attunement at his web site- http://woodlandsattunement.com

For those of you who are aspiring writers, thank you for reading this book and joining me in my journey. Perhaps you have gained some new ideas. My advice is, "Follow your dreams." Laura Ingalls Wilder was 65 when her first book *Little House in The Big Woods* was published in 1932. She was not well known at the time, except to a limited number of readers of the Missouri Ruralist Newspaper. She was hoping to generate a little income and had no idea how broadly popular her stories would become. None of us do. And what if our books only reach hundreds of readers instead of millions? Don't let these thoughts stop you. Trust the Spiritual Wind.

My friend and artist Cheryl Renee Long created an original watercolor painting, entitled *Sunseed's Dream*. She was excited to collaborate with me in recreating the essences of a dream, born many years before, into a visual form that could be shared with others. Her painting now hangs in my home, and it is reproduced on the cover of this book. This book would not be complete without it.

Thanks to Colleen Cayes, who visited us as I was struggling to finish this project. Her boundless energy and assistance in the final rounds of editing inspired me over those final weeks. It is amazing how the right person shows up at the right time; her visit was no accident.

Thanks also to Laura Shinn who applied considerable amounts of magic in the final steps of preparing this book for its release.

Sandra Smith and Loma Huh also provided earlier editing assistance. Loma helped me discover that parts of another book were hiding in plain sight in the midst of this book. Soon I will turn my attention to bringing those stories into another book. Its title will be *Sunseed's Quest— Discoveries Along the Journey Inward*. While this first book focused mostly on my journey outward, the opposite will be true next time. I'll talk more about the journey inward.

My brother played many parts, including being a dear friend for 65 years and counting. He drove Kathryn and me into West Fresno earlier in 2014 as we explored the location of Great-Grandpa Martin Oftedal's farm and then the acreage to which Great-Grandma Mary Oftedal moved with her children after Martin's passing. Before that, those farms had only been scribbled words on paper for me. Randy also encouraged me to include details in the book about the less happy days and some of the rowdier times. Thank you, Brother.

At first I was uncertain about including some of the most personal details of my life, particularly those about my experiences of Attunement. But I had great fun telling the stories. Now I am glad for all of it.

For those who think this book meandered too much, perhaps you are right. It thrills me, however, to see that you have persevered and read all the way to this last paragraph. All I can say is that some people think Virgil's epic poem *The Aeneid* meandered, and my book covered a much longer period of time. It tickles me to use the words "epic" and "my book" in the same sentence, but perhaps Sunseed's Dream and these stories should be described as epic. Our home planet Earth continues to circle the Sun. Sunseed and the fiery bird fly on.

# About the Author

It all started with a dream. At that time, in 1972, he had no thought of becoming an author.

Today Terry Oftedal is living quietly with his wife Kathryn in a small town near Portland, Oregon. After raising a family and retiring from a colorful business career which included trips to distant lands, Terry has found time to reflect and write. A life-changing dream he had as a young man in Ashland, Oregon serves as a backdrop for his first book *The Story of Sunseed.*

He says, "Read the book— it tells you all about who I am. I believe you will learn something new about yourself as well."

NOTE: Terry has pledged that 100 percent of the net proceeds from his writings will be donated to selected charities or gifted as "Sunseed Awards."

80
82
91
96